THE
TRUMP
TAX CUT

Your Personal Guide to the New Tax Law

EVA ROSENBERG, EA

Humanix Books

The Trump Tax Cut
Copyright © 2019 by Humanix Books
All rights reserved

Humanix Books, P.O. Box 20989, West Palm Beach, FL 33416, USA
www.humanixbooks.com | info @humanixbooks.com

Library of Congress Cataloging -in-Publication Data is available upon
request.

Humanix Books is a division of Humanix Publishing, LLC. Its trademark,
consisting of the word "Humanix," is registered in the Patent and Trademark
Office and in other countries.

Disclaimer: The information presented in this book is meant to be used for
general resource purposes only; it is not intended as specific financial advice
for any individual and should not substitute financial advice from a finance
professional.

Portions of this book originally appeared in *Deduct Everything* by
Eva Rosenberg (978-1-63006047-3).

ISBN: 978-1-63006-105-0 (Trade Paper)
ISBN: 978-1-63006-106-7 (E-book)

Printed in the United States of America
10 9 8 7 6 5 4 3 2 1

Contents

THE
TRUMP
TAX CUT

CHAPTER 1

The Tax Cuts and Jobs Act

How Trump's Tax Plan Benefits You

Dᴜʀɪɴɢ Dᴏɴᴀʟᴅ Tʀᴜᴍᴘ's ʜɪsᴛᴏʀɪᴄ campaign for president, he promised to reduce and overhaul America's tax system. President Trump delivered, signing the 185-page Tax Cuts and Jobs Act into law on December 22, 2017. President Trump's Tax Cuts and Jobs Act is among the largest tax cuts in history, including the largest corporate tax cut ever. The nonpartisan Tax Foundation says the Trump tax law will reduce federal revenues, that is taxes paid by individuals and businesses, almost $1.5 trillion over the next decade.

If you worried about adjusting your plans before you filed your 2017 returns, the good news is the Tax Cuts and Jobs Act did not affect your returns for last year. For the most part, the changes will start to affect your 2018 tax return and beyond. If anything does affect 2017, such as the following changes, your tax bill will be reduced.

TOP CHANGES THAT AFFECTED 2017
(However Briefly)

1. **Charitable contributions.** Still deductible, but must be backed up by receipts.

2. **Medical expenses.** Lowers medical expense threshold for 2 years, 2018 and 2019, allowing you to deduct any medical expense over 7.5 percent of adjusted gross income, after it reverts to 10 percent.

3. **Aircraft transportation fees.** Federal transportation taxes are eliminated for private plane owners whose aircraft is operated by a management company. Effective December 22, 2017.

4. **Bonus depreciation for business.** For qualified property placed in service between September 28, 2017, and December 31, 2022 (or by December 31, 2023, for certain property with longer production periods), the first-year bonus depreciation percentage increases to 100 percent. In addition, the 100 percent deduction is allowed for new and used qualifying property.

While you proceeded with your 2017 tax return as usual, it is important that taxpayers begin to understand how the Trump tax law changes their tax situation on a personal and a business level.

This book is an excellent starting point. If you have significant changes to your tax status, especially for business owners, you may seek out expert advice to fully benefit from the new law. The changes to the Tax Code are sweeping and will affect every individual and business return in 2018. This purpose of this book is to offer you tax strategies that will help both individuals and small business maximize their benefits and reduce their tax payments under the Tax Cuts and Jobs Act.

KEY BENEFITS FOR INDIVIDUALS IN THE NEW LAW

1. Personal tax brackets are lower.

2. Child Tax Credit is increased.

3. Standard deduction is increased.

4. Charitable contributions limits are increased to 60 percent of income.

5. Medical expenses are easier to deduct with a lower threshold.

6. Unpaid 401(k) loans: There is more time to repay after job termination.

7. Estate and gifts tax lifetime exclusion rises.

8. Section 529 education funds may be rolled over.

9. Section 529 education funds may be used to pay for private elementary and secondary school tuition.

10. Student loans discharged due to death or disability will not generate cancellation of debt income.

Provisions for Individual Under the Law

If a deduction or tax break is suspended, it means the change is only temporary. Most of the changes in the tax law affect the years starting on January 1, 2018, and expire on December 31, 2025 unless otherwise specified. Here are several key changes:

The ACA mandate is repealed. In January of 2017, President Trump issued an executive order eliminating any penalties for individuals who did not get health insurance under the ACA mandate rules.

But the IRS itself felt the president's executive order did not give them the legal authority to wipe out the penalty for not having insurance. Thus, for the 2017 tax returns, all filers had to fill out the forms and answer the questions about their insurance coverage or exemption. Not answering the questions generated a penalty, approximately 2.5 percent of your annual household income. Under the new tax law the penalty will stay in effect for the full year 2018, and filers in 2019 must prove they had adequate coverage or an exemption; otherwise they will face an automatic penalty.

What if you totally cannot afford the cost of the health insurance? You have a couple of options to help you get coverage:

- If your income is below the poverty level, perhaps you qualify for assistance via state or local programs such as Medi-Cal (in California).
- Also, check the HealthCare.gov website to see if you qualify for any of the exemptions: https://www.healthcare.gov/health -coverage-exemptions/. Some of them require that you file paperwork. Get started on that paperwork immediately.

And if you simply, flat-out cannot afford the insurance, in your budget? Well, here's one way to get around the penalties. Reduce your withholding or estimated payments so you owe a small balance on April 15 (in 2018, the filing deadline is April 17).

There's an odd provision in the ACA rules regarding how the IRS can collect these ACA penalties. It may only take the penalties out of your refunds. The IRS is not permitted to garnish your wages or levy your bank accounts or other assets. So if you don't have a refund for the next 10 to12 years, you will never have to pay the ACA penalties. (*Note: The IRS can collect balances due for 10 years after the balance is assessed. The last penalty will be assessed in 2019 for the 2018 tax return.*)

There are new tax brackets for individuals (see chart).

If taxable income is:	The income tax equals:
Single Individuals	
Not over $9,525	10% of the taxable income
Over $9,525 but not over $38,700	$952.50 plus 12% of the excess over $9,525
Over $38,700 but not over $82,500	$4,453.50 plus 22% of the excess over $38,700
Over $82,500 but not over $157,500	$14,089.50 plus 24% of the excess over $82,500
Over $157,500 but not over $200,000	$32,089.50 plus 32% of the excess over $157,500
Over $200,000 but not over $500,000	$45,689.50 plus 35% of the excess over $200,000
Over $500,000	$150,689.50 plus 37% of the excess over $500,000
Heads of Households	
Not over $13,600	10% of the taxable income
Over $13,600 but not over $51,800	$1,360 plus 12% of the excess over $13,600
Over $51,800 but not over $82,500	$5,944 plus 22% of the excess over $51,800
Over $82,500 but not over $157,500	$12,698 plus 24% of the excess over $82,500
Over $157,500 but not over $200,00	$30,698 plus 32% of the excess over $157,500
Over $200,000 but not over $500,000	$44,298 plus 35% of the excess over $200,000
Over $500,000	$149,298 plus 37% of the excess over $500,000
Married Individuals Filing Joint Returns and Surviving Spouses	
Not over $19,050	10% of the taxable income
Over $19,050 but not over $77,400	$1,905 plus 12% of the excess over $19,050
Over $77,400 but not over $165,000	$8,907 plus 22% of the excess over $77,400
Over $165,000 but not over $315,00	$28,179 plus 24% of the excess over $165,000
Over $315,00 but not over $400,000	$64,179 plus 32% of the excess over $315,000
Over $400,000 but not over $600,00	$91,379 plus 35% of the excess over $400,000
Over $600,000	$161,379 plus 37% of the excess over $600,000

If taxable income is:	The income tax equals:
Married Individuals Filing Separate Returns	
Not over $9,525	10% of the taxable income
Over $9,525 but not over $38,700	$952.50 plus 12% of the excess over $9,525
Over $38,700 but not over $82,500	$4,453.50 plus 22% of the excess over $38,700
Over $82,500 but not over $157,500	$14,089.50 plus 24% of the excess over $82,500
Over $157,500 but not over $200,000	$32,089.50 plus 32% of the excess over $157,500
Over $200,000 but not over $300,000	$45,689.50 plus 35% of the excess over $200,000
Over $300,000	$80,689.50 plus 37% of the excess over $300,000

Personal exemptions are suspended until December 31, 2025. For 2017, you still got your exemption of $4,050 for yourself, your spouse, and each qualified dependent on your tax return.

In 2018, you would have had a personal exemption of $4,150 for each member of your family. The TCJA suspends the exemption until December 31, 2025. However, you still need to know that $4,150 amount. If a potential dependent (other than your qualified child or student) earns more than that amount, you may not claim that person as a dependent.

Who is a potential dependent? Your parent (*Note: Social Security income doesn't count*), your live-in lover, your girlfriend's child living with you, your unemployed brother, or anyone else who has lived with you for the whole year. (See Tip #80.)

Child Tax Credit and personal credit are increased. Higher child and personal credits are intended to replace the personal exemptions until—December 31, 2025.

- The Child Tax Credit rose from $1,000 per child to $2,000 per qualifying child under age 17.
- The credit is refundable up to $1,400 per child.

- The taxpayer must earn at least $2,500 to qualify to receive any part of this credit (down from $3,000).

- The child must have a Social Security number to qualify for this credit.

- The additional personal credit is $500 for each nonchild member of the taxpayer's household. This credit applies to the taxpayer, spouse, and any dependent that doesn't qualify for the Child Tax Credit. This credit is nonrefundable.

- The credits phase out when adjusted gross income reaches $400,000 for married filing jointly, and $200,000 for all other taxpayers.

The kiddie tax is simplified. Reporting and paying taxes on certain earnings of your children has been simplified, and the tax rates have become easier to understand. Unearned income (all income except wages and self-employment income) will no longer be tied to the parents' tax rate. It will now be taxed at the rates in effect for estates and trusts. Since that table reaches the 37 percent tax bracket when unearned income hits $12,500, it is less of an advantage to transfer investment assets to your children than it was before. On the other hand, earned income (wages and self-employment income) will still be taxed at the child's rate in the single tables (see earlier chart).

Deduction for alimony payments is suspended for new divorce agreements. Alimony payments for divorce agreements signed after December 31, 2018, will not be deductible. This new rule doesn't start for another year, giving people time to sort out their divorce disputes in 2018. For divorce agreements in effect before December 31, 2018, the alimony is still a deduction to the payer and income to the recipient.

That's bad news for the ex-spouse paying the alimony, but good news for the person receiving the money—who still won't be paying any income tax on it. But it may reduce the amount spouses can pay in alimony when the new taxes are figured in. Expect this provision to shake up the divorce system.

The standard deduction is increased. The standard deduction is raised from $13,000 to $24,000 for married individuals filing a joint return, from $9,550 to $18,000 for head-of-household filers, and from $6,500 to $12,000 for all other taxpayers. The deduction is also increased for inflation starting in years after 2018.

Good news: the additional deduction for seniors and the blind is still available. This means, in addition to the standard deduction amount above, a person who is blind or disabled will get an extra deduction of $1,300 (if married) or $1,600 (all others) for each condition, as shown in the chart.

Filing Status	Basic Standard Deduction	Senior Deduction	Blind Deduction	Potential Total Standard Deduction
Single	$12,000	$1,600	$1,600	$15,200
Head of Household	$18,000	$1,600	$1,600	$21,200
Qualified Widow(er)	$12,000	$1,600	$1,600	$15,200
Married Filing Jointly	$24,000	$1,300	$1,300	$26,600
Married Filing Separately	$12,000	$1,300	$1,300	$14,600

The Pease phaseout of itemized deductions is suspended. The ACJA suspends the Pease limitation on itemized deductions and exemptions when certain income levels are reached.

Educator expenses deduction continues. The TCJA continues this tax break allowing qualified educators to deduct up to $250 of their unreimbursed expenses for school supplies. If both spouses are educators, the maximum deduction on the tax return is $500. (See Tip #219 for more details.)

Deductions for employee business expenses are suspended. The new provision suspends current business expense deductions made on individual returns until December 31, 2025. You will not be able to use any deductions for your job-related expenses, including travel, meals, union dues, supplies, etc. (See Tip #189 for more details and some options you might have to salvage the situation.)

New limit is set on deductions for state and local income taxes, sales taxes, and property taxes. The new law imposes a new limit of $10,000 on the deductibility of these taxes combined. This provision begins for the taxable year beginning 2018 and will sunset at the close of business December 31, 2025.

In the past, individuals could deduct all their real estate property taxes, personal property taxes on such things as your car and boat, and either your state income taxes or your state sales taxes. Before the TCJA there was no limit on the deduction.

Starting in 2018, the TCJA gives you a limit of $10,000 for all those taxes combined for single taxpayers and married taxpayers filing jointly, and half of that for married couples filing separately. (See Chapter 3 for some strategies that might help you.)

New limits are set on mortgage interest deduction. Interest may be deducted on mortgages for up to two residences based on acquisition debt (debt used to buy a home rather than a home equity line) up to $750,000. This provision begins for the taxable year beginning after December 31, 2017, and ends December 31, 2025.

- No interest deduction is permitted for home equity lines of credit—unless the funds are used to build, repair, or replace part of the home.

- Loans in place before December 15, 2017, are grandfathered in the law. That means you may still claim deductions for the interest on these loans up to a loan balance of $1 million for up to two homes.

- If married couples file separately, they may only use interest deductions on loans of up to $375,000 in place after December 14, 2017, or on loans of up to $500,000 in place before December 15, 2017.

The new law affects taxpayers who have new loans and does not apply to those grandfathered in at the time TCJA became law. We talk more about this in Chapter 5.

Moving expense deduction is suspended. The deduction is suspended until December 31, 2025.

- Members of the Armed Forces may still claim moving expense deductions for themselves, their spouses, and dependents, as long as the move is for someone on active duty, and the move is pursuant to a military order and due to a permanent change of station.

- Businesses may still use the deductions for moving the business and related assets on their respective business returns or schedules.

- Employer reimbursements to employees for their qualified moving expenses are now subject to taxation. This is no longer a tax-free employee benefit.

Gambling loss deductions are limited to gambling wins. Professional gamblers are those whose livelihood comes from gambling income. Until now, professional gamblers were able to deduct all the cost of operating their "business." That included more than just their wagering losses. It included travel to and from the casino, lodging at or near the facility, and other out-of-pocket expenses. Under the TCJA, their deductions are limited to their gambling winnings for the year. These provisions sunset on December 31, 2025.

Changes are made to charitable contributions deductions. Three provisions affecting itemized tax returns are effective starting in 2018 and remain permanent:

- Cash contributions to public charities are permitted up to 60 percent of filer's modified adjusted gross income.
- No deductions are allowed for money paid for seating rights to college athletic events beginning with 2018.
- Donors must have substantiation for their deductions whether or not the recipient organization files a report showing that it received the donations. This is in effect for the taxable year beginning after December 31, *2016*, and affected your 2017 tax return and beyond.

We'll talk more about charitable contributions issues and updates in Chapter 8.

Student loan interest deduction is not changed. TCJA keeps the deduction at $2,500 per tax return. For related information, see Tips #172 to 175.

Student loans discharged due to death or disability do not result in taxable income. This provision begins for the taxable year beginning after December 31, 2017, and ending December 31, 2025.

Under the present tax laws, anytime a debt is discharged or forgiven, the unpaid debt gives rise to a Form 1099-C (or 1099-COD) as cancellation of debt income. The TCJA has added a provision that if a student loan is forgiven when someone becomes disabled or dies, it will not generate taxable cancellation of debt income.

For tips on another way to get student loan debt discharged tax-free, see Tip #172.

Section 529 qualified tuition programs (QTP) provisions are modified. Effective for distributions made after December 31, 2017. (For more information on how Section 529 plans work and how much you may contribute to them, read Tip #165.)

Here are the new rules for Section 529 distributions:

- Up to $10,000 from these accounts may be used to pay tuition for elementary and secondary schools, per year, per student. *Note: If there are distributions from more than one Section 529 plan for the student, the total of all tax-free distributions for that student in any given year must still be no more than $10,000.*

- The funds may be used for public, private, or religious elementary or secondary schools.

- The funds may be used for certain homeschooling costs (see Tip #184).

Section 529 funds may be rolled over to Achieving a Better Life Experience (ABLE) accounts. Rollovers are permitted between qualified tuition programs (Section 529 accounts) and qualified ABLE programs. This provision begins in 2018 and sunsets on December 31, 2025.

ABLE accounts are special tax-free accounts for those with disabilities. Tax-free rollovers are permitted from IRC Section 529 tuition accounts to IRC Section 529A ABLE accounts. The rollovers must go to ABLE accounts with the same beneficiary as the Section 529 account or a member of that beneficiary's family.

For more information about ABLEs, see Tips #166 and 167.

Deduction for medical expenses is reduced by only 7.5 percent of adjusted gross income. Under TCJA taxpayers not only keep their itemized deduction for medical expenses, but will see it expand. The law lowers the threshold for deduction of medical expenses from 10 percent of adjusted gross income (AGI) to 7 percent. To a filer with an AGI of $100,000, this increases your medical deduction amount by $2,500. This provision applies immediately to your 2017 tax return and will continue through December 31, 2019.

Personal casualty and theft loss deduction is suspended. The suspension begins in tax year 2018, and this rule will sunset on December 31, 2025. TCJA does allow you to deduct casualty losses resulting from federally declared disaster areas. Such losses, however, will still be reduced by 10 percent of the filer's adjusted gross income plus $100.

Changes to the personal casualty and theft losses mean that if you invest in a Ponzi scheme, or other vehicle that turns out to be fraudulent, are a victim of identity theft, or even suffer a house fire, you won't be able to get any tax relief for those kinds of personal disasters. Taxpayers should consider these new changes in calculating the amount of insurance coverage they need for their home and person.

Business casualty losses are still fully deductible. Business casualty losses are not reduced by a percentage of AGI or other amount.

IRA to Roth IRA conversions or vice versa are no longer permitted. Recharacterization of a regular IRA to a Roth IRA, or a Roth IRA to a regular IRA, is no longer permitted. In other words, once you transfer money from your regular IRA to a Roth, you may not unwind that transfer. This rule primarily applies to transfers, not original contributions to IRAs.

However, if you simply open a Roth IRA during the year and decide you would rather fund a regular IRA account, you may still switch before the filing deadline.

This permanent provision begins with the 2018 tax year.

More time is allowed to repay or roll over 401(k) loans upon termination of employment or termination of the plan. The (former) employee has additional time to roll over the outstanding loan amount into the employee's own IRA or new employer's retirement account, as long as the outstanding balance is rolled over by the due date for filing the tax return, including extensions, for the taxable year in which such amount is treated as distributed from a qualified employer plan. Under the old law, employees who left a job, for any reason, had to repay all loans from their retirement plans within 60 days after leaving the job. If they didn't pay the loan back, the loan would be treated as a taxable distribution. For employees under the age of 59½, they would also be subject to the IRS penalty of 10 percent and state early withdrawal penalties. For more information about retirement plan loans, see Tip #155.

Plans include all qualified plans, including a Section 403(b) plan or a Section 457 government retirement plan.

This is a permanent provision beginning in 2018.

Changes to Alternative Minimum Tax (AMT). This is an extra tax imposed if you take advantage of certain tax loopholes. It kicks in when income reaches $109,400 for couples filing jointly (half of that if they file separately) or $70,300 for all other individual taxpayers (except trusts). When income rises above $1 million for couples filing jointly, or half that for all other individual taxpayers (except trusts), the two thresholds ($109,000 and $70,300) start to phase out. This is in effect beginning after December 31, 2017, and ending December 31, 2025.

The good news is, the AMT is totally repealed for businesses—permanently. We'll talk more about this in the chapter on the business changes.

Estate and gift tax exclusions are increased. The value of the assets excluded from estate taxation will be $11.2 million per person and will be adjusted yearly for inflation. This is effective starting in 2018 and sunsets at the end of 2025.

This effectively doubles the amount of assets that are not taxed upon death. Essentially, over 99 percent of taxpayers will be able to pass their assets to their heirs without gift tax concerns. This is a major benefit for individuals and families who own businesses that might have a high market value but low cash reserves. That means the business, farm, buildings, or assets don't have to be mortgaged to cover estate taxes.

The Impact for You as a Taxpayer

While greatly reducing the number of deductions you will be able to deduct, this is offset by a dramatic increase of the standard deduction. Only 30 percent of taxpayers itemized deductions, so most Americans will benefit from this.

The big losers are taxpayers who live in high-taxed states like California and New York. Many will see the $10,000 cap on their state and local tax deduction as simply not enough, and they could see a dramatic increase in their taxes.

But the fact is, TCJA will simplify tax filing for millions of people. You won't be able to file your taxes on a "postcard," but most will find both the process and paperwork greatly reduced.

GOOD THINGS THAT TAKE EFFECT IN 2019

1. ACA penalties for not having insurance coverage have been eliminated.

2. Alimony is no longer a deduction to the payer, nor is it income to the recipient—on new divorce contracts.

Even before the TCJA was passed, the IRS claimed that about 100 million taxpayers qualified to file their tax returns for free using the Free File Alliance program (https://freefilealliance.org). With the new increases in the standard deduction and Child Tax Credit, you may qualify to use that service yourself.

If you have a job, don't own a home, don't pay high state income taxes, and are healthy, you probably won't have to itemize on your federal tax return at all. As a result, your tax return will be simpler.

Don't forget, many of the deductions (Schedule A) you no longer need on your federal tax return might still be useful on your state income tax return. Be sure to enter all the deductions into your tax software, or bring that data to your tax professional, as usual.

MOST COMMONLY USED DEDUCTIONS THAT ARE CHANGING WITH TCJA

1. State and local tax deduction capped at $10,000

2. Mortgage interest deduction capped at $750,000

3. Home equity loan interest deduction eliminated

4. Casualty loss deduction can be claimed only if a federally declared disaster

5. Moving expense deduction for career opportunity eliminated

CHAPTER 2

Trump's Bold Tax Plan for Business

A T THE HEART OF the President's Tax Cut and Jobs Act (TCJA) is the most sizeable business tax reduction in American history.

The White House stated the main goals of Donald Trump's tax plan is to "grow the American economy by discouraging corporate inversions, adding a huge number of new jobs, and making America globally competitive again."

In the immediate aftermath of the passage of the TCJA, business confidence in the economy soared to record levels, as the stock market hit all-time highs. Major corporations led by AT&T began offering employees a $1000 bonus or more. And other companies raised their minimum wage, some to $15 an hour.

The impact of the Trump tax plan for business is nothing short of breathtaking. Consider a company with $10 billion in annual profits. Under the old tax regime, this company would pay $3.5 billion in taxes. At the new rate of just 21 percent, this same company will see its profits soar, as that tax bill declines to $2.1 billion, putting an additional $1.4 billion into corporate coffers for re-investment, hiring, salary increases and dividends for shareholders.

The Trump tax cut doesn't just help Fortune 500 companies. It will boost companies of every size, but especially small businesses, the true engine of the US economy.

According to the U.S. Census Bureau, there are over 27 million businesses in the U.S. and just 655,587 of them employ 20 or more employees. This means 21 million of those businesses do not have employees at all!

Most small business owners file their taxes using the personal income tax code. These small business owners will benefit from the new, lower individual rate structure. They too will benefit from the higher standard deduction and lower tax rates. And many will directly benefit from a special 20 percent deduction allowed by small business operators who qualify.

The changes in the TCJA will go into effect for the 2018 tax year, unless otherwise noted here.

First of all, what is a small business under the Tax Cuts and Jobs Act?

In most of the provisions, TCJA defines a small business as having under $15 million in gross receipts or $25 million for family farming corporations. (That takes into account an average of the last three years' gross receipts.) Other provisions also establish $25 million as the gross income level before other obligations become effective.

That's great news for you. Why? Because it exempts you from some of the more complicated record-keeping and reporting requirements.

We will only be covering the TCJA changes that affect small businesses as defined by the TCJA.

Business Tax Reform

Corporate tax rates have dropped from a high of 35 percent to a flat rate of 21 percent. There is no longer a 15 percent tax rate on the first $50,000 of income. The 21 percent rate applies to ordinary and capital gain income for all C corporations, and personal service corporations (PSC).

What are PSCs? These are C corporations generating income from a service provided by the owner: accounting, actuarial science, architecture, consulting, engineering, health (including veterinary services), law, and the performing arts.

The 20 Percent Deduction

Most small business owners use pass-through entities like S Corporations, partnerships, and limited liability companies or LLCs that move their company profits easily onto their personal income tax. Others are simply sole proprietorships where individuals declare their income directly on their personal tax returns. Pass through entities have allowed small businesses to maintain a corporate shield for liability purposes while avoiding double taxation—first at the corporate level and then again at the personal level.

Since the reduction of corporate taxes from 35 percent to 21 percent largely benefit C corporation owners and shareholders, the TCJA remedies that by offering a special deduction to individuals who use pass-through entities to do business.

The Tax Cuts and Jobs Act offers a 20 percent deduction for qualified business income from so-called pass-through entities, which include S corporations and limited liability companies. But it doesn't apply to everyone.

To fully qualify for the 20 percent deduction, a single person's taxable income must fall below $157,500 and married and file jointly must be below $315,000 of taxable income. If you make less than these threshold amounts, and use a pass-through entity, you are eligible for the deduction.

Once you go above those thresholds, many are still eligible for the 20 percent deduction, however, there are limitations. For example, the TCJA specifically excludes owners of specified service businesses like accountants, attorneys and healthcare practitioners with income exceeding $207,500 for single taxpayers and $415,000 for married taxpayers.

The special 20 percent deduction will be an incentive for many individuals to consider forming LLCs or other pass-through entities to conduct business, even if they are salaried employees. For example, if you are an independent sales person, you may be eligible for the 20 percent deduction.

Some large privately held companies are in the form of S corporations or other pass through entities.

Such owners may believe even with the 20 percent deduction, the TCJA does not treat them as beneficially as C corporation owners. With the 20 percent tax deduction, those individuals who use pass-throughs and typically pay at the highest end of the tax law, that is 37 percent, will find their business income, minus the 20 percent deduction, yields an effective rate of 29.6 percent.

Add on top of this the Medicare tax, small business owners with pass-throughs will find they are paying significantly more than the 21 percent rate C corporation owners pay.

As a result, some business owners are contemplating changing their status to C corporations to reap the lower rates. Since they can't distribute income without paying additional taxes at normal rates, they would have to use their profits within their C corporation for re-investment or acquisitions.

Many employees of existing companies are currently paying normal income taxes and may think they can simply become a 1099 contactor and take advantage of the tax loophole allowing for the 20 percent deduction.

Switching from "employee" status to one of an independent contractor is possible, but the IRS lays out requirements. Here is what the IRS website says:

People such as doctors, dentists, veterinarians, lawyers, accountants, contractors, subcontractors, public stenographers, or auctioneers who are in an independent trade, business, or profession in which they offer their services to the general public are generally independent contractors. However, whether these people are independent contractors or employees depends on the facts in each case. The general rule is that an individual is an independent contractor if the payer has the right to control or direct only the result of the work and not what will be done and how it will be done. The earnings of a person who is working as an independent contractor are subject to Self-Employment Tax.

If you are an independent contractor, you are self-employed. To find out what your tax obligations are, visit the Self-Employed Tax Center.

You are not an independent contractor if you perform services that can be controlled by an employer (what will be done and how it will be done). This applies even if you are given freedom of action. What matters is that the employer has the legal right to control the details of how the services are performed.

If an employer-employee relationship exists (regardless of what the relationship is called), you are not an independent contractor and your earnings are generally not subject to Self-Employment Tax.

However, your earnings as an employee may be subject to FICA (Social Security tax and Medicare) and income tax withholding.

The IRS also notes that employers have the responsibility to make sure their contractors are not employees.

IRS cites 3 Common Law rules that provide evidence of the degree of control and independence fall into three categories:

1. **Behavioral.** Does the company control or have the right to control what the worker does and how the worker does his or her job?

2. **Financial.** Are the business aspects of the worker's job controlled by the payer? (these include things like how worker is paid, whether expenses are reimbursed, who provides tools/supplies, etc.)

3. **Type of Relationship.** Are there written contracts or employee type benefits (i.e. pension plan, insurance, vacation pay, etc.)? Will the relationship continue and is the work performed a key aspect of the business?

The IRS notes: "Businesses must weigh all these factors when determining whether a worker is an employee or independent contractor. Some factors may indicate that the worker is an employee, while other factors indicate that the worker is an independent contractor. There is no 'magic' or set number of factors that 'makes' the worker an employee or an independent contractor, and no one factor stands alone in making this determination. Also, factors which are relevant in one situation may not be relevant in another. The keys are to look at the entire relationship, consider the degree or extent of the right to direct and control, and finally, to document each of the factors used in coming up with the determination."

If you are an employer or contractor and it is still unclear whether a worker is an employee or an independent contractor, the IRS provides Form SS-8, Determination of Worker Status for Purposes of Federal Employment Taxes and Income Tax Withholding.

The form may be filed by either the business or the worker. The IRS will review the facts and circumstances and officially determine the worker's status. (Be aware that it can take at least six months to get a determination, but a business that continually hires the same types of workers to perform particular services may want to consider filing the Form SS-8.)

Deduction of Business Debt Interest

In the past all business interest from debt was fully deductible. The new act limits business interest deduction to 30 percent of adjusted taxable income.

Certain businesses with average annual gross receipts over the last three years of less than $25 million are exempt from these rules. Farming businesses and Real property trades or businesses can elect out of the provision if they use ADS to depreciate certain property.

Changes to Deductions and Exchanges

The TCJA provides for numerous changes to certain business deductions and exchanges. These include:

- **Sec 1031 Tax-Free Exchanges** are limited to real estate not bought primarily for sale or resale.

- **Deduction for lobbying expenses** is eliminated effective December 22, 2017, including any portion of dues paid to an organization that are used for lobbying purposes.

- **Entertainment expenses** are no longer deductible. Under the terms of the TCJA, there will be no deduction for the costs for entertainment that are directly related to a business activity, this includes sporting tickets and boxes, theatre and other events.

- **Business meals** are still partially deductible at 50 percent of cost. Transportation industry workers who are subject to the "hours of service" limits may deduct 80 percent of their meal costs or per diem. Free meals provided by employers, at a company cafeteria or restaurant, are still deductible but are no longer exempt from the 50% limitation, but this provision will sunset at the end of 2025.

- **Transportation fringe benefit** is no longer deductible, with an exception. The part of the TCJA that disallows entertainment deductions also, "disallows a deduction for expenses associated with providing any qualified transportation fringe to employees of the taxpayer, and except as necessary for ensuring the safety of an employee, any expense incurred for providing transportation (or any payment or reimbursement) for commuting between the employee's residence and place of employment." Thus, money to support commuting costs will no longer be deductible. However, expenses are deductible if the employer provides those qualified employee transportation fringe benefits like parking, bus passes, etc. if they comply with the requirement that help to ensure employee safety.

- **Self-created property** such as patents, inventions, models or designs (whether or not patented), and secret formula or processes will no longer get capital gains treatment when sold by the creator or inventor, or by someone who was gifted these assets. The seller will pay taxes at ordinary rates. The same ordinary income rule applies if you try to trade a patent, especially if you enter into an agreement to receive installment payments over many years. That will generally be treated as a royalty, subject to ordinary income tax rates.

Expansion of disallowed deductions for fines, penalties, and settlements. Fines and penalties paid to government agencies have never been deductible. This provision does not apply to private lawsuits and settlements.

Congress has allowed deductions for payments that the taxpayer establishes are either restitution (including remediation of property) or amounts required to come into compliance with any law that was violated or involved in the investigation or inquiry, that are identified in the court order or settlement agreement as restitution, remediation, or required to come into compliance.

This is effective December 22, 2017, for all new settlements.

Deductions are not allowed for sexual harassment settlements subject to a nondisclosure agreement. No deduction is allowed for any settlement, payout, or attorney fees related to sexual harassment or sexual abuse if such payments are subject to a nondisclosure agreement. This is effective for all amounts paid or incurred on or after December 22, 2017.

Depreciation and Expensing

Depreciation is a big topic with lots of moving parts.

Taking the highest deduction is not always the best in the long run for your business. There three depreciation systems—GDS (General Depreciation System), ADS (Alternative Depreciation System) and MACRS (Modified Cost Accelerated Recovery System). We will be using these acronyms as we give you an overview of the changes to the various types of depreciation that may affect your business.

Note: ADS must be used for all properties outside the United States. It is highly recommended that you work with an experienced Enrolled Agent or Certified Public Accountant if you have depreciable property. The IRS Publication 946 is over 100 pages long!

Also known as "additional first-year depreciation," bonus depreciation has increased to as high as 100 percent of the cost of the property purchased during the year.

Bonus depreciation is a huge boon to small business and has been expanded to include used property. In the past, bonus depreciation was only permitted if the property you bought was new.

Note: This is not a permanent provision. It is effective for property purchased after September 27, 2017, through 2026 (through 2027 for longer production period property and certain aircraft). There's a special transition rule to allow businesses to opt to use the 50 percent deduction instead of 100 percent for the first tax year after September 27, 2017.

All property purchased before September 27, 2017, will still use the prior bonus depreciation tables. As a result, there are two different sets of bonus depreciation rates (see chart).

Placed in Service Year	Bonus Depreciation Percentage	
	Qualified Property in General/Specified Plants	Longer Production Period Property and Certain Aircraft
Portion of Basis of Qualified Property Acquired before September 28, 2017		
Sept. 28, 2017–Dec. 31, 2017	50 percent	50 percent
2018	40 percent	50 perfect
2019	30 percent	40 percent
2020	None	30 percent
2021 and thereafter	None	None
Portion of Basis of Qualified Property Acquired after September 27, 2017		
Sept. 28, 2017–Dec. 31, 2022	100 percent	100 percent
2023	80 percent	100 percent
2024	60 percent	80 percent
2025	40 percent	60 percent
2026	20 percent	40 percent
2027	None	20 percent
2028 and thereafter	None	None

The general definition of assets that qualify remains basically the same—tangible business-use assets with a life of 20 years or less. This includes commercial software, vehicles, office equipment, warehouse equipment, and certain improvements to business buildings.

Bonus depreciation can also be used by farmers. It applies to specified plants planted or grafted after September 27, 2017.

In addition, this law expands the additional first-year depreciation to apply to film industry costs—qualified film, television, and live theatrical productions placed in service after September 27, 2017, and before January 1, 2027.

"Placed in service" means the bonus depreciation may only be claimed after the time of initial release, broadcast, or live staged performance (i.e., at the time of the first commercial exhibition, broadcast, or live staged performance of a production to an audience).

There's one little drawback to all this bonus depreciation generosity. Pre-TCJA, taxpayers could accelerate their AMT credits instead of taking bonus depreciation. (See the explanation of the repeal of the AMT.)

Luxury Car Depreciation

The annual depreciation limits for luxury cars have risen substantially. See the chart for the allowable annual limits.

	Luxury Depreciation Limits	
	TCJA	Old Law 2017
Year 1	$10,000	$3,160
Year 2	$16,000	$5,100
Year 3	$ 9,600	$3,050
Year 4 and subsequent years until fully depreciated	$ 5,760	$1,875

Cars and Depreciation

Under the previous law, approximately $15,000 was the base value used to determine the maximum annual depreciation allowance on a car.

Frankly, that has been outdated for more than a decade. You can barely even buy a subcompact for $15,000. The new depreciation numbers are based on costs closer to $40,000.

What is considered a "luxury vehicle"? Any passenger vehicle, truck, or sports utility vehicle meant to be used on public roads (i.e., not farm vehicles or forklifts), rated as having a gross weight of 6,000 pounds or less. (For the 6,000 pound vehicles, see our explanation of Section 179 depreciation.)

This provision doesn't address the depreciation for trucks or vans. Those vehicles have generally been granted an extra $400 depreciation in the first year, $600 in the second year, $300 in the third year, and $200 in all subsequent years.

However, since the limits have increased so dramatically, it's possible that Congress intended to apply the same limits to small trucks and vans.

Bottom line: Under the Trump plan, you can take an $18,000 deduction for a new car the first year you own it. If you buy an SUV or a truck for business (over 6,000 pounds), the vehicle is 100 percent deductible. In the old days, leasing was the way to go. But under the Trump plan, you are probably better off buying a new vehicle.

Depreciating Computers

Computers and peripherals are no longer listed property. Listed property has been subject to more scrutiny and bookkeeping required to claim deductions. It has been generally is defined as (1) any passenger automobile; (2) any other property used as a means of transportation; (3) any property of a type generally used for purposes of entertainment, recreation, or amusement; (4) any computer or peripheral equipment; and (5) any other property of a type specified in Treasury regulations.

Under TCJA any computers used in a home-based business where the computer was also used for non-business matters, there is no longer a need to maintain a usage log, but it's still a good idea to approximate the percentage of business use and deduct the purchase price accordingly on your tax return.

Farm Depreciation

The TCJA shortens the recovery period (depreciable life) from seven to five years for any new farm machinery or equipment (other than any grain bin, cotton ginning asset, fence, or other land improvement) used in a farming business. This does not apply to used machinery or equipment.

For property having a recover life of 3, 5, 7, and 10-years, farmers won't have to use the 150 percent declining balance. They will be able to use the higher 200 percent rates. You can see how the different types of depreciation work in early and later years in the following chart, taken from the Congress's explanation of the three depreciation methods.

Recovery Method	Year 1	Year 2	Year 3	Year 4	Year 5	Year 6	Year 7	Total
200 percent declining balance	285.71	204.08	145.77	104.12	86.77	86.77	86.77	1,000.00
150 percent declining balance	214.29	168.37	132.29	121.26	121.26	121.26	121.26	1,000.00
Straight line	142.86	142.86	142.86	142.86	142.86	142.86	142.86	1,000.00

Under the declining balance method, the depreciation rate is determined by dividing the appropriate percentage (here 150 or 200) by the appropriate recovery period. This leads to accelerated depreciation when the declining balance percentage is great than 100. The table illustrates depreciation for an asset with a cost of $1,000 and a seven-year recovery period under the 200 percent declining balance method, the 150 percent declining balance method, and the straight-line method.

Real Estate Depreciation

This is where tax planning and working with an experienced tax professional is important to determine the most strategic deduction for your business.

Most businesses use the MACRS (Modified Accelerated Cost Recovery System) for real estate. Nothing has changed if you're going to use MACRS. It's still 39 years for nonresidential real estate and 27.5 years for residential real estate.

Long-Term Rentals

A long-term rental agreement (LTRA) is defined as a rental contract that spans at least 75 percent of the recovery life of a building. The TCJA defines the recovery life applicable to LTRAs as 25 years.

Strategy tip: If you're going to enter into a long-term lease on a building, include an option to buy the building. This may protect you from having to relocate due to a huge rent increase when the lease expires.

Qualified Leaseholds

Under the old law, there were three types of qualified leasehold improvements, each with a separate definition. The TCJA eliminates the separate definitions of qualified leasehold improvement, qualified restaurant, and qualified retail improvement property, lumps them all together as "qualified leasehold improvements," and provides a general 10-year recovery period for qualified improvement property.

It no longer matters if the building in which these improvements were made is leased or owned. The general recovery period drops from 15 years to 10 years.

This is where tax planning and working with an experienced tax professional is important to determine the most strategic deduction for your business because there two other depreciation systems—ADS (Alternative Depreciation System) and MACRS (Modified Cost Accelerated Recovery System) you can use.

The recovery period used for qualified leasehold improvements is 20 years for ADS and 15 years for MACRS.

Improvements to restaurant buildings that don't meet the definition of qualified restaurant improvements will be depreciated over 25 years, using the straight-line method.

To qualify as a restaurant building, more than 50 percent of the building's square footage must be devoted to preparation of meals and seating for on-premises consumption of prepared meals.

Section 179 depreciation. Internal Revenue Code Section 179 allows businesses to deduct 100 percent of the cost of new or used equipment used in their business. Qualifying property is defined as depreciable tangible personal property that is purchased for use in the active conduct of a trade or business. Qualifying property also includes off-the-shelf computer software and qualified real property (i.e., qualified leasehold improvement property, qualified restaurant property, and qualified retail improvement property). It also includes passenger vehicles with a gross weight rating of more than 6,000 pounds and less than 14,000 pounds.

You may use Sec 179 depreciation on the furnishings in lodgings (residential rental properties). For certain improvements to a non-residential property, you may only use Sec 179 if these were added or replaced after the building was put into use: roofs; heating, ventilation, and air-conditioning property; fire protection and alarm systems; and security systems.

Sec 179 also applies to passenger vehicles with a gross weight rating of 6,000 pounds or more. The deduction for those vehicles (usually SUVs) is still limited to $25,000. However, it just might be possible to use bonus depreciation on these vehicles if you really want a bigger deduction.

But beware! Writing off all the costs up front means you have lower costs in coming years—when your income just might increase.

The annual limits on the amount you may deduct have nearly doubled—and they are adjusted for inflation. You can see what the limit was under the old law (2017) and under the TCJA (2018) in Chart 6.

You may now deduct up to $1 million worth of business property a year, as long as you don't spend more than $2.5 million on all qualifying property. If you do, your Sec 179 deduction is reduced by every dollar over the limit.

	Section 179 Depreciation Limits	
	2017	2018
Regular 179 limits	$510,000	$1,000,000
SUV limits	$25,000	$25,000
Investment phaseout begins	$2,030,000	$2,500,000

When you use the Sec 179 deduction, you must keep that business asset in active use until the recovery life of the asset expires. If not, you will have to pick up part of the Sec 179 deduction for the shortfall.

For instance, you claimed a $10,000 Sec 179 full deduction for a business-use 3D printer which had a an expected five-year life. After three years, however, you were able to get a better 3D printer with more functionality. Because you never completed the 5-year depreciation period, you have to add $4,000 back on your filings as revenue for the last two years that were not depreciated.

The AMT

The tax reform bill permanently adjusts the AMT (Alternative Minimum Tax) exemption, starting in tax year 2018.

The AMT was originally conceived of to make sure that regardless of how may deductions an individual could claim, affluent Americans would pay their fair share of taxes.

Under the previous code, high-income households had to figure out their taxes twice—once with the standard tax system and then again with the AMT. They then had to pay whichever tax calculation was higher.

Problems arose because the AMT exemptions were not indexed for inflation. As years passed, the AMT started ensnaring more and more taxpayers.

Now, the TCJA permanently adjusts the AMT exemption amounts for inflation. The exemption starts higher initially in 2018. The Single or Head of Household exemption has gone from $54,300 in 2017 to 70,300 in 2018. And Married Filing Jointly has gone from $84,500 to $109,400 in 2018. Married Filing Separately from $42,250 to $54,700 in 2018.

The new law significantly raises the income thresholds when the exemption amounts begin to phase out—at $1 million for joint filers and $500,000 for individuals.

Investments and Dividend Income

There are changes in the new tax law for C corporations that own stock in other C corporations.

In order to avoid double taxation on the dividends the corporation receives from its investments in those other corporations, there is a special "dividends received deduction" (DRD). Until now, if a corporation owned 20 percent or more of the stock of another corporation, 80 percent of the dividends it received from that corporation were deducted from income. That deduction has been reduced to 65 percent of the dividends received.

When a corporation owned less than 20 percent of the stock of another corporation, 70 percent of the dividends it received from that corporation were deducted from income. That deduction has been reduced to 50 percent of the dividends received.

This lower DRD also applies to the dividends received when a corporation invests in the stock market. For more information on DRDs, read this section of IRS Publication 542, Corporations: http://iTaxMama.com/DRD.

Accounting Rule Changes

More businesses will be able to use the cash method of accounting since the threshold allowing the use of the cash method is raised to a $25 million gross receipts test (average annual gross receipts for prior three years).

Using the cash basis means you report your income when you receive it and report expenses only when you pay them. Also eligible businesses are excused from the chore of doing inventory accounting for tax purposes.

Operating Loss Carryback

No carryback of net operating losses (NOL). You lose the two-year carryback of net operating losses, unless you're a farmer, for losses incurred after December 31, 2017. Victims of a presidentially declared disaster may still carry losses back for up to three years.

NOLs generated after December 31, 2017 must be carried forward to future years and may be carried forward indefinitely, for up to 20 years. In the year that you deduct the NOL (or any part of it), you may only deduct the NOL up to 80 percent of taxable income (without taking the NOL into account).

The same ordinary income rule applies if you try to trade a patent, especially if you enter into an agreement to receive installment payments over many years. That will generally be treated as a royalty, subject to ordinary income tax rates.

Partnership technical terminations provision is repealed. Before the TCJA, if, in any 12-month period, there was a sale or exchange of 50 percent or more of the total interest in partnership capital and profits, the partnership would be considered over—even if the business continued. This transfer of 50 percent or more might be the result of a death and inheritance, replacing a partner, getting an investor, or other reasons. This created a number of complicated tax transactions. The good news is, this provision is repealed. Now, if you don't want a partnership to end, it won't end just because some of the partnership interests changed hands.

New procedures for taxable year inclusion for accrual method businesses. There are new procedures allowing you to put off reporting certain types of advance payments until the following year, as long as you treat that income the same way on your financial statements.

You will definitely want to work with your CPA or EA on this issue. This deferral may help defer taxes on a substantial amount of income for one year. But if the company's income is essentially level each year, you will only get a benefit for the first year. For companies with growing revenues, this is a valuable benefit. You will need to file Form 3115 with your tax return.

Credit for Medical or Family Leave

This is a new credit allowing employers to get a tax credit for providing their employees with paid medical or family leave for up to 12 weeks. The credit is 12.5 percent of the employees' wages if they are being paid at least 50 percent of their usual wages. The credit can increase up to 25 percent of the employees' compensation if they are paid 100 percent of their usual wages.

The employer must have a written leave policy in place, and there are a number of other administrative conditions to take into account. For companies that already provide paid leave, this is a winner, albeit temporary—this provision is in effect from December 31, 2017, and ends on December 31, 2019.

Excess Business Losses

For tax years beginning after 2017 and before 2026, the Act provides that "excess business losses" of a taxpayer other than a C corporation are not allowed for the taxable year, but rather are carried forward and treated creating (or adding to an existing) net operating loss carry forward in subsequent taxable years.

Tax Reform—Business Provisions

An "excess business loss" is the excess of aggregate trade or business deductions over the sum of aggregate trade or business gross income plus a threshold amount. The threshold is $500,000 for joint filers and $250,000 for other taxpayers.

These are the provisions of the TCJA that will have the most impact on small to medium sized businesses. As stated before, you should seek advice from a tax professional before making any changes to your business, as this chapter has only provided a brief overview. The American economy is already showing positive signs of growth and demand for labor due to the belief that the TCJA will incentivize domestic production and companies start to bring their operations back to the United States. The following chapters will provide tax strategies and tips that will help you make the most out of the TCJA on your individual tax returns.

CHAPTER 3

Homeownership: What's the Same and What's New

DESPITE CHANGES TO THE Tax Code, it's still the American Dream to own your own home—and/or a car or two, a big-screen television, and several mobile communications devices. It's true, not everyone ends up buying a home; but those who do are still entitled to a whole raft of itemized deductions and, perhaps, even tax credits. First, let's take them in the order they appear on Schedule A. Then we'll explore the potential credits and how to snag them.

Tip #1: Real Property Taxes

Deduct the real estate taxes you pay on all your properties, unless some of those taxes are deducted elsewhere. This split deduction might happen if you use a home partially for business (Form 8829) or rent out a room or half a duplex (Schedule E). Read your property tax bill carefully because not all the charges are deductible as property taxes. For instance, your bill might include special assessments for bonds, or might include sewer fees or payments for city or county improvements. While you pay for those things along with your property taxes, they are technically not deductions. (Shhh . . . I have never seen the IRS adjust for this on audit.) Some states might have special charges that look like nondeductible assessments or fees but are deductible. For instance, California has something called Mello-Roos fees. In February 2012, the IRS ruled that these are deductible as property taxes. *Note: If you pay your taxes to your lender as part of your monthly payment, the lender will give you a year-end statement showing the taxes, property insurance, and PMI (mortgage insurance) paid on your behalf during the year.*

Tax Act change. The TCJA limits your total combined property tax, sales tax, and/or state and local income tax deduction to $10,000 for tax years 2018–2025.

Tip #2: Who Is on the Title?

In order to deduct the property taxes, you must own the property and you must be the person making the payments. Not as obvious as it seems. Sometimes people don't have enough of their own credit to buy their homes. Someone else needs to get the loan for them (like a parent, a relative, or an amazingly good friend). So their name isn't on the title—or on the loan. That means the person on the title doesn't get the property tax deduction because that person wasn't the one paying the property tax. And you don't get the deduction because you're not on the title. Is there a solution to this dilemma? Yes, there is. Stay tuned to Tip #15, when we talk about this situation.

Tip #3: Fees You Can Deduct

What are the most overlooked, but deductible, property taxes? Property taxes assessed as part of your time-share fees and as part of your community's common area fees are deductible. Some sets of fees are pretty low, but in other areas, common area fees are quite high, and you can pick up several hundred (or thousand) dollars by getting the reports from your management company.

Tip #4: Escrow

Escrow is another source of real estate taxes paid. When buying or selling real estate, read the HUD-1 summary (or escrow closing statement). You may find that you have paid taxes through the escrow by repaying the sellers for taxes they paid for part of the year. On the other hand, you might learn that they are paying you in advance for their share of the taxes due later in year. For example, many states collect taxes around April and December. The April payment covers the period from January through June. The December payment covers taxes due from July through December. So if the sale takes place in September, the buyer ends up paying the June–September property taxes as part of the December bill. In escrow, the seller makes up for that by paying the buyer for those June–September property taxes. That means the buyer reduces his or her property tax expense at the end of the year. The opposite happens if the property is sold in the first half of the year. The buyer reimburses the seller for the taxes he or she paid in the beginning of the year and gets an extra property tax deduction as a result. Here's where you find this information on the HUD 1 statement: https://portal.hud.gov/hudportal/documents/huddoc?id=1.pdf (see image).

Tax Act change. The TCJA limits your total combined property tax, sales tax, and/or state and local income tax deduction to $10,000 for tax years 2018–2025.

100. Gross Amount Due from Borrower		400. Gross Amount Due to Seller	
101. Contract sales price		401. Contract sales price	
102. Personal property		402. Personal property	
103. Settlement charges to borrower (line 1400)		403.	
104.		404.	
Adjustment for items paid by seller in advance		Adjustment for items paid by seller in advance	
106. City/town taxes to		406. City/town taxes to	
107. County taxes to		407. County taxes to	
108. Assessments to		408. Assessments to	
109.		409.	
110.		410.	
111.		411.	
112.		412.	
120. Gross Amount Due from Borrower		420. Gross Amount Due to Seller	
200. Amount Paid by or in Behalf of Borrower		500. Reductions In Amount Due to seller	
201. Deposit or earnest money		501. Excess deposit (see instructions)	
202. Principal amount of new loan(s)		502. Settlement charges to seller (line 1400)	
203. Existing loan(s) taken subject to		503. Existing loan(s) taken subject to	
204.		504. Payoff of first mortgage loan	
205.		505. Payoff of second mortgage loan	
206.		506.	
207.		507.	
208.		508.	
209.		509.	
Adjustments for items unpaid by seller		Adjustments for items unpaid by seller	
210. City/town taxes to		510. City/town taxes to	
211. County taxes to		511. County taxes to	
212. Assessments to		512. Assessments to	

Tip #5: Personal Property Fees

Personal property taxes. Typically, these are the annual fees you pay to your state's department of motor vehicles (DMV) based on the value of your auto, boat, ATV, Jet Ski–type things, motorcycles, snowmobiles, and other such toys and vehicles. If the fee is not based on value but is simply a processing fee, the cost is not deductible. Often your license fee includes such base fees or special fees for vanity plates. Those costs are not deductible either. Incidentally, in the many decades that I have been preparing tax returns, this is one of the most often overlooked deductions. For some folks, it may not be much. But for others, when you look at all the vehicles . . . it adds up. Especially since motor home and RV licenses can be deducted on this line (line 7 of Schedule A). Incidentally, if you are leasing the car, the annual DMV fee may be included in the monthly lease payment. Remember to pick that up as a deduction, if you're not writing the lease fee off as a business expense. *Note: If you use the car for business, only report the personal use percentage of these taxes. For instance, if you* *use the car 80 percent for business and the tax is $75, only report $15 on Schedule A.*

Tax Act change. The TCJA limits your total combined property tax, sales tax, and/or state and local income tax deduction to $10,000 for tax years 2018–2025.

Tip #6: Sales Taxes

Sales tax strategy. Although sales taxes aren't around-the-house-type taxes, let's talk about them anyway—especially since we buy things for the home and pay sales taxes. There's a strategy to use with these deductions. If at all possible, deduct your sales taxes instead of your state income taxes. Why? There are several reasons:

- When you deduct your sales taxes, you don't have to report your state income tax refund as income on the following year's tax return.

- You don't have to track all the sales taxes you paid. Just use the IRS's Sales Tax Calculator: https://www.irs.gov/Individuals/Sales-Tax-Deduction-Calculator.

- Your tax software might even have the information for your state—just add in the extra sales tax percentage your county or parish charges.

- In addition to the sales tax tables, where the tax is based on your AGI, you can add the sales taxes paid on big-ticket items like cars, boats, RVs, expensive electronics, Rolex watches, and so on.

- Some states don't even have income taxes, so sales taxes are your only option. And then there are those states that have no sales taxes either—Delaware, Montana, New Hampshire, and Oregon. Surprised not to see Alaska on the list? That's because there are some areas of Alaska where there are local taxes. You can find the list of all the state sales tax information at the Tax Foundation: http://iTaxMama.com/State_SalesTax.

Note: The sales tax deduction is one of those tax provisions that have been expiring every year. **Although this became a permanent part of the Internal Revenue Code as Section 106 of the PATH Act of 2015, the law has been changed again. Tax Act change: The TCJA limits your total, combined property tax, sales tax, and/or state and local income tax deduction to $10,000 for tax years 2018–2025.**

Tip #7: State Income Taxes

If your state income taxes are much higher than the sales taxes you paid, use this deduction. When you end up getting a refund on your state tax return, after itemizing the taxes on Schedule A, you will need to report all or part of your state refund as income. Why only part of it? Well, if you didn't get any benefit from the state income tax deduction, you don't need to pay taxes on the refund either. There are detailed instructions for line 10 of Form 1040. Generally your software will do this computation for you if you give it enough information about last year's tax return.

Tax Act change. The TCJA limits your total combined property tax, sales tax, and/or state and local income tax deduction to $10,000 for tax years 2018–2025.

Tip #8: When Your State Refund Is Not Taxable

Good news: If you did not itemize in the year for which you received your refund, the state refund is not taxable. For instance, let's say you filed several years' tax returns in 2017—you filed 2013, 2014, and 2015. Suppose you didn't itemize in 2013 and 2014, but your state refund is $10,000. None of that refund is taxable. But let's pretend that you itemized in 2015 and got the full benefit of your state income tax deduction. In that case, the $5,000 refund you received for 2015 is income to you in 2016 even though you may have a received a total of $15,000 in state refunds during 2016.

Tip #9: Overlooked State Tax Deductions

Here are three commonly overlooked state tax deduction opportunities:

- If you were making state estimated tax payments, remember the January payment for the fourth quarter. Even though the payment you made in the tax year you are filing was for last year, you get to deduct it. Why? You paid it in the current tax year.

- Did you have a state overpayment on your tax return that you applied toward the following year's taxes? That's considered a payment you made in the current year. For instance, you applied your 2016 state tax refund to your 2017 state taxes. That payment is considered made in 2017.

- Did you pay a balance due to the state when you filed your tax return? Remember to add that to your total state taxes paid. For instance, you paid your state $532 when you filed your 2016 income tax return in April of 2017. That payment is made in 2017. Oh, and do remember to add it to your total estimated payments for 2017. A lot of people forget to include that.

Tax Act change. The TCJA limits your total combined property tax, sales tax, and/or state and local income tax deduction to $10,000 for tax years 2018–2025.

Tip #10: Tribal/Foreign Tax Deductions

Here are two more "state" tax deductions that many people don't know about:

- Taxes imposed by Indian tribal governments are deductible, including income taxes, real estate taxes, and personal property taxed imposed by the tribal government.

- Foreign income taxes paid are deductible. You may have paid them as deductions from dividends, from your pension, or from the foreign equivalent of Social Security income. Be sure to convert the foreign currency to US dollars. You can look up the IRS's approved currency conversion rates on its website here: https://www.irs.gov/Individuals/International-Taxpayers/Yearly-Average-Currency-Exchange-Rates. Or you can use the Oanda site to get values on specific days or averages for a year or so: http://www.oanda.com/currency/.

  › Incidentally, you have a choice about those foreign taxes. You may take them as a deduction here on Schedule A, or you may choose to take them as a tax credit using Form 1116, Foreign Tax Credit. When your total foreign tax credit for the year is $300 or less ($600 when married filing jointly), you can skip Form 1116 and just deduct your credit directly on page 2 of Form 1040.

  › What if you are not reporting your foreign income at all because you are working overseas? If you have the privilege of using Form 2555, the Foreign Earned Income Exclusion, then you don't need to worry about losing the cost of foreign taxes you have paid as either a deduction or a credit. After all, if you don't pay taxes in the United States, you don't get any US tax benefits.

Tax Act change. The TCJA limits your total combined property tax, sales tax, and/or state and local income tax deduction to $10,000 for tax years 2018–2025.

Tip #11: Making the Most of Deduction Limits

Here is a strategy for getting the most out of the $10,000 limit on deductions for taxes. While the TCJA established a temporary ceiling on the itemized deductions for taxes, there is no limit to taxes deducted for business purposes. This is the time to look at the viability of picking up an office-in-home deduction, if you work or run a business from home. You could consider renting out a room or two and deducting part of your property taxes on Schedule E. Of course, you could double this $10,000 deduction by getting divorced. Naturally, this deduction isn't worth your marriage. But when we get to the mortgage interest deduction (next tips), some people with million-dollar homes might start thinking about divorce.

Tip #12: Mortgage Interest

Mortgage interest deduction is limited in several ways.

- You may only deduct the interest on acquisition debt—the amount of the mortgage you took out when you bought the house. Plus any mortgage you took out to pay for major repairs or remodeling.

- **As a result of the new Tax Act, you may no longer deduct the mortgage on up to another $100,000 of a home equity line of credit (HELOC).**

- Often, when the value of the home increases dramatically or interest rates plunge, people refinance. **Under the new Tax Act, when you refinance, your mortgage interest deduction is limited to the interest on the balance of the loan at the time of the refinancing.** For instance, your original loan was for $200,000 five years ago, and today the loan balance is $175,000. The house is now worth $400,000. You get a new 80 percent loan for $320,000 and include the points and refinance fees in the new loan, taking the balance to $325,000. Since the interest rates are lower, your payments don't go up very much—but you're able to pull out $145,000 in cash. Suppose this is the only loan on the house. You may deduct the interest on only the $175,000 balance left on the original loan—period. What happens to the interest on the other $150,000 ($325,000 loan less the deductible mortgage value of $175,000)? Nothing. No deduction. No carryforward. Nothing. So please take this into account when refinancing. If you are ever audited, the IRS will catch this error and may go back for up to three years to recover taxes due.

- **Under the new Tax Act, $750,000 is the limit on the total amount of mortgages on which you may deduct interest ($375,000 for couples filing separately).**

- The new Tax Act limits the total amount of mortgage balance on which you may deduct interest to $1 million—**but only if you already owned your home and had a mortgage in place before December 15, 2017. That's good news for people who already have mortgages in place This limit is only up to two homes.**

- Yet another limit: Unlike real property taxes, where you may deduct the property taxes on all your properties, **you are only entitled to deduct the interest on up to two homes.** So people who have multiple homes must pick the **two homes** producing the highest interest deduction for the year. But you may switch your choices each year. A good strategy is to use the homes with the highest interest rate or highest total interest expense.

- One more limit has been suspended until 2025—the Alternative Minimum Tax (AMT). **It no longer matters due to the new Tax Act. Since we can no longer deduct the interest on home equity loans, there is no AMT effect on the mortgage interest.**

- Can you get around these deduction limits by moving some of the interest to your office in home (Form 8829) or to the rental form (Schedule E) when you rent out space in your home? No. **No matter where you try to move that interest on your personal residence(s), you are still limited to the acquisition debt or to the $750,000 ($1 million if you have a grandfathered loan) total loan balance.**

- To top it all off, if you managed to get a loan with a really good interest rate, like 4 percent or less—a married couple might not have enough interest expense to allow you to itemize in the first place. **Especially with the new, higher standard deduction for a couple of $24,000.** (Average US mortgage debt is around $156,000 [https://www.nerdwallet.com/blog/credit-card-data/average-credit-card-debt-household/] × 4 percent = $6,240. Add in about $2,000 in property taxes, and your potential itemized deduction is under $10,000, including state taxes. As I mentioned, the new standard deduction for a couple filing jointly is $24,000.)

Tip #13: Refinancing

Good news—here's how you can increase the deduction for mortgage interest after you refinance. Suppose you realized that you had $200,000 in equity that you could pull out of your mortgage. This is a great way to get your hands on some cash without having to pay tax on the earnings. You decided that you can use that money as a down payment on a rental property. There is a special provision (http://iTaxMama.com/MtgIntDebt_Election) that lets you choose to treat that loan not as being secured by your home, but as a loan on the new rental property (deduct the loan on Schedule E). Or you can use that money to invest in your business (deduct the loan on Schedule C or on your business tax return). In any case, the money from the loan must go directly to the business account or property purchase escrow or seller. Try to make sure these funds never hit your personal bank account at all. If the funds must get deposited into your bank account first, consider opening a separate account that you only use for that property or business and deposit this money there. Under no circumstances should these funds get mixed in with your personal funds. Otherwise the IRS does something called tracing. It traces each check or debit that cleared after the deposit and treats that deposit as being spent on those things (like the dry cleaner, groceries, credit cards, etc.) instead of on your investment. You might want to consider sitting down with a tax professional who is experienced with this area of taxation to work out the details. And consider writing loan documents between yourself and your business or yourself and the rental property to make sure the transaction is kosher. A good real estate attorney can be worth the investment of a consulting fee to ensure you are able to claim these interest deductions in full.

Tip #14: Time-Share Interest

Often overlooked mortgage interest is the interest on your time-shares. Since most people do not own two homes, they are not subject to all that nonsense we talked about before. But while you may not own an actual vacation home, you may own a time-share. Those loans tend to run about 10 or 20 years. That is considered a second home. You're entitled to deduct the interest on it.

Tip #15: Equitable Owner

The mortgage is not in your name. We started talking about this in Tip #2. You didn't have enough credit to get the loan, so your parents are named on the loan and on the title. Technically you are not allowed to deduct the mortgage interest or property taxes since you don't own the house on paper. You probably get a notice from the IRS each year saying that it doesn't have a Form 1098 reporting any mortgage interest in your name, and you have to duke it out in the mail, year after year. But this is such a common phenomenon these days that there is a solution. (Tax professionals struggle with this problem. Many don't know this definitive solution. They know there should be one, but don't know what the solution is. Now you will know!)

- You are what is called an equitable owner, or beneficial owner. When you respond to the IRS, say that you are the beneficial owner under Treasury Regulation §1.163-1(b) (https://www.law .cornell.edu/cfr/text/26/1.163-1) and the owner on the title will not be taking the deduction. (Feel free to read the regulation.)

- It might not be a bad idea to also get some paperwork drawn up. Have an attorney draw up a contract between you and the owner on the title, spelling out that you are the actual owner and that the person just helped you out for credit purposes.

- Have a deed prepared showing the title in your name. Better yet, have your name added to the title with the named owner. (It's not wise for the person who is responsible for the loan to be removed from the title. After all, if you default on the payments, it's his or her credit on the line. Without being on the title, the person won't be able to get control of the house and won't be notified if you default on the loan.)

- If you ever face a tax battle, there's a really good article about this topic in the *Journal of Accountancy* based on Tax Court cases that were won (http://www.journalofaccountancy.com/issues/2008/ oct/equitableownerequalsdeduction.htm).

Interest You Paid	10	Home mortgage interest and points reported to you on Form 1098	10
	11	Home mortgage interest not reported to you on Form 1098. If paid to the person from whom you bought the home, see instructions and show that person's name, identifying no., and address ▶	
Note. Your mortgage interest deduction may be limited (see instructions).		--	
		--	11
	12	Points not reported to you on Form 1098. See instructions for special rules	12

Tip #16: Interest to Private Lenders

Mortgage interest paid to private lenders. Generally, when you pay a bank or financial institution, it sends you Form 1098 at the end of the year showing how much you paid in interest. It might also include your property taxes, PMI, and insurance payment information. The IRS gets a copy of that and matches it to your tax return. But when you pay a private lender, that person doesn't generally send you Form 1098. And most individuals do not think of sending the private lender Form 1099-INT to tell the IRS how much interest you are paying to that person. Instead, there is line 11 on Schedule A. That's where you give the name, address, and Social Security number (SSN) or other Taxpayer Identification Number (TIN) to the IRS. If you don't have that information, send the lender Form W-9 to request it (https://www.irs.gov/pub/irs-pdf/fw9.pdf). If you think the lender will resist providing you with that information, send it certified, with return receipt requested, so you can prove that you tried to get it. Then enter all the information you do have with "REFUSED" as the SSN or TIN. *Note: You don't mail the completed W-9 to the IRS. You just keep it in your records for as long as you pay that lender plus four years.*

Tip #17: Unpaid Interest

Unpaid interest. Some loans start out with the buyer's monthly payments being less than the amount of monthly principal and interest. Those are called negatively amortizing loans. While you get a lower payment in the beginning, the unpaid interest gets added to the loan balance. Your year-end mortgage statement will show the total amount of interest generated on the loan and the amount that you actually paid. You may only deduct the interest you pay. The unpaid portion will only be deductible when you pay it, perhaps several years later.

Tip #18: Reverse Mortgages

Reverse mortgages. A reverse mortgage is a loan where the lender pays you (in a lump sum, a monthly advance, a line of credit, or a combination of all three) while you continue to live in your home. You don't have any mortgage payments. What a relief. With a reverse mortgage, you retain title to your home. Depending on the plan, your reverse mortgage becomes due, with interest, when you move, sell your home, reach the end of a preselected loan period, or die. Because reverse mortgages are considered loan advances and not income, the amount you receive is not taxable. Any interest (including original issue discount) accrued on a reverse mortgage is not deductible until you actually pay it, which is usually when you pay off the loan in full. **However, since the loan keeps increasing the longer you live in the home, most of the interest will not qualify as acquisition debt at all. So neither you (if you move out while alive) nor your heirs are likely to benefit from this interest deduction.**

Tip #19: Reverse Mortgage Warning

Reverse mortgage warning. While you might be relieved not to have to pay a monthly mortgage payment anymore, beware, and read everything carefully. Anything you don't understand, have the lender explain, slowly, until you do understand. The interest on the reverse mortgage is generally higher than interest you would normally pay on a regular mortgage. There are a lot of fees that get added to your loan balance. You cannot get any additional cash out of the home if you need it in an emergency. Your reverse mortgage lender controls your equity. If you are married, or have someone you care about (like your child or a friend) living in the home, make sure that person is on the title before getting the reverse mortgage. Otherwise, if you are forced to move out into a convalescent facility or senior home, the person may be kicked out of the house. The lender will demand payment or force the sale of the home when the "owner of record" no longer lives there. So if the person is on the title before the loan is issued, he or she will be protected. But . . . watch out for potential gift and estate tax issues if you add someone to the title. It would be a good idea to discuss the details about, and alternatives to, reverse mortgages with a tax professional and/or tax attorney.

New warning: Someone contacted TaxMama about her reverse mortgage problem. BB and her husband needed a reverse when he retired. The mortgage broker, at the last minute, insisted that she sign documents removing her from the title. She didn't understand why, but signed, under pressure. Her husband died a few years later—and she is facing eviction. Ultimately, she won't have to leave. But the fight to keep her home spans more than a year of frustrating battles with attorneys and bureaucrats—and a fortune in legal fees. The warning? Do *not* allow anyone to remove you or your spouse or your caretaker from the title to get that reverse mortgage. (If people try, report them to your state authorities.)

Tip #20: Personal Residence Points

Personal residence points. These are the extra fees you typically pay when you get a mortgage. When you buy the home, they are fully deductible. Incidentally, if the points are added to your mortgage and you do not actually pay them, there is no deduction. What if the seller pays your points to help you buy the house? Do you get a deduction? No again. If you don't spend, you don't deduct. If you did pay the points, how can you prove that you paid them? Deposit a check for the amount of the points into escrow, or pay it directly to the lender or loan broker. Otherwise . . . there is no deduction at all. Incidentally, if the points are not reported to you on Form 1098 from your lender, read the instructions to Schedule A and enter those points on line 12 instead of including them on line 10.

The TCJA doesn't mention points at all. So check with your tax professional to see if the IRS has issued any guidance before

deducting points on qualifying loans. Or visit TaxMama.com and click on Ask a Tax Question if you incur points on a new loan.

Tip #21: Refinance Points

Refinance points. When you refinance that first mortgage, you must deduct the cost over the life of the mortgage. That is called amortization. If the mortgage is for 30 years, the points are deducted over 360 months. Let's say you refinanced in the beginning of September. That first year, you will deduct 4/360th of the points (September to December = 4 months). From then on, you will deduct 12/360th until the last year when you deduct whatever is left over.

The **TCJA doesn't mention points at all. So check with your tax professional to see if the IRS has issued any guidance before deducting points on qualifying loans.** Or visit TaxMama.com and click on Ask a Tax Question if you incur points on a new loan.

Tip #22: New Points

Refinanced again points. You have already refinanced once, right? You paid $3,000 and have been able to deduct about $250 so far. But you found a better interest rate (or your credit improved) and you can refinance again. OK, you will amortize the new points as we have described. But what do you do about the old points? You still have $2,750 that hasn't been deducted, right? Great news! You may deduct that entire balance, since that loan has been paid off.

The TCJA doesn't mention points at all. So check with your tax professional to see if the IRS has issued any guidance before deducting points on qualifying loans. Or visit TaxMama.com and click on Ask a Tax Question if you incur points on a new loan.

Tip #23: Whose Points?

Someone else's points. Sometimes we use incentives to sell our properties. For instance, to close a sale, you offer to pay the buyers' closing costs, including their points. Is that a deduction to you, as the seller? Nope. That is part of the selling price. You add this to your selling costs, and it reduces your overall profit on the sale. So you think this comes out the same in the end? Think again. If the profit on your home is under $250,000 (or $500,000 when you file jointly), you won't be paying taxes anyway. So this doesn't matter. And you didn't get the deduction for the points, since it wasn't your loan obligation. But at least you finally got to sell the home and stop paying for that mortgage.

The TCJA doesn't mention points at all. So check with your tax professional to see if the IRS has issued any guidance before deducting points on qualifying loans. Or visit TaxMama.com and click on Ask a Tax Question if you incur points on a new loan.

Tip #24: PMI

Private mortgage insurance (PMI) (http://iTaxMama.com/IRS_PMI). This is insurance that you must pay for if your down payment is too low. It's designed to protect the lenders in case you default. This expense became an allowable deduction sometime around 2007 (https://www.law.cornell.edu/uscode/text/26/163#.Vh_JqivSmSY). However, this is one of those political footballs (like the huge $250 deduction for educators' costs). Each year, Congress needs to reconsider this deduction and extend it—or not. At the time of this writing, the PMI deduction was only valid through December 31, 2016. There is a Tax Extender Bill pending in Congress. That includes restoring this deduction through December 31, 2018.

What's the fuss all about? After all, when your AGI is higher than $100,000 ($50,000 if married filing separately), your deduction phases out. So why can't Congress make this permanent? Write to your legislators and ask them (http://taxmama.com/special-reports/call-to-action). Meanwhile, before claiming this deduction, please Google the deductibility of PMI each year. That said, just how much is deductible?

- You may deduct the premiums you paid in the current year for the current year. In other words, if you paid a large lump sum in advance that covers several years, you may only deduct the premium for the current year.

- You may only deduct PMI on acquisition debt—that is, loans used to buy, build, or improve a home. You may not deduct it when you refinance.

- For veterans who get loans from the Department of Veterans Affairs, it is commonly known as a funding fee. If it is provided by the Rural Housing Service, it is commonly known as a guarantee fee. Regardless of what it's called, it follows all the same rules as private mortgage insurance.

Tip #25: No More PMI

Make your PMI payment go away! Whether you can deduct this cost or not, as soon as you can, make this financial drain disappear. When your mortgage balance is 80 percent or less than the value of your home, you can make a written request to your lender to cancel the PMI premiums. How can the mortgage balance get that low? Several ways:

- Market conditions have improved since you bought the house. If you think they have improved enough, get a formal, written appraisal to prove it. Submit that to your lender.

- You have paid down the principal balance. You can do this by paying a little more than the regular principal payment on your mortgage. For instance, consider adding $50 or $100 per month to your payment. This will bring the principal down slowly. If you can afford a few hundred dollars per month, that will help.

- You have made a lump sum payment on the mortgage to bring it down to below 80 percent of the fair market value of the home.

Combine that with the appraisal showing the increase in value, and you may be able to save yourself $50 a month or more.

Tip #26: Avoid PMI

Avoid PMI altogether. Don't try to handle your own mortgage application when buying a home. Find a solid, reputable loan broker to help you. Not only can loan brokers help you get the best interest rates possible; they can help you avoid paying the PMI in the first place. How? You are only required to pay the PMI if your mortgage loan is for more than 80 percent of the purchase price. A good loan broker can help you get a first mortgage for 80 percent of your purchase price and second mortgage for the rest of the loan. That way you aren't faced with any PMI costs at all. Naturally, it's a good idea to pay something down. People who didn't pay anything down ended up losing their homes when the mortgage industry collapsed. But by getting the first and second mortgages, if you can avoid the extra $50 to $100 (or more) premium per month, you can use that money to pay your mortgage loan more quickly.

We have covered a wealth of details about taxes, interest, and insurance and learned a variety of special tips to help you address common problems. Let's move on to tax credits we can find around the house.

CHAPTER 4

Tax Credits
Around the House

A SIDE FROM BEING A great place to live, your home can provide you with a wealth of credits if you know how to go after them. The credits can come from a variety of sources, not just from the IRS.

Tip #27: Beyond the IRS

Look beyond the IRS for tax credits and rebates. Great places to look are your state, your city, your utility, and even your various appliance manufacturers. You may get access to rebates and refunds in addition to tax credits. Let's start with the simplest kind of credit.

Tip #28: State Credits

State renter's or homeowner's credits. Some states provide some kind of credit to low-income renters and/or seniors, since their rent covers a portion of the landlord's property taxes. For instance, California offers renters $60 (single or married filing separately) or $120 (all other statuses) (https://www.ftb.ca.gov/individuals/faq/ivr/203 .shtml). Pennsylvania offers a property tax/rent rebate program worth up to $650 depending on your income, age, and disability level (http://www.revenue.pa.gov/generaltaxinformation/propertytax rentrebateprogram/pages/default.aspx#.WNwMXhPn99A). To find out if your state offers anything similar, just Google "[*state name*] property tax credits," "[*state name*] renter credit," and "[*state name*] renter rebate." One of those searches should get you what you want. Of course, you can always go directly to your state's website to search that. Go to http://www.taxadmin.org/state-tax-agencies, and look up state tax forms here: http://www.taxadmin.org/state-tax-forms.

Tip #29: Think Local

Before we look at what the IRS offers you, it's important for you to find the benefits that your state, city, or utilities can provide. They can provide rebates, tax credits, or special financing. The https:// energy.gov/ site is maintained by the US Secretary of Energy and his or her staff. You can look up available benefits by selecting your state. Using this as a starting point, you can see what cost reductions you have available to you before getting to the IRS tax credits. Bear in mind you need to reduce the costs you report on any IRS or state forms by any benefits you get from these sources. In other words, if something costs you $5,000 and your utility gives you a rebate of $2,000, you will only report a cost of $3,000 to the IRS. You don't generally have to pick up the rebates as income, since you are reducing the cost of repair or improvements. Read your state's rules to find out how your state wants such rebates reported on its forms.

Tip #30: Alternative Energy

Depending on your location or your income level, you might qualify for local or federal subsidy programs that will give you

grant money or low-interest loans to help pay for your alternative energy devices. The previous administration made renewable energy a major goal, so there was money flowing to communities. In particular, seek out federal funding from the PACE (property-assessed clean energy) program as long as the program lasts (https://energy.gov/eere/slsc/property-assessed-clean-energy-programs). One of the interesting things about this is that the repayment for the loan becomes part of your property tax rather than a mortgage lien on your property. The two benefits to this are that the loan balance doesn't affect your FICO score, and when you sell the house, the buyer continues to make the payment. So you get more cash out when you sell. You don't have to pay off the loan. Be sure to disclose this to all potential buyers.

The budget proposed by President Trump slashes funds for renewable energy resources by 50 percent. Much of that is in funds provided to state programs.

Tip #31: Nonbusiness Energy Property Credit

The Nonbusiness Energy Property Credit, Form 5695, Part II (https://www.irs.gov/pub/irs-pdf/f5695.pdf). I've seen people work themselves into a frenzy to nab this credit. This is for adding insulation to your home or replacing windows, doors, or roof components designed to reduce heat loss or gain. While doing those things might reduce your utility bill or improve the appearance of your home, the IRS tax credit for it is minimal. The entire lifetime credit amount is limited to $500 for all these improvements. (I have seen new windows costing more than $5,000.) By "lifetime," Congress means that once you have used all $500 of this credit, you may never get it again. If you are only making these improvements to get the tax benefits, think again. But do look to see if your state or utility offers any rebates.

Note: This is another of those credits that expire. This was extended through December 31, 2016. There is a Tax Extender Bill pending in Congress. That includes restoring this credit through December 31, 2018.

Tip #32: Residential Energy Property Credit

The **Residential Energy Property Credit, Form 5695, Part I**
(https://www.irs.gov/pub/irs-pdf/f5695.pdf). This is the credit worth
snagging. This gives you back 30 percent of your entire expenditure
on installations of solar, geothermal, or wind energy power units and
power cells. As we write this, this IRC Section 25D (https://www.
law.cornell.edu/uscode/text/26/25D) credit is good for all installations paid through December 31, 2016. Naturally, the devices must
meet the specifications for allowable units (https://www.energystar.
gov/about/federal_tax_credits). Make sure you have all the receipts
and paperwork from the contractor, including written verification
that the devices meet the standards for this credit. Allowable costs
include "any labor costs properly allocable to the onsite preparation,
assembly, or original installation of the residential energy efficient
property and for piping or wiring to interconnect such property to
the home" (quoted from the instructions—that's why the wording is
so stilted). Incidentally, this credit is only good on your main home
or second home (like a vacation cabin), not rental property.

*Note: This is another of those credits that expire. Presently, the credit is
valid through December 31, 2021.*

Tip #33: Labor Costs?

**If you or a close family member is capable of doing installation
of practically anything, you will undoubtedly save a lot of money.**
(But if you are not, please be realistic and hire a professional.) Be
aware, though, that the value of your labor for the installation work
does not count as an installation cost. However, all the parts, supplies, and expendable tools you buy specifically for this project may
be taken into account. But don't include the tools you buy that you
will be able to use in the future. If you hire casual (unlicensed) help,
you can't add those costs to the installation either.

By hiring professionals, you will save a lot of time and money getting the installation and setup done correctly. Besides, they are also familiar with the paperwork and can answer many of your questions. They can probably help you fill out the paperwork or give you forms that are already filled in. They might even be able to get you discounts on the materials and supplies.

As a result of the new Tax Act, the federal tax credit may not even exist—but the state credit might!

Tip #34: Energy Star

Most of the allowable units will have the Energy Star certification. But not all Energy Star units will qualify for the credit. The Energy Star website will help you find acceptable products, credits, and perhaps even local builders: https://www.energystar.gov.

Tip #35: Energy Reality Check

Let's do a reality check. Why do you want to install this alternative energy system in your home? Do you live off the grid or far from the nearest town? Do you live in an area where there are frequent power outages? Are your electricity bills outrageously high due to the constant need for air conditioning in the summer and heating in the winter? Then this probably makes sense. Are you a Green advocate and want to make a statement? Alternative energy is a great goal, but you may want to to think twice before you make this major expenditure for the wrong reasons. Although you might get excellent tax benefits, you will still be out of pocket for several thousand dollars. So please do a financial analysis of this decision. For instance, many of the components only last for about 10 years, then need to be replaced. So when doing your financial analysis, it's important to factor in the expected life of each part of your system and the costs to replace the parts, as well as the costs for routine maintenance of the system.

Tip #36: Residential Energy Credit

Good news and bad news about this Residential Energy Credit.
First the bad news—two facts:

1. When using this credit, you must reduce the basis (tax cost) of your home.
2. This is a nonrefundable credit. So if your tax liability is not high enough to use all or part of the credit, you don't get any money back at all. So you might have seriously underestimated the cost. Someone just wrote to TaxMama about this very issue. The solar panel salesman promised him a tax credit of $8,500. But John's total tax liability is only $408. You can read about the reality of the credits here: http://taxmama .invisionzone.com/topic/8208-solar-panels-credit-vs-refund/.

The good news? While the credit is not refundable, it can be carried over to the following tax year. (One year only.) Make sure you have enough income and tax liability to use up the credit. If you don't expect to have enough income, this is a good time to get an extra job; start a quick, profitable hobby; collect a bonus; sell some securities or assets at a profit; or roll over retirement or IRA funds to a Roth IRA. Do some tax planning to see how the numbers balance before doing anything. And please take this into account when doing your computations.

Tip #37: Cost Analysis

Here's a proposed cost analysis form for you to consider using—whether you can get tax credits or not:

Step A
Add all the following amounts:

1. System cost, including all components: _____

2. Permits from city, county, or local authority: _____

3. Installation costs: _____

4. Depending on the length of time to finish the installation, how much will it cost and what will it cost if you need to spend any nights in a hotel or with family or friends. *Note: Staying with family or friends is never free. Factor in costs of gifts, chipping in on groceries, and getting on each other's nerves, and remember that you will have to repay the favor at a time most inconvenient for you.* _____

5. Cost of routine maintenance and how often this must be done. (Remember, the panels need to be cleaned regularly or they lose their efficacy.) _____

6. Monthly costs (add them in × 12): _____

7. Cost of major repairs or parts replacement and how often parts need to be replaced (divide the costs by the number of years in the life of the parts): _____

8. How long you are planning to live in this house. If less than the life of the parts, divide your costs by the number of years you plan to be there to use the system. _____

9. The cost of financing. How much interest will you pay for the loan you take out to install all this? Divide the total interest you will pay over the life of the loan by the number of years the loan will run. That will give you an average annual interest cost.

10. Anything else that crops up (add as many lines as you need).

_____

TOTAL STEP A _____

Step B
Add all the following amounts (if applicable). These are good things:

1. Rebates from your vendors or manufacturers: _____

2. Rebates from your utility companies: _____

3. Rebates from local government units: _____

4. Rebates or credits from your state: _____

5. Any other rebates or credits you get that reduce your cost:

   _____

6. Amount you expect to earn each year if your utility company wishes to buy your excess power to use in its grid. (Reduce whatever the system sales folks tell you by at least 50–70 percent.) _____

7. Any other goodies that come your way (use as many lines as you need): _____

TOTAL STEP B _____

Step C
Deduct the total rebates and discounts you received in **Step B** from your **Step A** costs. This will be the net cost you can use to determine your IRS energy credit. _____

Step D
Deduct your federal (IRS) energy credit (30 percent × **Step C**) from the net costs you arrive at in **Step C**.

This will give you your net cost for the use and installation of your new energy system after all rebates and credits. Divide this by the number of years your system is expected to last, before you have to replace most of it. _____

That's your annual cost.

Step E

Add up the utility bills that you realistically expect the system to replace. Review your utility bills carefully to see what it really covers. For instance, an alternative energy unit will not reduce your cost of trash pickup, use of the sewage system, water usage, or certain other costs that may be buried in your water and power bill. It is likely to reduce the cost of gas and/or propane and the need to pay for deliveries. (Did you know there were this many things you pay for in that single utility bill?) Once you determine how much you really *will* save by installing this system, compare it with the annual cost you arrived at in **Step D**.

Are you going to save any significant dollars? If it turns out that the installation will end up costing you more than you will save, you have to decide if you want to do it anyway for ecological, emotional, or other reasons. But at least you will make the decision with your eyes open. *Note: In most cases, we learned the costs were higher than the benefits.*

Step F

One last consideration to take into account if this is a financial loser. Will adding this system increase the market value of the home when you ultimately decide to sell it? If so, by how much? Alternatively, how much will it reduce the sales price of your home if the system looks ratty and shabby by the time you're ready to sell?

Tip #38: Lease or Buy?

What about leasing these systems instead of buying them? That could be a great alternative. There are lower paperwork demands, the leasing company handles the maintenance, and you just sit back and enjoy the reduced utility bills, right? You generally have to pay for the privilege. Expect to pay about $3,000 or so for the company to set it up (even if the company says it's free). You will not get any tax credits. The leasing company will keep them all. If this is installed on a rental property, you will not be depreciating the cost of the unit(s) because you didn't pay for it. Ask questions. If your house or property generates excess power and sends it to the grid, who gets the money—you or the solar company? If you will start paying the solar company for your utilities instead of the local utility company, what protection do you have against price increases? Read all contracts very carefully so you understand all your obligations. If you don't understand some clause—ask. Do not let salespeople bully you or charm you away from answers. The contract will generally run for 10 to 20 years. You need to make sure it is transferable to a new owner and disclose the terms to any potential buyer. Make sure you are not hampered from selling the home because of this. Find out if the company will put a lien on your home, and if so, for how long? You don't want this affecting your credit. What are your obligations to maintain the roof and other adjacent parts of your home or property? For instance, if there is a tree overhanging the roof, how often do you have to trim it back (or will the leasing company do it)? What costs or penalties will you face if your tree damages the solar panels? Will your homeowner's insurance cover this, and how much extra will it cost? Will the solar company carry insurance? What are the company's obligations if its installers are careless or sloppy and create roof leaks or other damage to your home? If the installers open up part of the roof or wall, or cut into your patio or yard, do they pay to close it up or to fix, repaint, or replant? And what if they go out of business, go bankrupt, or sell the company? Who owns your system then? Who takes care of it? So if you are considering the leasing option, be sure the company is financially solid and not planning to go public or sell the business while you live in the house (if possible).

Tip #39: Appliances

Energy credits are not limited to alternative power systems. You can also get credit for installing Energy Star appliances (https://www.energystar.gov/products). While these credits don't come from the IRS, you can probably get them from your city, utility, or state. Generally, the stores selling these appliances can tell you all about the rebates in your area. After all, that's a powerful sales incentive. The rebates can be minor or substantial. In addition, some states have sales tax holidays that allow you to buy these appliances without paying sales taxes on certain days of the year. You can look up your state in advance so you can schedule your purchase to take advantage of that extra discount (http://www.salestaxinstitute.com/resources/sales-tax-holidays). Be careful to identify specifically what you're buying and that it qualifies for the Energy Star rebate. And verify that the qualified model and unit numbers you bought are on the paperwork with the delivered machines.

Tip #40: Disabled Access Credit

Disabled access credit. This might not necessarily be a residential credit. But . . . when you run a business from home, it just might be. The credit can be as high as $5,000 (50 percent of up to $10,000 of eligible expenses). Use Form 8826 (https://www.irs.gov/pub/irs-pdf/f8826.pdf). It applies to businesses with gross receipts of less than $1 million that employed no more than 30 full-time people in the past year. Most home-based businesses are likely to qualify. The expenditure can be for the purpose of removing barriers to accommodate employees, customers, clients, or the business owner. Naturally, expenditures in areas that are not used for business cannot be taken into account for this tax credit. Aside from the construction costs, here are some expenses that might surprise you (from IRC 44):

> The term "eligible access expenditures" includes amounts paid or incurred—
>
> (A) for the purpose of removing architectural, communication, physical, or transportation barriers which prevent a business from being accessible to, or usable by, individuals with disabilities,

(B) to provide qualified interpreters or other effective methods of making aurally delivered materials available to individuals with hearing impairments,

(C) to provide qualified readers, taped texts, and other effective methods of making visually delivered materials available to individuals with visual impairments,

(D) to acquire or modify equipment or devices for individuals with disabilities, or

(E) to provide other similar services, modifications, materials, or equipment (https://www.law.cornell.edu/uscode/text/26/44).

Incidentally, this only applies to modifications to existing buildings. Expenditures for new construction do not qualify.

Tip #41: Disabled Access Deduction

Disabled access deduction. While this isn't a credit, it is a tax break. These costs might be useful as medical deductions. Sometimes it is necessary to make modifications to entrances, hallways, bathrooms, bedrooms, and even the patio area to make the home accessible for someone with physical disabilities. The adjustments may be minor, like adding handholds to bathtubs, showers, and certain walls. Or they may be extensive, like remodeling rooms, making doors wider, putting molding or railings on walls as handholds, installing ramps, or installing special pools or spa systems. Be sure to get paperwork from the physician spelling out what improvements are needed and why. Without a physician's order, you will not be able to claim any medical deductions. Keep copies of all the receipts in a permanent file as well as the tax file for the year the improvements were made. The deduction is a little tricky, especially if the costs are high. The IRS has a worksheet in Publication 502 to help you (https://www.irs.gov/publications/p502/ar02.html). You may only deduct the costs to the extent that they did not increase the value of the home. So if there is a lot of money at stake (like tens of thousands of dollars), it's worth the investment to get a professional appraisal on the home—before the improvements and afterward—to be able to prove how much the value increased, if at all. Remember, not all improvements increase a home's worth.

CHAPTER 5

Putting Your Home to Work

I F YOU ARE SMART and creative, there are several ways to put your home to work for you so it pays for itself . . . and more.

Tip #42: Rental Income

A solution for someone who is no longer able to afford the mortgage. If you have extra space, getting a roommate can be a better alternative than selling the house. It might require sacrificing a little space. Be very, very careful about screening the roommate or tenant for both financial stability and compatible personality (and noise-level preferences). Do not rent to family or friends. They are apt to skip payments when convenient. And it's hard to kick them out—on so many levels. Besides, you might end up losing the friend or alienating the family member and other family members, as you end up being the villain when they don't pay you.

Tip #43: Short-Term Rental Loophole

A 14-day rental loophole. Did you know that you could rent your home or vacation property for up to 14 days each year without reporting any of that income (http://iTaxMama.com/FreeRentalIncome)? This is perfect for time-shares you can't really afford to use right now. Depending on your home, you can probably rent the property for $100–$300 or more per night depending on the configuration of the property and the number of people. That's worth $1,400–$4,200, tax-free. You don't get to deduct any of the costs. After all, you're not reporting any income. Beware: Rent the property for 15 days or more overall during the year and all the income becomes taxable. *Note: Check to see if your state follows this rule. Most do.*

Tip #44: Film Location

Film location. Does your home or property have some interesting or unique quality that might make it attractive to a film company? Consider listing it with a service used by location managers. California, where many films are shot, has a State Film Commission website where you can find reliable places to list your home (http://film.ca.gov/locations/market-your-property/). The New York City's mayor's office offers a way to "make your home a star" (http://www1.nyc.gov/site/mome/production-in-nyc/make-home-star.page). A recent venture from the Airbnb folks called PeerSpace is also designed for film location scouts and business location scouts (https://techcrunch.com/2014/09/17/peerspace/). So far, they are just in New York and California (https://www.peerspace.com). But you know their locations will be expanded. Many other states and Canada are becoming more attractive for film production. Googling turned up several other services, but I couldn't find any evidence that they had successfully helped people get their homes rented. So search your state's website to see if your state offers a directory, which will list reputable location services. Incidentally, my brother's very ordinary home was used for filming. The filmmakers repaired his 10-foot glass patio door, replaced his worn-out rug, and make some other repairs, since they had the tools and materials handy. So your home doesn't have to be fancy or unique to be useful to a production company. What are the advantages? Here are just a few:

- High compensation. You might get more than $1,000 per day. All of it is taxable.

- Permanent improvements to your home—like new carpeting or drapes, repairs, and certain upgrades—at no charge to you. These repairs don't constitute taxable income, since they are tenant repairs or improvements. *Note: Some things are just brought in for the film and removed when the filmmakers leave, like plants, furniture, accessories.*

- Short-term usage of the property. For a couple of weeks' use, you might earn enough money to pay your mortgage for a year. Several people I have known over the years have earned more than $50,000 in a month or less this way and have gotten some nice improvements to their homes.

Tip #45: Before You Rent

General short-term rental thoughts. If you're going to rent your home out for a week here, another week there, particularly as an absentee landlord, you need to take sensible precautions. Even more so if you have a home or property that you want to rent out full time.

- Turn off your landline phone service. Let people use their cell phones. If they don't have them for here in the United States, point them to the nearest 7-Eleven or local store where they can get cheap, use-based cell phones for short-term use. *Note: Simply removing the phone from the plug won't prevent someone from plugging in another phone.*

- Turn off all pay-per-view features on your cable or satellite system.

- Remove all computers that contain *any* personal information or passwords. Consider leaving an inexpensive computer there just for visitors to use.

- Do you have personal items that are special to you, especially family pictures and such, that would not be easy to replace? Either lock them away safely (off the premises) or take good scans of them so you can reproduce them if they are inadvertently lost, misplaced, or destroyed. Naturally, any jewelry, furniture, or knickknacks of value should be removed from the home entirely.

- Stop your mail. You don't want strangers snooping through your mail, getting your checks, opening your credit card offers, getting your replacement credit cards, or potentially stealing your identity. In fact, if you are going to rent your home out frequently, get yourself a PO box service—preferably not from the US Postal Service. Why? Because with private services, you can call them up, reach a live person quickly and easily, and ask them what mail has arrived. If you have made prior arrangements, perhaps they can even open and scan your time-sensitive mail for you. However, if you have newspaper delivery, let that continue. Your guests will enjoy the local news and information about local events, attractions, films, television schedules, and so on.

- Folks with pools should consider not renting to anyone with children. If you do rent to families with children, make sure you have a strong fence around the pool—one that cannot be climbed over by small children—and be sure to put a solid lock on the fence. Have the parents sign a statement when they get that key, agreeing that they will be with the children and watching them at all times when they use the pool. Make sure you have insurance that covers rental use!

- If you are leaving town, make sure that you have a reliable local friend or associate drop by and check on the visitors. This person should have a key to the place. The visitors should be informed that he or she will be dropping by to make sure they find everything they need, or to see if they need help operating washing machines, dishwashers, cable televisions, and so on.

- Make sure your contract includes a provision to get reimbursed for stolen linens or other personal items. A reasonable security deposit would work. In this case, make sure you provide an inventory of all key items that the visitors can sign when they arrive. The same number of towels, linens, and so on should be there when they leave.

- If you install cameras so you can look in on your place remotely, be sure to tell your guests in advance, in the listing. Show them how to turn off the cameras so they have privacy.

- Check the rental laws with your city, community association (if you have one), and so on. At what point do you have to register and collect/pay hotel taxes? After a certain number of days, a certain level of income, or what? Legitimate hotels and bed and breakfast locations are screaming about the lack of registration by online hosts. New laws are being considered or passed to require hosts to pay fees like all other hostelries.

All these costs that are specifically related to your rental activities will be deductible. Of course, the question is: Where on your tax return will you be reporting this income?

Tip #46: Airbnb

Airbnb rentals. They have become quite the craze. Over the years there have been other sites, worldwide, making it possible for people to list their homes, rooms, vacation properties, and so on for rent to strangers without the need for rental agents to act as intermediaries.

But Airbnb has become one of the top markets (https://www.airbnb .com). One of the attractive features of the service is that it doesn't charge any fees to list your property. You only pay when Airbnb gets you a paying guest. OK, so guests are giving you money. How do you report the income from Airbnb and any other rental sources? You have three different ways to handle the income. You may be able to decide whether to use option 1 or 2. When it comes to option 3, even if you don't select it, the IRS might—in an audit. So I'll give you some tips on how to avoid that problem. Let's explore the differences among the following options:

1. As regular residential real estate rentals on Schedule E
2. As hotel-type rentals on Schedule C
3. As casual rentals, not rented for profit

Note 1: Airbnb still does not post a phone number on its contact page or anywhere else on the website. Although its Twitter team recommended that I email the press office, the press office did not respond, despite repeated requests and alerts that I was working on deadline. As a result, I am not able to provide you with the specifics about how Airbnb handles its income reporting to you, its management of long-term rentals, or other key information I had hoped to provide for you. The fact that the company was so unresponsive might be a concern when you place your properties and trust in its hands.

However, Airbnb has added a tax information section to its website. Airbnb will provide Americans with Form 1099-K if you generate $20,000 or 200 transactions or more for the year. Or you will get Form 1099-MISC if you generate $600 or more in revenues. Read more information here: https://www.airbnb.com/help/topic/247/ how-taxes-work.

Note 2: Both visitors and hosts have had problems reaching Airbnb according to the Better Business Bureau and PissedConsumer.com (https:// www.bbb.org/greater-san-francisco/business-reviews/rental-vacancy

-listing-service/airbnb-inc-in-san-francisco-ca-375521/reviews-and -complaints; https://airbnb.pissedconsumer.com/). Based on the volume of activity in the overall Airbnb system, the percentage of problems does seem to be quite low.

Tip #47: Residential Rental

Residential rental. What are the considerations for treating vacation traveler rental income as Schedule E rentals (https://www.irs.gov/ pub/irs-pdf/f1040se.pdf)? Read IRS Publication 527 for in-depth information about rentals (https://www.irs.gov/publications/p527). Typically, Schedule E is used to report income from long-term rentals—in other words, income from tenants who move in and stay more than a month at a time. When you have a long-term tenant, someone who signs a lease and lives in the room or the home for a year or more, Schedule E is the way to go. The IRS considers this passive income. There are all kinds of special limits when it comes to deducting losses. (Congress simplified the US Internal Revenue Code with the Tax Reform Act of 1986. Consider reading IRS Publication 925 about passive losses (https://www.irs.gov/publications/p925/index .html). The advantage of using Schedule E comes into play when your rentals are profitable. Although you pay income taxes on the profits, you don't pay the self-employment taxes of 15.3 percent on the profits. The problems and complications arise when you have losses. In fact, owning rental property could probably be an entire book all by itself. There are so many complicated rules, nuances, and traps, they could fill volumes.

Tip #48: Hotel-Type Rentals

Hotel-type rentals. These are short-term rentals generally reported on your Schedule C, like a business (https://www.irs.gov/pub/irs -pdf/f1040sc.pdf). Tenants typically stay for a few days, or a week or two. (Some tax professionals treat this as a Schedule E, passive rental, regardless. The decision will be on a case-by-case basis.) In addition, it's important to learn your locality's definition of a hotel. (For instance, in the City of Los Angeles, the Transient Occupancy Tax applies to any rental for 30 consecutive calendar days or less: http://finance.lacity.org/tax-information-booklet.) Be sure to look up your city's rules to determine if you are subject to the hotel taxes and rules. Incidentally, it's not just potential taxes and licensing fees you might face. There may also be zoning prohibitions against short-term rentals. Folks who live in a community with CC&Rs (Covenants, Conditions, and Restrictions) might have to get written clearance from the homeowners' association board of directors. When it comes to tax issues, the bad news is you pay income taxes and self-employment taxes of 15.3 percent on the profits, if your activities are considered hotel-like. The good news is, if you have profits, these profits will count as earned income in case you want to make contributions to your IRA or other retirement plan. And when you have legitimate losses, there is no limit to the losses you can deduct (except for office-in-home deductions). And when you have losses, those losses will reduce your AGI without being limited by the Alternative Minimum Tax.

Tip #49: Casual Rentals

And then there are the casual rentals, not rented for profit. Often, this revenue comes from renting at deep discounts to family or friends, renting out rooms for extremely low fees, or just renting the house or rooms out if someone happens to ask, with no active attempt to try to attract paying guests. Avoid finding yourself in this last category. This is the worst of all worlds. You must report all the income on line 21 of your Form 1040 (the Other Income line), but your deductions face several limits. The first is that you may only deduct your expenses up to the amount of your gross rental income. Then you must report the expenses on Schedule A as Miscellaneous Itemized Deductions, which means you must itemize. If you own a home with a mortgage, you're probably already using Schedule A, so that may not be a major obstacle. But the deductions are reduced by 2 percent of your AGI. And if your income is really high, your itemized deductions might be limited by the Alternative Minimum Tax (AMT) and the itemized deduction phaseout. Often, you will only get the benefit of half of your expenses or less.

Tip #50: Proving Profit

Proving that your rentals really are for profit. This is especially important in two circumstances:

1. When your Schedule E or Schedule C for your rental activities shows losses consistently for more than a couple of years.

2. When you end up with very few days of paying visitors during a given year. If this is the case, how can you prove your intention to make a profit? One of the best ways is to list your rental everywhere you possibly can, including a Facebook page, Twitter account, your own website, and perhaps some videos to put on YouTube. Another suggestion is to keep track of all people who called to rent and what the disposition was of each query. After all, no one closes 100 percent of potential sales opportunities. Sometimes the time, availability, or amenities won't suit the person. Sometimes you will have legitimate objections and won't accept the potential visitor or tenant. Or your area may become undesirable for a while due to storms, earthquakes, sudden local violence—whatever the reason for not being able to rent your place, keep records and document that you tried to get tenants. In addition, create a business plan (a good idea regardless!)—a plan that describes steps you will take to attract tenants. Use that as a checklist throughout the year, showing what steps you have taken each month. The goal is to prove that you have a profit motive and are not just sporadically renting out your home.

Tip #51: Follow the Rules!

Incidentally, when it comes to working with companies like Airbnb, follow their guidelines. When they tell you not to accept payment outside their system, don't think you're putting one over on them by pocketing money without paying them their fee. By bypassing their rules, you will have cost yourself all protection related to that guest (and perhaps get booted out). If that guest does damage, you will have to handle the conflict yourself. The company won't be there to intervene for you.

Tip #52: Highly Deductible

Deduct it all. Renting out your home gives you an excellent opportunity to deduct everything. It's smart to track every single receipt and detail about every possible expenditure. The great thing about this obsessiveness is that you present your tax professional with all your costs. The tax pro can review them and decide what is and what is not deductible. Often, because clients have tracked every detail, I will notice valid deductible expenditures that they might not have thought to show me on their own. Not everyone has the patience for all that record keeping, so at least track as many of your expenses as possible. Naturally, you can fully deduct all costs for expenses directly related to the photographing, displaying, advertising, and management of the rentals. But on Schedule E or Schedule C of your tax return, you will be able to deduct the business-use percentage of many of your costs that don't change very much when tenants move in—long or short term. What things can you deduct that you spend money on anyway? See the following four lists.

1. Costs you can fully deduct now but can move to Schedule E or C to reduce your adjusted gross income (AGI) and/or your self-employment taxes:

    • Mortgage interest

- Property taxes

- Mortgage insurance premiums

2. Costs you pay every month but never get a deduction for because the IRS considers them personal expenses:

    - Community association fees

    - Gardener

    - Homeowner's insurance

    - Pool maintenance service

    - Utilities (except the ones you've turned off while you have paying guests)

    - Newspapers

3. Costs you pay especially because you have guests or to attract a higher class of guest but that might benefit you anyway:

    - Housecleaning

    - Groceries and goodies bought specifically to welcome guests

    - New towels and linens

    - New carpets or drapes

    - Wide-screen television

    - Shiny new dishes and cutlery

    - Other stuff you bought to make the place appealing—to "stage" the photos and the experience

4. And there's a cost you don't pay at all but can be a substantial deduction—depreciation.

Tip #53: Depreciation

Depreciation. This is a phantom deduction for the wear and tear of the home due to business use. You don't actually spend any money on it for tax purposes. In reality, the idea was for people to put some money in reserve each year to repair and replace things that tend to wear out, like roofs, driveways, plumbing, walls that need cleaning and painting, carpets and drapes that need replacing, and so on. That concept has been forgotten, but the deduction stays behind. How do you depreciate your home? Well, you need to know your tax basis in your home. You also need to know the breakdown between the value of the building and the land. You may not depreciate the land—just the building. Warning: If the value of your home has declined since you bought it, you will be using the fair market value instead of the tax basis. Frankly, when it comes to setting up the correct values for depreciation, go see a tax pro. You should not be doing this yourself. Get a worksheet on this with the backup data and documentation that was used to establish the correct depreciation schedule. With that, you might be able to do this yourself in future years. If you live in a condominium or co-op, you don't really own any land directly, but you do own a share of the overall land that belongs to your community. So don't think there is no land value. There is.

Assuming you will be renting out your entire place to each set of guests, you will use the following ratio for depreciation:

1. Start with the building's basis or the lower fair market value of the building only (not the land).
2. Multiply that by the number of days rented divided by 365 days (366 days in 2020, the next leap year).
3. This gives you the percentage of rental use.

If you are only renting out some rooms and you're staying there, it gets more complicated because you will have to take the rented area into account. Definitely get a tax pro to help you!

IRS Publication 946 explains depreciation and provides the tables and number of years to use for various assets (https://www.irs.gov/publications/p946). When it comes to renting your home, you will

Table A-6.   Residential Rental Property
            Mid-Month Convention
            Straight Line—27.5 Years

Year	Month property placed in service											
	1	2	3	4	5	6	7	8	9	10	11	12
1	3.485%	3.182%	2.879%	2.576%	2.273%	1.970%	1.667%	1.364%	1.061%	0.758%	0.455%	0.152%
2–9	3.636	3.636	3.636	3.636	3.636	3.636	3.636	3.636	3.636	3.636	3.636	3.636
10	3.637	3.637	3.637	3.637	3.637	3.637	3.636	3.636	3.636	3.636	3.636	3.636
11	3.636	3.636	3.636	3.636	3.636	3.636	3.637	3.637	3.637	3.637	3.637	3.637
12	3.637	3.637	3.637	3.637	3.637	3.637	3.636	3.636	3.636	3.636	3.636	3.636
13	3.636	3.636	3.636	3.636	3.636	3.636	3.637	3.637	3.637	3.637	3.637	3.637
14	3.637	3.637	3.637	3.637	3.637	3.637	3.636	3.636	3.636	3.636	3.636	3.636
15	3.636	3.636	3.636	3.636	3.636	3.636	3.637	3.637	3.637	3.637	3.637	3.637
16	3.637	3.637	3.637	3.637	3.637	3.637	3.636	3.636	3.636	3.636	3.636	3.636
17	3.636	3.636	3.636	3.636	3.636	3.636	3.637	3.637	3.637	3.637	3.637	3.637
18	3.637	3.637	3.637	3.637	3.637	3.637	3.636	3.636	3.636	3.636	3.636	3.636
19	3.636	3.636	3.636	3.636	3.636	3.636	3.637	3.637	3.637	3.637	3.637	3.637
20	3.637	3.637	3.637	3.637	3.637	3.637	3.636	3.636	3.636	3.636	3.636	3.636
21	3.636	3.636	3.636	3.636	3.636	3.636	3.637	3.637	3.637	3.637	3.637	3.637
22	3.637	3.637	3.637	3.637	3.637	3.637	3.636	3.636	3.636	3.636	3.636	3.636
23	3.636	3.636	3.636	3.636	3.636	3.636	3.637	3.637	3.637	3.637	3.637	3.637
24	3.637	3.637	3.637	3.637	3.637	3.637	3.636	3.636	3.636	3.636	3.636	3.636
25	3.636	3.636	3.636	3.636	3.636	3.636	3.637	3.637	3.637	3.637	3.637	3.637
26	3.637	3.637	3.637	3.637	3.637	3.637	3.636	3.636	3.636	3.636	3.636	3.636
27	3.636	3.636	3.636	3.636	3.636	3.636	3.637	3.637	3.637	3.637	3.637	3.637
28	1.97	2.273	2.576	2.879	3.182	3.485	3.636	3.636	3.636	3.636	3.636	3.636
29							0.152	0.455	0.758	1.061	1.364	1.667

use the residential real estate life of 27.5 years. See IRS Table A-6, above (https://www.irs.gov/publications/p946/ar02.html).

Note: There are a variety of permanent changes to depreciation deduction rules in the Internal Revenue Code as Part 3 of the PATH Act of 2015. Please see Tip #230 for more details.

In fact, the new Tax Act has increased the depreciation deductions for a variety of different assets. See Chapter 2 on business tax changes in the TCJA.

Tip #54: Pet Hosting

Pet hosting. More than 43 million households have dogs living within. Thirty-six million homes are ruled by cats. Where do all these animals stay when their parents are at work or away on a trip? Pet care places are popping up all over the country, from commercial places like PetSmart to high-end salons. These offer much better and more personalized care than old-fashioned kennels seem to, where animals are simply held in cages and fed on a schedule. You can join the fun, too, by signing up as a pet-sitter for Rover (https://www .rover.com/become-a-sitter/). It's almost like a dating service for pet fanciers. You get to meet the pets and owners before agreeing to care

for the animals, before the owners reluctantly relinquish care of their
dearly beloved family member to you. You get to decide how many
pets you will accept for a single day, overnight, or multiple-day stay.
It's a great way to earn extra money without leaving the house. You
don't need a college degree or specialized skills. Just patience, attention to detail, and an honest-to-goodness affection for the animals
in your care. It doesn't hurt to get some specialized training, which
Rover provides. The company provides insurance coverage and a 24/7
emergency phone number in case you need help, and the company
helps you negotiate costs when the pet causes damage to your home.

Tip #55: Income from Pet Care

Income from pet care. Naturally, you report all your income as business income on Schedule C. Rover's position is that it is acting as
your banker and collecting the credit card payments. It sends you the
money, less the company's fees. So you will get Form 1099-K from
Rover, not Form 1099-MISC (https://www.irs.gov/pub/irs-pdf/
f1099k.pdf). Rover only issues that form if you have had more than
200 transactions or earned $20,000 or more. The amount shown will
only be the net amount that you receive after Rover takes its cut. So if
you don't meet that level of income or transactions, it's important for
you to maintain your own income records. Most likely, you will be
able to look up a summary of your transactions online. Just in case,
it's wise to record or download the data into your accounting system.

Tip #56: Pet Care Direct Costs

Tracking doggy-kitty daycare direct costs. The actual costs of the
animal's food and supplies should be relatively easy to track. When
shopping for groceries, the smart way to separate the cost of personal
groceries from pet guest groceries is to separate them on the checkout
conveyor belt. Just put that little plastic spacer between your groceries and the guest's supplies. In fact, it would also be smart to use

a separate check, debit card, or credit card. Using a separate bank account or credit card to pay for business-related expenses makes it easier to track them.

Tip #57: Pet Care in the Office

Pet daycare office in your home. With animals running around your entire home and yard, how do you determine your office-in-home-type costs? First of all, you will take into account all the expenses above. Again, this is a good time to speak to your tax pro about how to get the maximum depreciation deduction. But if you want a guideline for how to handle this, read the IRS depreciation explanation for daycare facilities in Publication 587 (https://www.irs.gov/publications/p587/ar02.html). Your issues are essentially the same as if you were providing care for children or seniors, except that the special food and meal tables described won't apply to dogs and cats. You will have a special area on Form 8829, the Office in Home form, to enter both the square footage of your home and the number of hours it was used for day (or night) care. See the top of Form 8829: https://www.irs.gov/pub/irs-pdf/f8829.pdf.

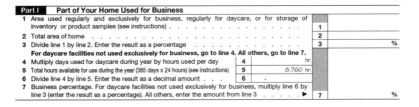

Part I	Part of Your Home Used for Business			
1	Area used regularly and exclusively for business, regularly for daycare, or for storage of inventory or product samples (see instructions)		1	
2	Total area of home		2	
3	Divide line 1 by line 2. Enter the result as a percentage		3	%
	For daycare facilities not used exclusively for business, go to line 4. All others, go to line 7.			
4	Multiply days used for daycare during year by hours used per day	4	hr.	
5	Total hours available for use during the year (365 days x 24 hours) (see instructions)	5	8,760 hr.	
6	Divide line 4 by line 5. Enter the result as a decimal amount . . .	6	.	
7	Business percentage. For daycare facilities not used exclusively for business, multiply line 6 by line 3 (enter the result as a percentage). All others, enter the amount from line 3 . . . . . . ▶		7	%

Tip #58: Paying for Services

Paying for services. Generally, when a business pays an individual who provides services or rental facilities $600 or more in any year, it must issue Form 1099-MISC to that freelance worker by January 31 of the following year. If you've ever tried to get a worker's Social Security number in January, you may have been faced with a variety of unproductive reactions. They range from complete indifference (ignoring your request), to hostility, to outright violence. You might be surprised to learn how many people have no intention of reporting what you pay them—and become infuriated when you tell them, after the year is over, that you are reporting their income to the IRS. You can avoid this problem by having service providers give you a filled-out and signed Form W-9 before you hire them—and certainly before you issue the first check (https://www.irs.gov/pub/irs-pdf/fw9.pdf). Get this form signed even before you pay them anywhere close to $600. Once you like a person's services, the dollars add up. Pretty soon the service providers have earned more than $600, and you can ruin a beautiful relationship by springing this on them in the middle of the year. Making it clear that you need this form from service providers up front means they know they will be paying taxes on this stream of income. They can factor the taxes into their fee for the services they provide to you. You will need this from the housekeepers, repair folks, gardeners, and other people who have been providing services to you for years without ever being 1099'd. That may cause a bit of a stir.

Several years ago, Congress was playing around with the 1099-MISC rules and rescinded the rule requiring rental property owners who report their rentals on Schedule E to issue 1099-MISCs. However, some tax professionals still insist on it. And if you're reporting your rental income on Schedule C, you must issue the 1099-MISC to all service providers to whom you pay $600 or more during the year.

Tip #59: 1099-MISC

Filing the 1099-MISC. Not filing carries a penalty of $250, or 10 percent of the total amounts on all 1099-MISCs that should have been filed (https://www.irs.gov/irm/part4/irm_04-023-009.html). It's best to file these forms online. You can use the IRS's service. It's called FIRE (Filing Information Returns Electronically). There are also several inexpensive services that can do this for you such as Intuit Payroll, tax1099.com, and efile4biz.com.

Tip #60: Use PayPal

Want to avoid filing the 1099-MISC altogether? All you need to do is pay all your service providers by credit card or by PayPal. If you do that, the credit card company or PayPal will send them a 1099-K, and you're off the hook (https://www.irs.gov/uac/General-FAQs-on-New-Payment-Card-Reporting-Requirements)! If transactions are already reportable on other information returns, must they be reported again by payment settlement entities (PSE)? No. If a transaction is reportable by a PSE both under Section 6041 or Section 6041A(a) and under Section 6050W, the transaction must be reported on Form 1099-K and not Form 1099-MISC.

CHAPTER 6

Auto Deductions

THESE DAYS EACH HOUSEHOLD has at least one car. Some people are sharing the single car, driving each other to work. Others have multiple cars. Whatever your situation, this chapter cover tips for getting the most out of this necessary expense.

Tip #61: Vehicle Use

One of the most common sources of tax breaks comes from the use of vehicles. There **used to be** four ways to take advantage of vehicle-related deductions:

1. Charitable mileage
2. Medical mileage
3. Moving mileage

4. Business or job-related mileage

5. **As a result of the new Tax Act, employees may no longer deduct moving expenses or job-related expenses (including mileage) until after 2025. Individuals are left with business and charity, although employers may reimburse employees for qualified moving expenses. (See Tips #66–71.) At the end of each year, the IRS issues the mileage rates for the coming year. (See Tip #64.)**

Tip #62: Charitable Mileage

Charitable mileage. This comes in at 14 cents per mile. The mileage rate is set by Congress, so it has not changed since 1998. (In 1997 it was 12 cents per mile.) Keep track of all charity-related driving. That includes going to meetings, doing volunteer work, driving your charitable charges to doctors' offices, meetings, events, campgrounds, and so on. **Interestingly enough, the IRS finally got the right to control the charitable mileage rate. Yet, for 2018, it left the rate at 14 cents per mile.**

Tip #63: Charitable Parking

Charitable parking. Be sure to track all parking costs. If you don't get a receipt (due to meters or other mechanical payments), write a note with the date, time, and amount of the parking fee and the charitable purpose.

Tip #64: Annual Mileage Rates

Business, moving, and medical mileage rates change annually. For 2017 the rates are:

• Business: 53.5 cents per mile
• Moving and medical: 17 cents per mile

For 2018, the rates are:

- **Business: 54.5 cents per mile**
- **Moving and medical: 18 cents per mile**

The IRS computes the new rates based on cost of living increases and some other factors. Generally, the rates only change in January. However, in years when gas prices rise or drop dramatically, the rates may change two or three times during the year. Most recently, in 2008 and 2011, we had two rates. You can look up the most current mileage rates and the history since 1997 on this IRS page: https://www.irs.gov/tax-professionals/standard-mileage-rates.

Just in case the IRS changes the page's URL, this page on the Small Business & Management website is consistently available: http://www.smbiz.com/sbrl003.html#smr.

Tip #65: Start Recording

Make a note of the mileage shown on your vehicle(s) odometer(s) as early as possible in the beginning of the year so you have the starting point to track your annual mileage. Remember to write down the mileage at the end of year. You will need to know the total miles driven on each car each year when you deduct mileage for anything. If you didn't start January out with this annual tradition, you can work backward to extrapolate the mileage in six easy steps:

1. Find a service or tune-up receipt for each car from the earliest date this year, or the latest date last year. It will show the mileage at the time of the service. Write that down.

2. Write down the mileage on your odometer today. Subtract the earlier mileage from today's mileage. For example, say the mileage on January 18 was 56,117 and the mileage today is 58,326—the difference is 2,209 miles.

3. Count the number of days between the two dates. Suppose the service was done on January 18 and today is February 26, making it 39 days.

4. Divide the miles you've driven by the number of days. 2,209 divided by 39 = 56.64 miles per day.

5. Multiply the daily mileage by the number of days in the year so far. For example, if you are doing this on February 26, there have been 57 days so far this year = 3,228 miles driven this year.

6. Subtract the result from today's odometer reading to get the beginning mileage for the year. Voila! 58,326 minus 3,228 = 55,098 is your approximate mileage on January 1.

Tip #66: Moving Mileage

Track your moving mileage. That's pretty easy. You generally won't be doing this more than once a year. In order to deduct moving expenses at all, you must meet the distance test: "Your new main job location is at least 50 miles farther from your former home than your old main job location was from your former home" (https://www.irs .gov/publications/p521/ar02.html). What mileage counts? Only the mileage you drive to move your household to the new location. If you are driving several cars (yours, your spouse's, your teen's, etc.), record the mileage on each car—and identify the car for the tax records. You may not use the mileage to drive to the new location to scout out a new home, or a job, or anything else. Just the pure moving-related mileage. However, if you rent a moving van, no need to worry about mileage. (Though keep the receipt because that is excellent proof of the distance driven.) When using a moving van, you deduct the cost of the rental and the fuel you bought throughout the trip—including the last fuel fill-up before you returned the rental car. Deduct all your moving expenses on Form 3903 (https://www.irs.gov/pub/irs-pdf/ f3903.pdf). This will carry the allowable deduction to the front page of your Form 1040. You will be able to use these expenses even if you cannot itemize.

The TCJA no longer allows employees to deduct moving expenses until after December 31, 2025—except for members of the US Armed Services and their families. There is also a provision allowing for tax-free reimbursements to members of the US Armed Services.

Tip #67: More Moving

More about moving. As long as we're talking about moving mileage, let's outline some of the other moving costs that are deductible. Naturally, if you pay a moving and storage company to move all your goods, you can deduct the full amount you pay. Deduct your travel expenses—hotels, motels, or campgrounds along the way—for yourself and your moving helpers. Incidentally, be aware that someone might break into your rented moving conveyance. Please take appropriate precautions and keep irreplaceable valuables with you at all times.

Tip #68: Moving Insurance

Moving insurance. Beware of theft. I have heard of several instances where people woke up and found that that the lock on their moving vehicle had been broken and many of their possessions had been stolen or ransacked. Or that their moving vehicle had been stolen outright. Stay in places where there is security or someone at the lodging's desk at night. Try to get a room where the desk clerk can see your room and your car. Get moving insurance—the cost will be deductible. Ask your present homeowner's insurance agent for information about a policy, or search online for moving insurance. If you are working with a moving and storage company, it helps to understand the company's terminology and what your coverage does and doesn't offer. The Spruce has a page with good definitions: https://www.thespruce.com/should-you-purchase-more-moving-insurance-2435989.

Tip #69: Moving No-Go's

Moving costs you may not deduct. New law or old—there is no deduction for meals. Not yours, not your moving companions'. If you don't drive directly from your old home to your new home, there is no mileage deduction for side trips and touring around while making the move. So if you have taken this travel opportunity to indulge your curiosity, print out a Google Maps or MapQuest page showing what the direct mileage would have been. Store it in your tax file for the year.

Tip #70: Reimbursements

Reimbursements. Lots of large or wealthy employers provide full reimbursements for all your moving expenses. In fact, if you're lucky, some employers even reimburse you for the costs of selling your old residence and buying your new one. Keep in mind that most of those reimbursements are taxable income, since they are far beyond the actual deductible moving costs. The good news is those extra reimbursements have already been added to your wages and withholding has been taken. It would be wise to review your overall income with a tax pro in the year of your move to make sure you have had enough taxes withheld to cover the extra income. On the other hand, if you have only been reimbursed for moving and mileage, it's not added to your income and you don't need to report anything on your tax return. Remember, you may have gotten reimbursed for some costs, but not all of them. Report all the costs on Form 3903 and deduct the reimbursements you did receive. The difference will be a deduction you can use even without having to itemize.

Tip #71: Time Test

Doing time. In order to be allowed to use the moving expenses at all, you must meet the second test, the time test (https://www.irs .gov/publications/p521/ar02.html). Employees and self-employed business owners have to meet different tests about their working period after the move. When you're married, only one spouse must meet one of the tests for the moving deductions to qualify. Let's get the information straight from the IRS.

Time Test for Employees

If you are an employee, you must work full time for at least 39 weeks during the first 12 months after you arrive in the general area of your new job location (39-week test). Full-time employment depends on what is usual for your type of work in your area.

For purposes of this test, the following four rules apply:

- You count only your full-time work as an employee, not any work you do as a self-employed person.
- You do not have to work for the same employer for all 39 weeks.
- You do not have to work 39 weeks in a row.
- You must work full time within the same general commuting area for all 39 weeks.

Time Test for Self-Employed Persons

If you are self-employed, you must work full time for at least 39 weeks during the first 12 months and for a total of at least 78 weeks during the first 24 months after you arrive in the general area of your new job location (78-week test).

For purposes of the time test for self-employed persons, the following three rules apply:

- You count any full-time work you do either as an employee or as a self-employed person.
- You do not have to work for the same employer or be self-employed in the same trade or business for the 78 weeks.
- You must work within the same general commuting area for all 78 weeks.

Incidentally, if you haven't met the time test at the time you file your tax return, don't worry. Go ahead and file as if you had worked for the required number of months. You will only have to amend and take back this deduction if it turns out that you did not keep working long enough. Otherwise, you're just fine.

Read IRS Publication 521 for more information about moving expenses (https://www.irs.gov/publications/p521).

Note: Although moving expenses have been suspended by the TCJA, for now, expect this deduction to return within the next few years.

Tip #72: Business Mileage

Business mileage. This is the big deduction for employees and business owners. Be sure to track all your business or job-related miles. These miles count:

- Going from your home to a client's location
- Going from one client's location to another in the same day
- Going from your office to a client's location in the same day
- Going from your main office to a second office
- Educators going from your school to a second school location in the same day
- Running business-related errands, like picking up office supplies, going to your PO box to pick up or drop off your mail, going to the US Post Office to drop off mail, and so on
- Driving to airports for trips that are primarily work related
- Driving to conferences, seminars, workshops, and classes
- Anything else that is specifically work or business related

The miles that don't count? Commuting miles—driving to and from your home to your business. The nice thing about working from home for yourself or your employer's benefit is that all mileage starts at your front door.

Tip #73: Track Carefully

Track your mileage carefully by hand or using any other tools you can find. In Appendix B on record keeping, we suggest some tools that can help you with this. Or you can create your own Excel spreadsheet. It doesn't hurt to back up your mileage log with a printout from MapQuest (https://www.mapquest.com/) or Google Maps to prove the mileage for each trip. The image below shows a suggested Excel template heading and MapQuest record. Naturally you can create your own with headings that define your business or job-related travels.

	A	B	C	D	E	F	G	H
1		Year		Business or Job Mileage				
2								
3	Date	Starting Point-address	Destination	Business Miles	Business Contact	Business Purpose	If Personal-Enter Miles Here	Map Saved
4								
5	1/15/20XX	1515 Hi Point, Burbank, CA 91501	Huntington Library, 1151 Oxford Rd, San Marino, CA 91108	16.85 miles				Y
6								

Tip #74: More Deductions

When you use the mileage method, you may still deduct all the parking lot, parking meter, and toll fees that you must pay when you drive for business. In addition, if you have to pay a separate fee to garage your vehicle (think New York, Chicago, and other places where space is at a premium), you may deduct a portion of that. Use the business percentage of your car use. For instance, let's say you drive 12,000 miles a year and drove the car for 8,325 miles for business. You may deduct 69.375 percent (8,325/12,000) of the garage rental.

Tip #75: Hidden Depreciation

The hidden depreciation in the mileage. Most people don't realize it, but the mileage rate includes a depreciation component. In year-to-year usage, it's not a factor. But when you sell the car, you need to reduce the basis of the car by the amount of depreciation you have deducted on your tax return. So be sure to save your Form 4562 worksheets for all the years you use each vehicle for your job or business. You will need to prepare a spreadsheet showing the number of miles you have claimed each year. In the next column, show the depreciation per mile value. In the final column, show the total depreciation taken that year. Folks who run up the miles during the vehicle's life may find that the depreciation has wiped out their basis altogether. See the example at the end of this tip.

To read more about how to deduct auto expenses, and using the actual expenses instead of mileage, read chapter 4 of IRS Publication 463, "Travel, Entertainment, Gift, and Car Expenses" (https://www.irs .gov/publications/p463/ch04.html).

	A	B	C	D	E	F	G
1							
2		Depreciation used in mileage method					
3	YEAR		2012	Cost of Vehicle:	$28,000	Adjustments:	0
4	Vehicle:	Model	Kia	Make	Optima		
5							
6	Year	Dep/cents mile	Total Miles	Business Miles	$ Value of Deprec		
7	Begin Odometer		57				
8	2015	0.24	11353	7625	1830		
9	2014	0.22	13287	8418	1852		
10	2012–2013	0.23	28466	17654	4060		
11	2011	0.22			0		
12	2010	0.23			0		
13	2008–2009	0.21			0		
14	2007	0.19			0		
15	2005–2006	0.17			0		
16	2004–2003	0.16			0		
17	2001–2003	0.15			0		
18					------------------		
19					7742		
20							

Tip #76: Billboard Your Car

Turning your car into a billboard: http://www.wrapify.com/about/. What a great way to generate income and get a complete makeover for your car. The company wraps your car in advertising. You get paid based on two criteria:

- How much of your car is covered—just panels or the full car
- How many miles you drive

You don't have to pay any fees or invest any money. All you need to qualify is to be over age 21, have a clean driving record, and have a car that is a 2008 model or newer (due to insurance considerations). Oh yes, one more thing—you need an iPhone or device that runs IOS applications. If you qualify, and the company has an advertiser in your area, the company will wrap the ad around your car . . . and awaaaaaay you go!

The interesting thing about this revenue is that since it is based on the number of miles you drive, you can suddenly turn your commuting mileage into business mileage. You will report the income on Schedule C and deduct the mileage there as well.

Alas, you are not allowed to drive for Uber et al. when your car is wrapped.

Tip #77: Rider Services

Uber, Lyft, Sidecar, and related quasi-cab services. The news is full of lawsuits by drivers, cities, and cab unions, as well as conflicts about whether the drivers are employees or independent contractors. Here is a website with a summary of the current state of those lawsuits, which were still pending—http://uberlawsuit.com/. For now, the general consensus is that drivers are independent contractors. That means you are running your own business. You need to do everything a normal business would do with respect to record keeping, cost tracking, mileage tracking, and so on. The good thing is these major companies provide a mileage tracker. Be sure to download the information at least monthly. In fact, it's a good idea to check your data every few days to make sure you get paid for all your passengers. Uber, Lyft, and Sidecar take care of all payments from riders. Sometimes, though, riders will pay you tips. If they pay by credit card, fine. Your company will track that. But if you get paid by cash, it's up to you to track the income. You could, of course, skip reporting the cash. But when the IRS runs audits, it will compare your income to that of other drivers for the same company. If they typically show that they receive tips and you don't, you may get a deeper audit.

Many drivers sign up for all the services that operate in their town when they need the hours. Others are only driving part time around their regular jobs, classes, or homemaking tasks. Incidentally, this is a terrific job for retirees. It gets you out of the house and talking to people. Who knows, you might even make new friends.

Tip #78: New (to You) Car

Getting a new car. My brother decided to drive for Uber a couple of years ago. His car was a bit too old and worn-out looking. So he bought a new (**gently used**) car that he uses primarily for Uber and Lyft driving. It's a good idea to buy a slightly used car and avoid paying for the value that drops the minute you drive off the dealer's lot. Consider buying the dealer's loan car, a salesman's demo car, or one of the dealer's leased vehicles. Why? It has been serviced by the dealer who is selling it. You can see the full maintenance record. You can get a substantial part of the warranty that's left. Through the dealer, you can buy an extended warranty and keep the dealer's maintenance crew at your beck and call. And if you get a nice dealer like I did when I bought my Infiniti, the dealership will totally clean up and detail your "new" car, replacing soiled carpeting and giving you a car that is just like new. If you don't get your used car from a dealer, please run a CarFax report on the car before buying it (https://www .carfax.com/) or have it inspected by an AAA (American Automobile Association) mechanic.

With a newly purchased car, you will need to decide if you want to depreciate the car and use actual expenses or use the mileage method. Frankly, with the severe limits on depreciation deductions, you're better off using the mileage method. Think about it—if you drive about 50–100 miles each workday, you'll end up with more than 18,000 miles. Multiply that by 53.5 cents for 2017 (**and 54.5 cents in 2018**) and you end up with nearly $10,000 in mileage deductions. Your actual expenses, even in a car that gets about 23 miles per gallon will be about $8,000 or less.

CHAPTER 7

Medical Deductions

U NDER THE TCJA, THE medical expense deduction also has been changed. Under previous law, taxpayers whose unreimbursed medical expenses exceeded 10 percent of their adjusted gross income (AGI) could deduct that excess. Starting tax year 2018, taxpayers may deduct unreimbursed medical expenses that exceed **7.5 percent** of their AGI. This new threshold means fewer taxpayers will qualify for medical deductions. As a rule of thumb, for an average household with two jobs earning about $40,000 combined, if unreimbursed medical costs are $3,000 or less, this household will not be able to deduct unreimbursed medical expenses. Yet there will still be opportunities for some taxpayers to use this deduction.

Tip #79: Taxable Year Only

You can only include in medical expenses those amounts that were actually paid during the taxable year, for which the taxpayer received *no* insurance or other reimbursement during the year.
Some common examples of such expenses include:

- Health insurance premiums (or the excess that was not claimed as a self-employed health insurance deduction). Remember to look at your year-end paystub for medical insurance you paid from your paycheck using after-tax dollars.

- Medicare insurance premiums, often deducted from the Social Security checks. Look at the year-end statement from the Social Security Administration for the amount.

- Medical mileage at **18 cents per mile in 2018**.

- Tolls and parking fees for medical care or treatments.

- Medical copays—watch out, they add up.

- Prescribed drugs. Even with low copays, they can add up. Especially if you take into account the prescriptions for everyone in the household.

- Medical travel. (Covered in more detail below.)

- Costly routine medical and dental treatments that are not reimbursed by insurance, like braces, Lasik surgery, dental implants, and so on.

- Eyeglasses, contacts, and all related solutions and paraphernalia. Our health insurance covers only the basics. You can end up spending $200 or more out of pocket for the frames/lenses you want.

- Breathing treatments, medicines, apparatus, and portable or stationary air compressors.

- CPAP machines, TENS muscle stimulators, and other medical devices prescribed by physicians.

- Cosmetic surgery for medical purposes—for example, to repair the body and skin after certain operations, fires, accidents, and such, and not purely for cosmetic reasons.

- Special tutoring, education, or therapy for a child or adult diagnosed with a variety of conditions, such as vision correction or speech therapy.

- Live-in schools/treatment programs whose purpose is specifically to help treat certain conditions. This cost is guaranteed to be high enough, so you can use your medical expenses deduction.

- Chiropractic, acupuncture, Reiki, and other alternative/naturopathic medical treatments if prescribed by your physician. At $75 per week for treatments, you are looking at nearly $4,000 worth of expenses.

- In-home nursing care. (Covered in detail below.)

- Nursing home and convalescent home fees. Wow. These can be significant.

This is just a small list of qualified expenses. IRS Publication 502 has a much longer list (https://www.irs.gov/publications/p502). It includes things that might surprise you.

Tip #80: Dependents

Deducting costs for a dependent who isn't a dependent. Sometimes, due to divorce, custody issues, separations, or other life-altering reasons, your child is filing his or her own tax return and you are not entitled to claim your child as a dependent. Despite that, if you pay your child's medical expenses, you can include medical expenses as deductions on your tax return. You can include medical expenses you paid for an individual that would have been your dependent except for the following:

- He or she received gross income of $4,050 or more in 2017 **or $4,150 in 2018.**
- He or she filed a joint return for the current year.
- You, or your spouse if filing jointly, could be claimed as a dependent on someone else's current-year tax return.

What constitutes a dependent for medical deductions if the person is a dependent? Both of the following requirements must be met:

- The person was a qualifying child or a qualifying relative (https://www.irs.gov/publications/p502/ar02.html).
- The person was a US citizen or national, or a resident of the United States, Canada, or Mexico.

Tip #81: Parking and Tolls

Speaking of parking fees and tolls. While you may not have your parking receipts from your doctor or hospital visits, most likely you have an appointment calendar showing which doctor, hospital, lab, that you have visited. (You can also use a Google Calendar and print it out at the end of each year.) If you have even one parking receipt from each location (get one now if you don't have any), then save that. Multiply the usual cost by the number of visits to each facility. You can enter all this information on a spreadsheet—by the end of the year, the amount may surprise you.

Tip #82: In-Home Care

In-home nursing care is expensive. Deduct the cost of wages and other amounts paid for nursing services. The services don't need to be performed by a nurse as long as the services are of a kind generally performed by a nurse. This includes caring for the patient's condition, giving medication or changing dressings, and bathing and grooming the patient. The services can be provided in your home or another care facility. Generally, only the amount spent for nursing services is a medical expense. If the attendant also provides personal and household services, amounts paid to the attendant must be split between the time spent performing household and personal services and the time spent for nursing services. For instance, someone works for eight hours a day. The person spends two hours in the morning bathing your mother, changing bandages, providing medication, making sure she's eating properly, and clearing away the evening's detritus. The next two hours are spent preparing lunch and tidying up the house. The following two hours are spent taking Mom shopping or to visit friends. The last two hours of the day are devoted to cleaning Mom, providing medications, serving dinner, and getting her ready for bed—even if she does stay up reading or watching television after the attendant leaves. Essentially, the care provider devoted half her time to medically relevant activities. So 50 percent of her entire compensation and payroll taxes count as a medical expense.

Tip #83: Overlooked in-Home Costs

Overlooked in-home nursing medical costs. Did you know that the cost of a caregiver's meals can be used as medical expenses? Also, if you had to pay additional amounts for household upkeep because of the attendant, you can include the extra amounts with your medical expenses. This includes extra rent or utilities you pay because you moved to a larger apartment to provide space for the attendant.

Tip #84: In-Home Payroll

In-home care means payroll or an agency. If you are paying someone directly, you probably have to put the caregiver(s) on payroll.

A person is considered a household employee if you pay him or her $2,000 or more in 2017 **or $2,100 in 2018**. You will have to register with the IRS and the state as an employer and issue W-2s to all the household workers each year. For the IRS, you report the wages and the taxes withheld on Schedule H, which is included in your tax return (https://www.irs.gov/pub/irs-pdf/f1040sh.pdf). However, your state may require regular quarterly payroll tax returns and deposits. The truth is, payroll reporting is as detailed, complicated, and time consuming for one employee as it is for 25–50 employees. If just reading this gives you anxiety, turn this task over to a payroll service or your tax professional. True, it will cost you about $75–$125 per quarter, but it's worth it to take the pressure off. (Search for "nanny tax.")

The other option is to hire attendants through an agency. The agency will put them on their payroll and take care of all the taxes, reports, and so on. Make sure the agency has a payroll. If not, use a different agency. But using an agency typically means paying at least 25 to 30 percent for the agency's costs and profits. Suppose this costs you an extra $25 per day. That could mean as much as $700 extra per month (25 × 365 divided by 12) when your mom or child needs daily care. Frankly, paying $125 per quarter for a payroll service is much cheaper than paying $2,100 extra per quarter to an agency.

If you are using the Schedule H route, remember to increase your federal withholding at work, or raise your quarterly estimated tax payments to cover the additional Social Security, Medicare, and Unemployment taxes that will be due with your ultimate tax return.

Tip #85: Nursing Home

Nursing home care is sometimes the best choice for your loved one. This could be due to extreme age or dementia or the need to provide rehabilitation after an accident or physical event. In this case, practically all the costs are deductible as medical expenses.

But the deduction is not always a given. Here is the fine print: "If an individual is able to perform at least two activities of daily living, the rental costs are not deductible. Activities of daily living are eating, toileting, transferring, bathing, dressing, medication management and continence" (https://www.irs.gov/publications/p502/ar02 .html#en_US_2014_publink1000178974). You should also note, though, that when someone is unable to perform at least two activities of daily living *without substantial assistance from another individual, or requires substantial supervision to be protected from severe cognitive impairment* (such as Alzheimer's), then qualified long-term care services will be necessary and deductible.

Even if your loved ones can take care of themselves, if they are getting medical or nursing care, those medical costs are deductible. In many cases, the nursing home provides all kinds of doctors, and residents receive treatments on the premises. It's a good idea to get paperwork from the facility that defines what part of the fee goes to medical care.

Tip #86: Medical Travel

Medical travel. Let's look at the basics. Medical travel includes the costs for the patient and a (one) companion/caregiver—up to $50 per night each (no deduction for meals). Medical travel for treatment outside the country is deductible. Remember to pick up the cost of medical miles if you're driving and the cost of airfare, shuttles, cabs, and so on if you are not driving.

Tip #87: Foreign Travel

Medical travel bonus. Did you know that medical travel outside the country is deductible? The same limits apply: the airfare to and from and $50 per night each for the patient and companion. The treatment may require the patient to stay in that country for several weeks until the full set of procedures is complete. The lodging for all those days is allowable if it is impractical to travel back and forth for the treatment. For instance, sometimes you need to get a series of operations or procedures (like dental implants, medical lap-banding, medical cosmetic surgery, or burn treatments). After each procedure, it's necessary to wait a few days before the next step can be taken safely. In some cases, the treatment, travel, and living expenses are still cheaper than it would cost here in the United States. Make sure you have a valid prescription or course of treatment, in writing, from a legitimate, licensed US medical practitioner.

Incidentally, some medical facilities around the world are aware of this tax deduction. They will make it easy for you to comply with US laws. Since their costs are so much lower, the foreign medical facilities attract patients by providing a full-service facility—medical services, lodging, and meals all rolled into the price. But do your research. While many facilities are highly qualified, beware that there are also charlatans who can do you great harm.

Tip #88: Not Quite Dependent

Not quite a dependent, but almost? These days, we often find ourselves in that sandwich generation—squeezed between helping to support our children and helping to support our parents, who are living longer than ever before. In order to claim someone as a dependent, we need to be paying more than half the person's support. But costs are so high that it might require several people to chip in to cover all the costs to support a particular person. The IRS has a solution for you. It's Form 2120, the Multiple Support Declaration (https://www.irs.gov/pub/irs-pdf/f2120.pdf). Enter the name and Social Security number of the person being supported. This person will not claim his or her own exemption on the personal tax return. Then get each person to sign this form every year that you are all jointly supporting someone. Allocate the deduction to you first, since you came up with the idea. Next year, and thereafter, take turns giving the dependency exemption to each person participating in the support.

Tip #89: IRA and Retirement Plan Strategies

When medical expenses are high, reduce regular IRA account and retirement plan balances. When someone dies, the heirs have to pay taxes on all the money in regular IRA accounts and most retirement accounts. Money held in Roth IRA accounts is not taxed to heirs or to the living (after the account has been funded for five years). There is a way to pull the money out of an IRA or retirement account while you (or your loved one) are alive without paying much, if anything, in taxes.

If you have a significant amount in your 401(k) or retirement account, and you have high medical expenses for yourself and/or a dependent, you can withdraw money from your retirement account in order to pay for the medical expenses. Then you can add that amount to your income and take a deduction for the medical expenses. Then, if you don't need that cash, just roll those funds into a Roth IRA. The deductions might offset the income. You can do this every year until all the retirement accounts are rolled over to Roth IRAs, or are used to pay medical expenses.

Tip #90: Gift/Estate Tax Strategy

This tip provides no tax deduction, but here's how you can avoid gift and estate taxes when paying someone else's medical expenses. You may pay anyone's medical expenses as a gift without any gift tax limitations providing you make the payments directly to the medical provider. Normally, gifts are limited to $14,000 per person per year in 2017 and **$15,000 per year in 2018** before the giver must face gift taxes. In this case, if you have a friend or family member who needs your help, pay the doctor, hospital, lab, or other medical provider directly. You won't need to file a gift tax return for these gifts, no matter how much you spend. Since this person isn't your dependent, you won't get a medical expense deduction, though. One warning: If the person for whom you are paying changes his or her mind and backs out of the medical services, gets a refund, or gets insurance reimbursements, he or she must pay you back. So of course you should use this strategy only with someone you know well and trust.

Tip #91: Getting Help

You need money to help pay your medical bills. Crowdfunding sites like GoFundMe, YouCaring, GiveForward, and others have cropped up all over the Internet. Generally, when you use sites like these, the funds you receive tend to be considered income by the IRS. How can you avoid causing tax problems when you help someone? Easy; set up the campaign properly. Here are four easy steps to keep you, and the friend in need, out of tax trouble:

1. When raising money for someone's medical expenses, set up the crowdfunding account and bank account in the name and SSN of the recipient—not yours!

2. Do *not* offer anything in return—no e-books, no T-shirts, no nothing! Doing that allows the IRS to think you've turned this appeal into a sales opportunity.

3. Do *not* promise the donors a tax deduction. Since you are not a registered nonprofit (exempt) organization, none of the contributions are deductible donations. They are all gifts.

4. For the recipient, use all the money to pay for things you said you needed to pay, so include living expenses while you cannot work and follow-up treatments. Otherwise you could be accused of defrauding the people who were kind enough to help you. Sometimes you raise more money than you requested. As long as you use the money for aforementioned living expenses or follow-up treatments, these funds are still not taxable, since all the contributions were voluntary gifts. Of course, you can opt to donate those excess funds to charity or to someone else's crowdfunding campaign—**and claim a**

contribution deduction, since you are now donating your own money. A great way to pay it forward.

Tip #92: When You Can Deduct

If your medical expenses were paid by others or via crowdfunding, do you get to deduct the medical expenses if you didn't pay them yourself? As it turns out, you may. There is a very clear and specific Tax Court Memo from 2010 that addresses this issue. Should you ever find yourself in this situation and get audited, use this citation to settle your audit. Consider reading it. It's quite interesting (TC Memo 2010-286, *Lang v. Commissioner*: http://www.ustaxcourt.gov/inophistoric/la5ng.tcm.wpd.pdf).

Tip #93: FSAs

Flexible Spending Accounts (FSAs). For tax year 2017, the FSA limit is $2,600, and for 2018, the limit is **$2,650**. When you know that your out-of-pocket medical expenses during the year will average $50 per month or more, it's worth signing up for the FSA. You should be realistic about your medical expense projection. You run the risk of losing your money if you overestimate your expenses. Assuming you figured correctly, it's a great deal, since you're spending the money anyway. How do you set it up? During open enrollment, when starting a new job, or whenever your company schedule permits, tell your payroll department to deduct up to $2,650 (you decide how much) from your paycheck over the 12-month period. As you pay for eligible medical expenses for yourself, family members, or dependents (or almost dependents; see Tip #80), just send in the receipts to the administrator and get your money back. Meanwhile, for tax purposes, your W-2 will show a lower income amount in all the boxes—Wages, Social Security income, and Medicare income.

What happens if you don't run up enough expenses to get your money back by the end of the year? It's important to understand this issue. Find out if your employer participates in the 2½-month extension, allowing you to get medical services and pay medical bills until March 15 of the following year. If it does, you will have 2½ extra months to get your money back.

There's also a carryover option. This means that if you have up to $500 left over at the end of the year, you can carry that balance over to the following year and use it that year.

If your employer doesn't offer these options, review your medical expenditures by October of each year. See how much money you have not yet gotten back. Are there receipts you have not submitted yet, for, say, prescriptions, contact lenses, or routine medical supplies? If yes, submit them immediately. If not, it's time to get new eyeglasses or contact lenses or visit the dentist. Your employer will have a list of qualified expenses. Read more about FSAs in IRS Publication 969 (https://www.irs.gov/publications/p969/ar02.html).

Tip #94: HSAs

Health Saving Accounts or Arrangements (HSAs). These are quite a bit more complicated, but they also allow you to stow away a lot more money. Individuals may contribute up to $3,400 and families up to $6,750 (https://www.irs.gov/pub/irs-drop/rp-15-30.pdf) for 2017 **and for 2018 individuals may contribute up to 3,450 and families up to $6,900 (https://www.irs.gov/pub/irs-drop/rp-17-37.pdf)**. Visit the IRS website for update information, since this amount changes each year due to inflation. The money may be funded by an individual or an employer. Once the money is in the HSA (set up as part of the Health Savings Arrangement), if you don't touch the money, you can leave it there to grow until you get old or face an emergency. Kind of like a second IRA. The contributions to this account can come off the top of your wages if you have a job. Or your employer can pay the money for you without you facing any taxes. If you are self-employed, it will be an adjustment to income. (So the contribution won't reduce your self-employment taxes.)

On the other hand, the HSA is designed to cover your out-of-pocket medical expenses when you have a high deductible insurance plan. So you are definitely allowed to use the account to pay for your medical expenses. In fact, the insurance provider can give you a debit card to use in pharmacies, hospitals, and other medical establishments. For 2017 (**and 2018**), a high deductible health plan means the plan has a deductible of at least $1,300 (**$1,350**) for individuals and $2,600 (**$2,700**) for families.

Tip #95: HSA Reporting

HSA reporting. The one drawback to this is that the HSA administrator will send you Form 1099-SA at the end of the year showing how much money you spent from the account (https://www.irs.gov/pub/irs-pdf/f5498sa.pdf). In order to avoid paying taxes and penalties on these expenditures, you must attach Form 8889 to your tax return (https://www.irs.gov/pub/irs-access/f8889_accessible.pdf). Ever since this form was created, taxpayer and tax professionals alike have struggled to get it to work so that all the penalties are cleared. Definitely see a tax pro if you used your HSA to pay for medical expenses. One more important thing to know about these debit cards: you can use them for anything at all in a pharmacy or certain other places. In other words, you can buy food, beverages, greeting cards, makeup, and so on. The IRS is wise to this. Just showing that the charge took place in a pharmacy, CVS, Walgreens, and so on is not enough. You must have the receipt for the purchase, and it must be for a legitimate medical expense. If not, you will be paying taxes and penalties on the noneligible purchase. Be sure to look at the receipt or invoice carefully.

Note: Not all states recognize the HSA, so find out if this works with your state tax laws. Otherwise, your contributions will be taxable on the state level.

There is more to HSAs than summarized here. In fact, there are a couple more medical-type tax breaks. Please read more about them in IRS Publication 969 (https://www.irs.gov/publications/p969).

Tip #96: Caregiver Income

Caregivers, get your money back! There are Medicaid programs that pay individuals to provide care to family members. You should be able to find information about these opportunities in your state by searching the Internet.

On January 3, 2014, the IRS issued a notice stating that this income is specifically not taxable (https://www.irs.gov/Individuals/Certain-Medicaid-Waiver-Payments-May-Be-Excludable-From-Income). The IRS "will treat these Medicaid waiver payments as difficulty of care payments excludable from gross income under §131 of the Internal Revenue Code."

What does this mean for you? It means that you don't have to report this income. Better yet, if you reported this income in the past, you might be able to file an amended return (Form 1040X) to get a refund for the taxes you paid on this income. You can amend a tax return to get a refund within three years of the filing date of the tax return. Or if you paid the taxes later because you were short of funds, you may get a refund within two years after you paid the taxes if that turns out to be later.

For instance, you finally finished paying $2,000 of your 2014 IRS balance due on September 12, 2017. You can recover this payment until September 11, 2019. Normally, if you filed the 2014 tax return on October 15, 2015, you could only get a refund until October 14, 2018. Sometimes there is an advantage to filing or paying late.

CHAPTER 8

Charitable Deductions

A MERICANS ARE REALLY GENEROUS people. Whenever there is a flood, earthquake, fire, disaster, or refugee situation anywhere in the world, Americans step up and chip in with money, time, and resources. We do this as individuals, through nonprofit organizations, and via our tax dollars as well.

Some of our donations generate charitable contribution deductions. Some don't. And some are outright thefts by scam artists. Let's sort through the noise and help you find the truth so you can continue to be generous and at the same time make sure your donations do what you intend.

Tip #97: Beware Fakes

Every time there is a major disaster or event, charities spring up to help out. But many of them are fakes designed to tap into the outpouring of love and money. Confine your contributions to established charities. If you've never heard of it, it probably isn't real. There are two ways to find out if a charity is legitimate via the IRS:

- Look the charity up on the IRS list of exempt organizations. This list will tell if you the charity exists, if it has been suspended or is active, how much of your deduction you can use this year, and if the charity has filed the Form 990-N postcard (for very small charities): https://www.irs.gov/Charities-&-Non-Profits/ Exempt-Organizations-Select-Check. This resource will let you see the data entered on Form 990-N, if the charity was small enough to file one.

- Call the IRS at 1-877-829-5500 if you think the charity is too new to be on the list.

Tip #98: Look 'Em Up

Learn how organizations use your money. Most exempt organizations (except "churches," which include all religious denominations) must file a version of Form 990 every single year. This is public information. You can go online and see their report. This can help you decide if they are using enough of your funds for the intended purpose—or using too much for the administrators' compensation, trips, and personal benefit. Or just wasting it. Here are some places you can find that information:

- GuideStar is one of the most established resources online and the one at the top of the search engines. It provides summary information about the organization's total revenues and expenses. To see the tax returns, you need to set up a free account and log in. For more detailed information, like tax reports going back more than three years and information about officers and more, you must pay for access: http://www.guidestar.org/Home.aspx.

- The Foundation Center allows you to look up your organization and gives you instant access to its tax forms for free without any log-ins. So you can look up your charity anonymously: http:// foundationcenter.org/findfunders/990finder.

  › To help you understand what the tax return means, let's take a look at a specific charity—Shelters for Israel (http://www .sheltersforisrael.com/about-us). It's a very small organization started by Holocaust survivors pooling their winnings at their weekly card game. The mission of the organization is to provide housing, daycare centers, playgrounds, and other facilities for children, students, disadvantaged youth, and immigrants. You can see the list of the projects it has funded since 1950 (http://www.sheltersforisrael.com/list-of -all-projects). The organization states that all its funds go toward its projects. Here's how to verify this claim.

  › First, look at the overview of the charity's Form 990 filings for the last three years. You can see the organization is in compliance and has been filing. Here is the summary:

ORGANIZATION NAME	STATE	YEAR	FORM	PAGES	TOTAL ASSETS	EIN
Shelters for Israel	CA	2015	990EZ	19	$102,306.00	95-6118813
Shelters for Israel	CA	2014	990EZ	16	$69,991.00	95-6118813
Shelters for Israel	CA	2013	990	20	$209,588.00	95-6118813
Shelters for Israel	CA	2013	990R	1	$0.00	95-6118813

Clicking on the link (under the name) to see the tax return (http://990s.foundationcenter.org/990_pdf_archive/956/9561 18813/956118813_201512_990EZ.pdf), we learn:

  › The charity spent less than it raised in 2015 (page 1 of Form 990).

  › It pays absolutely no salaries to any of the officers (Part IV and Part V of Form 990) or anyone else (line 12 on page 1 of Form 990).

› It charges no membership dues. Its fund-raising events (an annual banquet and advertising/tributes in the monthly newslet-
ter) raised $116,000, while it spent less than $9,000 on food
and related costs (page 15 of the PDF file of Form 990). That's
an astonishing 92.2 percent net return on the event.

› The organization spends a bit on rent "occupancy"—totaling
$1,410 (page 15 of the PDF file of Form 990).

› The organization's highest expenditures, besides the costs of
putting on events and funding its projects, are printing and
postage, about $16,000, which is less than 9.1 percent of the
contributions and funds it raised ($174,566) (page 1 of Form
990).

› Most importantly, over 95 percent of the funds raised from the
annual banquet were used for the charitable purpose intended.
The charity did reserve some funds at the end of the year (over
$100,000), but it used them in 2016 and 2017 to fund the
Desert Shanti House village, an at-risk youth education center
(http://www.sheltersforisrael.com/our-current-projects/).

• GrantSpace.org maintains a page where you can find a list of
sources providing information about exempt organizations:
http://grantspace.org/tools/knowledge-base/Funding-Research/
Forms-990-and-990-PF/finding-990-990-pfs.

Tip #99: Proper Receipts

Deducting money. While it should be straightforward to claim a
deduction for donations of money to legitimate exempt or religious
organizations, there are specific rules you need to follow. First and
foremost, it is important to get proper receipts from the organization
for each and every donation of $250 or more. The receipt must show
the following:

• The date of the donation.

- The legal name of the organization.
- Its mailing address. (It also helps to have a phone number.)
- The taxpayer ID number (TIN)—*very* important.
- The amount of the donation.
- A statement that says you did not receive any products or services for your donation, or a statement that spells out the value of products of services you received. (For instance, suppose you pay $250 per person for a fund-raising banquet. The receipt should show that you received an amount, say, $50 worth of food and goody-bag stuff.)

Not having all this information for every single donation means you can lose the deduction if you're audited.

Tip #100: Timely Receipts

Get receipts on time. You absolutely must have the receipt in your possession before you file your tax return or before the legal deadline to file your tax return (if you are filing late). The receipt must be dated before you file your tax return. This is imperative. When you are audited, even if you can prove that you paid $10,000 to your favorite charity—with all the cancelled checks and a letter from the charity dated during the audit—you will lose the deduction. The IRS auditor has no authority to approve it. IRS Appeals cannot grant you the deduction. Even the Tax Court cannot give you the deduction, though it will be sympathetic. Why is there no leeway? Internal Revenue Code Section 170 (Section 170(f)(8)(C)) has this rigid provision:

Contemporaneous

For purposes of subparagraph (A), an acknowledgment shall be considered to be contemporaneous if the taxpayer obtains the acknowledgment on or before the earlier of—

(i) the date on which the taxpayer files a return for the taxable year in which the contribution was made, or (ii) the due date (including extensions) for filing such return.

There have been many court cases where people did have proof that they made donations worth many thousands of dollars. But the verifications from the exempt organizations were dated long after the acceptable date.

To avoid the problem of gathering receipts for your many donations of $250 or more, consider contributing to a donor-advised fund. Read TaxMama's December 2015 article in her MarketWatch.com Tax Watch column: http://www.marketwatch.com/story/how-to-get -a-big-tax-write-off-while-doing-a-good-deed-2015-12-17.

Tip #101: Disguised Donations

No deduction for disguised donations. The IRS knows that the $2,000 per month tuition paid to your child's religious school isn't really a donation to the synagogue, church, temple, or mosque. It really is tuition—and is not a deductible contribution. What part of the tuition to religious schools may you deduct, if any? Naturally, none of the tuition itself. But what if the school calls part of it a donation, say $300 per month? If this is a mandatory payment for every student, it's not a donation. Donations are voluntary. It's just another way to disguise tuition. Sometimes the invoices have a line where you can add an amount as a donation. That would be deductible. Make sure the school totals that separately and provides a separate receipt monthly or a summary of the donations at the end of the year. The IRS audits religious schools all the time and "teaches" the administrators about how to separate tuition and donations—after making a list of parents to audit.

Tip #102: No Cash

Cash in the collection plate. Listening to an inspiring sermon, how can you help but contribute generously when the plate comes around? Please, don't restrain your enthusiasm. Instead, carry your checkbook and contribute on paper. This way, the organization has your information. It can create a report at the end of the year showing how much you contributed. Without that written receipt, you won't be able to deduct anything over $250.

Tip #103: The Truly Needy

Cash to street people. There are presently over half a million people who really are homeless in America living on the street or in temporary shelters, with many asking for money. It's impossible not to feel sympathy. But given the fact that there are con artists out there, you are better off donating to tax-exempt or religious organizations that help the homeless. Plus, you will get a tax deduction for your love and generosity.

Tip #104: Auctions for Charity

Cash for silent auctions, regular charity auctions, bazaars, and so on. It's fun to go to the special events where people donate things to help an organization raise money. You may not simply deduct the total amount of your purchase. If you bid on something and get it at less than the actual retail value of the item, there is no deduction at all. If you pay more than the retail value, be sure to get a receipt that shows that the excess amount is a contribution.

Tip #105: Donating Your Time

Donating time. Time is the most precious, irreplaceable resource there is. Unfortunately, there is no tax deduction for your volunteer time.

Tip #106: Strings Attached

Donating money to specific people. The Tax Code (IRC Section 170 (c)(2)(C)) has a prohibition against making a donation to benefit a specific person. People try to make a sizable donation to a college, for instance, so it will accept a particular student or provide that specific student with a scholarship. Not deductible. The donation may not have strings on it. Or someone in your community is about to lose her home and the pastor asks everyone to chip in and help her. Even if the donations go to the church, there is no deduction because it's specifically earmarked for an individual. To raise funds for people without any tax effect on the person receiving the money, read Tip #91. Regardless, there is no charitable contribution deduction.

Tip #107: Gently Used

Donating household items, starting with minor amounts. We all do the year-end thing where we clean out our closets and attics and take all the clean and usable clothing, small appliances, games, and knickknacks to our favorite charity or thrift shop. Make sure you get a receipt for your donations each time that you drop off your bags and/or boxes. You can get away with claiming a deduction of up to $500 without too much substantiation, aside from the receipts. Figure that each bag is worth about $25–$30 and each box is worth $50–$100, depending on what's in it.

Tip #108: It Adds Up

Donating your used items and getting a higher deduction for the minor stuff. If you take the time to carefully list all the items that go into those bags and boxes, you may find that those three bags and two boxes that were originally worth about $275 now prove to be worth well over $1,000. It's a good idea to take pictures of all the things you're donating, and take the time to make sure the items are clean and appealing. This will help support the value you are giving the items. One of the best free tools you can use to establish the current market value for each item is Intuit's ItsDeductible software (https://turbotax.intuit.com/personal-taxes/itsdeductible). The software has the values built in. True, it can take you an hour or two to enter each item one by one. But once you're done, you might be able to demonstrate that your so-so $275 bags and boxes really contain items that add up to $1,475. Do this before completing your tax return so you can put the printout and pictures into your tax file for the year. An extra $1,200 of deductions could net you anywhere from $180 to over $300 in federal and state tax savings. That's not too bad for an hour or two of work, is it?

Tip #109: High-Ticket Items

Donating expensive things. When you have something very special to donate, like a work of art, the rights to a piece of music, especially something worth $5,000 or more, you need to use a special tax form, Form 8283 (https://www.irs.gov/pub/irs-pdf/f8283.pdf). You must also get a formal, written appraisal, and the professional appraiser must sign Part III on page 2 of Form 8283. In cases like this, have the appraiser sign at least three copies of the form: one for the IRS, one in case the state wants an original, and a third copy for the taxpayer's own files.

- Sometimes you can get an objective valuation for some things from the retail or wholesale seller. But only do this if the item's value is under $5,000—and get the value in writing on the seller's forms.

- If you need an appraisal for probate, in California there is a special designation called a Probate Referee (http://www.sco.ca.gov/eo_probate_contact.html). This organization is empowered to provide valuations for items in estates for the Probate Court. Other states may have similar programs, so it pays to do your research.

Note: The IRS doesn't always accept appraisals at face value. If you don't get a professional appraisal done properly, it's quite likely that

*the IRS will audit and dispute your valuation (https://www.irs.gov/
publications/p561/ar02.html). Using someone unqualified who over-
states the value of your donation could get you penalties of 20–40
percent of your tax underpayments (https://www.irs.gov/publications/
p561/ar02.html#d0e1964).*

For more information on the IRS's perspective about putting a
value on your donations, read IRS Publication 561, "Determining
the Value of Donated Property" (https://www.irs.gov/publications/
p561).

Tip #110: Appraisal Fees

Appraisal fees. When you pay a professional for the valuation of
donated property, the fee is not a charitable contribution. You may
no longer claim the deduction on Schedule A as a miscellaneous
itemized deduction, reduced by 2 percent of AGI, as a result of the
TCJA. This option is suspended until after 2025 (http://iTaxMama
.com/IRS_Appraisal_Fees).

Tip #111: Vehicles

Donating vehicles. Think twice before deciding to donate a vehicle.
The process is more complicated than you might think, and you may
be better off selling the vehicle and donating the proceeds to a charitable organization. If you do choose to donate a vehicle, you will have
to jump through many hoops and get specific paperwork with the valuation of the vehicle. You need Form 1098-C from the organization
to which you donated the vehicle (https://www.irs.gov/pub/irs-pdf/
f1098c.pdf). You might not get the paperwork until after the organization sells it, which might not happen before you file your tax return—
which means you don't really know the value of your donation. P.S.:
If you donate your vehicle to one of those places that also gives you
money or trips to Las Vegas, you have to reduce your donation by the
face value of the money or products or services you received.

Tip #112: Gifting for Benefit

You love to make donations but get no tax benefit from them. I came across this situation because one of my favorite clients tithes—or more than tithes, actually. She donates more than $10,000 per year to her church. But since her income is mostly retirement, Social Security, and paper losses from her rental properties, she doesn't need to itemize her deductions. The donation is wasted on her as far as tax benefits are concerned. Do we want her to stop making the donations and supporting her church? Of course not. What's the solution? She can gift the money to her son and daughter-in-law. They make the donation to the church, now that it's their money. They get to claim the $10,000 deduction. See what a clean, elegant solution that is? Everyone wins.

Tip #113: Limits

Tax deductions are limited. Depending on what you contribute to what kind of charity, your charitable contribution deductions are limited to 20 percent, 30 percent, or **60 percent** of your AGI. The 20 percent and 30 percent limits only matter when you donate appreciated assets (things that are worth more now than when you bought them), when you donate to foundations, or in a couple of other special situations. If you are lucky enough to be in that position, you should be working with a tax professional to plan your giving. But do read what the IRS has to say about these limits in Publication 526 (https://www.irs.gov/publications/p526). **The 60 percent of the AGI limit on charitable contributions is for cash donations to public charities.**

Tip #114: Rolling Over

Speaking of limits, what do you do with the deductions you cannot use this year? Good question. You can take those deductions next year, or the year after that, and so on, for up to five years. Read about carryovers (https://www.irs.gov/publications/p526/ar02.html). That's why it was important to have my client stop tithing directly to her church. She already has enough contribution carryovers that it will take her a few years to use them up. This way they won't go to waste.

Tip #115: IRA Strategy

Why would you want to make a $100,000 nondeductible donation? There is a special provision in the Internal Revenue Code allowing senior citizens to make donations directly from their IRA accounts to the charity or charities of their choice (http://iTaxMama .com/RMD_Charity). This is targeted at folks ages 70½ or above who faced taking required minimum distributions (RMDs) from their retirement accounts—or face hefty penalties. This option requires that the withdrawal be transferred directly to the charity (called a qualified charitable distribution, or QCD). We'll talk a lot more about this in Chapter 9.

Tip #116: Volunteering

Services are not deductible, but volunteering can be profitable. Volunteering often comes with costs. As you know, we may deduct our volunteer mileage (14 cents per mile), but there are other costs as well. To participate in certain events, we might have to buy and wear uniforms. Those costs, as well as laundering costs, are deductible. We bring food or goodies to supply other volunteers. We print things to hand out, often at our own expense. We might need supplies, tools, and other things that we only use in association with our volunteer activities. We might take our charges (children, homeless people, seniors, etc.) out to lunch or dinner as part of our volunteer function. For camping with Scouts, we might need camping supplies that are only used for these events. How can you deduct these costs? Document, document, document! Keep excellent records (appointment books, logs, and such), receipts, and detailed notes about the odd or unusual expenses. If you can, submit an overall report to the charity or organization with a list of the costs. Have the charity write you a "Thank you" letter showing the amount of your out-of-pocket contributions. This will provide additional substantiation for the legitimacy of the costs, as they relate to the charity's activities.

Tip #117: Fun!

Volunteering can be fun, too! There are many intangible rewards: meeting celebrities, making new friends, and feeling good for a job well done.

Tip #118: Ideas for Helping

Here are some creative ideas for volunteering. They are not only fun; they are good exercise, you get to meet interesting people, and, who knows, you might even end up meeting your soul mate (if you're looking for one!).

The volunteer opportunities are limited only by your imagination. To meet writers, artists, and celebrities, find out which charities they run or those in which they actively participate. You can also search the web for local organizations that have put out the call for volunteers. Here's one such website: https://www.volunteermatch.org.

Tip #119: Resources

An amazing resource for exempt organization administrators and volunteers. TechSoup (http://www.techsoup.org). This is a great place to get free, or seriously discounted, software, refurbished computers, tools, and supplies for your entity. You can find entire suites from Microsoft, Intuit, Cisco, GoDaddy, NetSuite, Norton, and many, many more big-name vendors. It's free to register. So don't overlook this valuable resource. You will find more resources, like TechSoup and other goodies, at the Foundation Center's GrantSpace site (http://grantspace.org/tools/knowledge-base). As an exempt organization, you have access to government grants, cable television time, corporation foundation grants, and lots more free money—if you know where to find it.

Tip #120: Start Your Own

Start your own nonprofit. If you have a passion and time, why not start your own nonprofit organization? What do you love to do? With whom do you love to spend your time? How do you start your own charity or association? It will take effort. You will need the help of a tax professional who is experienced setting these organizations up. It all starts with two things:

- A solid business plan where you define what your mission is, how you plan to achieve your goal, whether you will fund it all or raise funds, how you will get volunteers to participate, and whom you will be serving.
- A tax form. Use one of these forms—Form 1023 (1023-EZ) or Form 1024 (https://www.irs.gov/Charities-&-Non-Profits/ Applying-for-Tax-Exempt-Status).

Incidentally, the IRS has an amazingly detailed website to walk you through the entire process, including online training materials (https://www.irs.gov/Charities-&-Non-Profits). You will find an entire area about the Life Cycle of an Exempt Organization that can take you from conception, to inception, to operation of your organization (https://www.irs.gov/Charities-&-Non-Profits/Life-Cycle-of -an-Exempt-Organization).

CHAPTER 9

Retirement Tax Issues for the Young at Heart

F WE HAD A real crystal ball, it would be supremely simple to know exactly how much to save and how much money we can spend enjoying the moment. After all, members of our baby boomer generation who are reading this right now most likely have many good years ahead of them. We're still here. Some of us are active and vital and pursuing life's pleasures with even more gusto than we did in our thirties and forties. So what's a person to do?

Tip #121: Never Too Early

Start setting aside money toward retirement as soon as you can. Your most obvious choices are:

- Open a savings account.

- Use an IRA—Individual Retirement Account with deductible contributions.

- Use a Roth IRA—Individual Retirement Account with nondeductible contributions now—but no taxes when you retire.

- Use one of the many retirement plans offered at work. See what your employer has to offer.

  › Some employers offer to match your contributions—definitely invest as much as you can in those plans. At least invest as much as your employer will match.

  › Some employers offer a Roth option to their retirement plans. That means you won't get a deduction when you invest. You will get the benefits when you retire. (That's called delayed gratification.)

- Buy US Savings Bonds.

- Invest in stocks, bonds, or securities.

- Buy a whole life insurance policy.

- Invest in real estate.

Tip #122: Roth vs. Regular

What do the Roth and regular IRAs have in common? Both have the same annual contribution limits.

- Presently for 2017 **and 2018**, the limits are $5,500 per person, or $6,500 if your age is 50 or over (https://www.irs.gov/ Retirement-Plans/Plan-Participant-Employee/Retirement -Topics-IRA-Contribution-Limits).

- Your contributions to all IRAs are limited to your earned income.

- Even though your spouse is not working, you may contribute to a spousal IRA (Roth or regular), as long as the total of all your IRA contributions does not exceed your earned income.

- Earned income consists of the total of all your wages and your self-employment profits, which can come from your Schedule C or your general partnership income from Form 1065 (reported on Schedule E, page 2).

- If you have self-employed losses that wipe out your self-employment income, you won't be able to make any IRA contributions.

- All earnings inside the plans grow tax-free.

- You are permitted to roll over balances from your other IRAs or pension plans into any of your IRA accounts, Roth or regular, without paying any early withdrawal penalties. (Rolling to a Roth will generate taxes.)

- You may roll over the money from an existing IRA or Roth IRA to another investment house only once per year (newly defined rule: https://www.irs.gov/Retirement-Plans/IRA-One-Rollover -Per-Year-Rule). When you do make a rollover, if the funds are not transferred directly from the first IRA account to the new (or second) account, you must finish moving the money within 60 days. Not two months. *Sixty days!* If you miss the deadline, the entire amount of the rollover becomes taxable immediately. Folks who are under age 59½ face all those early withdrawal penalties (unless they meet certain exceptions).

- Yes, you are permitted to establish self-directed IRAs. But they are very expensive and complicated and can easily end up being disallowed, which means that everything in the account can become instantly taxable.

- You may draw your money out when you reach age 59½ without facing early withdrawal penalties. If you take the money earlier, you will face an IRS penalty for 10 percent of the taxable balance plus whatever your state charges as a penalty.

Sounds good so far. So what are the differences?

Tip #123: The Regular IRA

With a regular IRA, you get to deduct your contribution in the year you make the contribution. So you get an immediate tax benefit, or instant gratification. When you pull money out of your IRA, all your distribution is taxable. Why? You got a tax deduction for your original contribution—and all the earnings grew tax-free. So none of the money in the account has ever been taxed. This is especially important to understand when it comes to estate planning. Whoever inherits your IRA will also pay tax on the full balance in the account. Unlike other assets you might own at death, IRAs do not get special treatment. And remember, if you are covered by a retirement plan at work, your IRA deduction is limited based on the amount of your modified adjusted gross income (MAGI). You can find the most recent limits at the IRS website (https://www.irs.gov/Retirement-Plans/IRA-Deduction-Limits).

Tip #124: You Paid Tax?

But, you say, you *did* pay tax on some of your IRA contributions! What then? First of all, under what conditions might you have paid tax?

- Your income was too high to qualify for a deductible contribution, but you contributed anyway. Keep track of those amounts on Form 8606: https://www.irs.gov/pub/irs-pdf/f8606.pdf. That way, you, your heirs, and the IRS will know how much of your contribution was made with after-tax dollars.

- You live in a state that has (or had) a lower IRA contribution allowance than the IRS permits. While all your IRS contributions might have been deducted, you might have made nondeductible contributions on the state level. If the state doesn't have a form that lets you track this number, keep a worksheet in a permanent file that allows you to track the numbers. Let your tax pro, your estate attorney, and key members of your family know about this worksheet. For instance, California has a Publication 1005 that helps identify the basis differences for years when California had lower contribution limits (https://www.ftb.ca.gov/forms/2016/16_1005.pdf—see page 5). What does your state have to help you?

Tip #125: The Roth

If you don't get a deduction for your Roth IRA contribution, what is the Roth IRA for? This is a perfect savings vehicle for people with long-term vision. You can stash away money, little by little, every year. Although you pay taxes on the money you deposit, you don't pay taxes on the earnings. However, you must leave the funds in the Roth IRA for five years before tapping it. The Roth IRA contributions are limited if your earnings are too high. Look up the MAGI earnings limits on the IRS website (https://www.irs.gov/Retirement-Plans/Roth-IRAs). Here are the rewards. When you finally retire, none of the money you draw out is taxable. You do not have to take any of those pesky required minimum distributions (RMDs) at age 70½ (see Tip #126). When you die, no matter how much money is in the Roth account, none of it will be taxable to your heirs. Isn't that a terrific benefit? In fact, some 401(k) plans at work allow you to make part of your contributions to a Roth 401(k) account. Remember how earlier I mentioned that you can roll over your pension balances to the Roth account? Yes, you can do this. And if you plan the rollovers properly, you can move the money while paying just a little tax on each rollover.

Tip #126: Which Is Better?

Which is better, a regular IRA or a Roth IRA? That's a great question. And the answer depends on your income and asset level while you are working and when you retire.

- For people who expect to have very low levels of income when they retire, the regular IRA is better for them. Especially since they get that very valuable tax break in the year they make the IRA contribution. They probably won't build up hundreds of thousands of dollars in their IRA. They will probably end up using all the money in their lifetime.

- The Roth is the perfect account for folks who expect to be in a higher tax bracket when they retire than when they were working. Believe it or not, I have seen this happen.

- You need to note that **the TCJA no longer permits us to recharacterize IRA rollovers to Roth IRAs** (https://www.irs.gov/Retirement-Plans/Roth-IRAs).

- In order to make sure your annual earnings are not too high to qualify for the Roth IRA, you should wait to fund Roth IRA accounts until November of your tax year. That way you will know how much your earnings are for most of the year and have an idea of how much bonus to expect. (Or wait until March of the following year when all the numbers are in.) You can still move your contributions for the current year from your Roth IRA to your regular IRA. Just make sure to do it before the April filing deadline for your tax return.

Tip #127: RMDs

RMDs explained. RMDs affect seniors age 70½ and older and their required minimum distributions (RMDs). What is an RMD (https://www.irs.gov/retirement-plans/plan-participant-employee/retirement-topics-required-minimum-distributions-rmds)? This is the least (minimum) amount of money you are required to withdraw from your IRAs and retirement accounts every year once you reach the age of 70½—give or take a few months.

Tip #128: Timing

Timing. When must you start taking the distributions? You must take the first distribution by April 1 of the year after you reach age 70½. You have a little leeway. It doesn't need to be *the* year you turn age 70½. But you must keep in mind:

1. Getting this extra time means that people put off taking the distribution and forget to take it on time. Forgetting is expensive.

2. The penalty for not taking a timely distribution is 50 percent of the amount that should have been distributed.

3. If you wait to take your first RMD until April 1 of the year after you turn age 70½, you must take two distributions during that year. One for the year you turned 70½, and the second one for the year in which you are age 71.

4. You can avoid the risk of forgetting and incurring penalties or duplicate income by simply taking the first distribution in the year you turn 70½.

Tip #129: Delay RMD

Legitimate delay for RMD. If you are still working for the company where you have your retirement account in the year you turn 70½, you can put off taking the first distribution from that account until you retire from that company. Retirement accounts that qualify for this delay include 401(k)s, profit-sharing, 403(b)s, or other defined contribution plans. But you will have to take a distribution from that account in the year you retire. *Note: You must still take all the required distributions from your IRAs and other retirement accounts.*

Tip #130: Distributions

Distributions from *all* accounts? No, you don't need to take a distribution from each and every account you have. You may add up the value of all the accounts and compute the overall RMD. Then you may choose to draw that year's distribution from one account, or several, as long as you draw at least the minimum amount. Naturally, you may withdraw more—just not less. Use this IRS worksheet to determine how much you must withdraw based on your age: https://www.irs.gov/pub/irs-tege/uniform_rmd_wksht.pdf. Do this each year, since account balances change based on investment returns and withdrawals. After all, you are entitled to draw money for your other needs. You are welcome to draw more than the minimums each year.

Tip #131: Reduce!

Reduce your IRA and retirement account balances as quickly as you can. The balance in your previously untaxed retirement accounts will be fully taxable to your heirs. So draw out more than the minimum amount if you can do that without raising your tax bill or moving up to a higher tax bracket.

Tip #132: No RMD?

No RMD required. If all your retirement funds are in Roth IRAs, you don't have to worry about taking any distributions at all. **If you do some freelance work, make new contributions to your Roth IRA. After all, the IRS says you're still allowed to contribute to your Roth IRA after age 70½ (https://www.irs.gov/retirement-plans/roth-iras).** The funds in your Roth IRA can continue to grow tax-free. You can use the money anytime you like without paying taxes when you take the money (as long as the Roth IRA has been open for at least five years). And your heirs will get all that money tax-free as well.

Tip #133: Avoid Taxes

Avoid taxes on your RMD altogether. Make a nondeductible charitable contribution to your favorite charity of up to $100,000. Why would you want to make a $100,000 nondeductible donation? There is a special provision in the Internal Revenue Code allowing senior citizens to make donations directly from their IRA accounts to the charity or charities of their choice (http://iTaxMama.com/RMD_Charity). This is targeted at folks ages 70½ or above who face taking required minimum deposits (RMDs) from their retirement accounts or incurring hefty penalties. This option requires that the withdrawal is transferred directly to the charity (called a qualified charitable distribution, or QCD) (see Tip #134). If that is done properly, seniors get two visible benefits and lose one benefit:

> **Benefit 1:** They can count this draw as their RMD for the year.
> **Benefit 2:** They don't have to pay taxes on the amount they have withdrawn and sent to the charity.
> **Drawback: They don't get to claim the charitable contribution deduction for this donation.** By this time, most folks this age are no longer itemizing anyway, unless they have large out-of-pocket medical costs. So it's no great loss.

Tip #134: More Benefits

Six more reasons for this nondeductible contribution. Here are the (sort of) intangible benefits of making a QCD donation:

1. This can be a terrific benefit for people whose draw might otherwise cause their Social Security income to become taxable. An RMD of $5,000 might end up costing the taxpayer several thousand dollars in taxes because it causes Social Security income to become taxable, too, raising the AGI.

2. This can keep someone out of Alternative Minimum Tax (AMT) territory. As your income rises, you could face AMT, based on a variety of tax loopholes you might be using on your tax return.

3. Not adding the RMD to income keeps the AGI lower, so a variety of credits and deductions are not lost.

4. This makes it possible to keep estimated taxes lower during the year.

5. For people who tithe anyway and couldn't otherwise use the deduction, this lets you keep tithing and hold your head up in the community as a generous donor.

6. By distributing much more money from your retirement than the minimum requirement, you can deplete this taxable asset without paying taxes on the draws.

In other words, this provision carries a lot of worthwhile benefits to the taxpayer. (There are probably several benefits I haven't even touched upon.)

Hooray! Congress made this provision permanent as part of the PATH Act of 2015. Since you like to make charitable contributions, make the donation. Here are two ways to take advantage of this:

• Wait until December to take your RMD, so you can keep the earnings on these funds for the year.

• Take the distribution earlier in the year and have it sent directly to your charity, so the charity has time to use the money or invest it.

Regardless, you will have drawn enough money to cover your RMD. Either way—you win!

Tip #135: Social Security Timing

Is it a good idea to start collecting Social Security benefits at age 62? Be careful when you start collecting early. Unless you have no other source of support and are not well enough to work, this is not a good idea. Most people cannot live on their SS benefits, so they still have to work to supplement those Social Security checks (especially after they deduct Medicare payments). What is the maximum amount you are allowed to earn? For 2017 (**2018**), you may earn up to $16,920 (**$17,040**) in wages or net self-employment income. (Use this chart to look up later years: https://www.ssa.gov/oact/cola/rtea.html.) When you earn any more than that, you must pay back the good old Social Security Administration to the tune of $1 for every $2 you earn past this limit. This is bad for at least two reasons:

- If you don't pay the money back in the same year that you received it, you will include the full amount of SS benefits in your income—even though you will have to repay some of it in the following year (see Tip #145).

- You started collecting SS benefits early, so you have locked in a lower monthly benefit than you would have gotten had you waited until age 66, or your minimum Social Security retirement age. And you now have to repay some of those lower benefits you have. Doesn't this seem like such a waste?

So review your needs carefully before applying early. Don't apply for Social Security benefits if you cannot afford to live on them and are still healthy enough to earn more than the allowable limits.

Tip #136: Nontaxable?

Understand when SS benefits and Equivalent Railroad Retirement Benefits are not taxable. *Note: Anytime you see anything about Social Security in this book, the information also covers "Equivalent Railroad*

Retirement Benefits." When all your income comes from the Social Security Administration, none of the benefits are taxable. This applies to seniors, folks on Social Security Disability, and children collecting survivor's benefits after a parent has died. There is no tax when you are single (S), the head of household (HOH), the qualifying widow or widower (QW) with a dependent child, or married individuals filing separately if all your income, plus half the Social Security income, stays below $25,000. For married couples filing jointly (MFJ), the limit is $32,000. Beware: When married couples live together and file separately (MFS), 85 percent of their Social Security benefits are taxed immediately. There is no exclusion for MFS.

Tip #137: Watch Limits

When your income is higher than the Social Security limits, what is the tax effect? When income rises above that, suddenly up to 85 percent of the SS income becomes taxable. You can use the IRS worksheets (they have examples) in Publication 915 to figure out how much of your benefits will be taxable (https://www.irs.gov/publications/p915/ar02.html). However, your tax software will also have tools to make these computations. In fact, it might just be easier to log into some live tax software and enter your income and Social Security benefits to see exactly where you stand.

Tip #138: AGI

Let's look at a tangible effect of adding RMDs or retirement rollovers to your AGI when you're collecting Social Security. You are married. The two of you collect a total of $23,000 from Social Security. Your interest income is $5,000. Your total AGI is $5,000 because none of your Social Security income is taxable. Now let's add an RMD of $15,000. Good news! No tax effect because half of your Social Security benefits ($11,500) plus your additional income are still less than $32,000. That means you can either draw this money or move it to a Roth IRA. What happens if you take $30,000? Adding this $15,000 to your income means that $8,125 of your Social Security benefits becomes taxable. So adding $15,000 actually means raising your income by $23,125. The good news is, after the standard deduction and personal exemptions for seniors, your taxable income is low enough that you end up paying less than $2,000 for the $30,000 you drew from your retirement account. That's less than 7 percent (plus whatever your state charges). Raising the distribution to $50,000 however, means $19,550, or 85 percent, of your Social Security benefits are taxable (the maximum level). You end up paying nearly $7,000 in IRS taxes (plus state taxes) on that $50,000. Actually, this is still not bad because you're paying less than 14 percent of the distribution.

- Do you see how you can test numbers in your live tax software account to see what the real tax effect will be? Remember, those live tax software accounts are free to play around in. You only pay when you actually file a tax return . . . though some of the services will charge you if you print the forms.

- Based on your comfort level with respect to paying no taxes or, say, up to a 15 percent tax rate, you can find the ideal amount of distributions to draw from your taxable retirement accounts.

- This can give you a good way to determine the highest amount to draw from all your taxable IRAs and pensions—or even how much you can afford to produce when it comes to capital gains.

- By working with an experienced tax professional, you can get even more guidance on how to manage the flow of funds to get the lowest tax hit on the most cash.

Tip #139: Medicare Fees

Social Security Form SSA-1099 also contains fees for Medicare benefits. Those amounts are deductible as health insurance costs.

In fact, if you are self-employed, you are entitled to take these into account for your self-employed health insurance deduction. This is often overlooked because many self-employed folks don't know it's allowed.

Tip #140: Lump Sums

Lump sum payments from Social Security. If you know anyone who ever applied for Social Security Disability, you probably know they got rejected at least two to three times before getting approved. This means that applicants often end up hiring an attorney to help get their claim approved—and lose 35–50 percent of their benefit after all fees and cost reimbursements are deducted. Yet they must pay tax on all the money they received, right? The taxable part of this is not as bad as you think.

1. When the SSA finally approves the claim, it pays you based on the date of your original claim. So you will get three to four years of benefits all at one time. Yes, you must report the entire amount in the year you get the money.

2. You must report the gross amount of your award even though your attorney gets that large chunk. Deduct the attorney's fees and costs on Schedule A as a miscellaneous itemized deduction reduced by 2 percent of your AGI (https://www.irs.gov/publications/p529/ar02.html).

3. There is a special computation (and worksheet) you can use that treats the money as though you received it over several years (http://iTaxMama.com/SSDI_LumpSum). If you are using commercial tax return software and can't figure out how to get the program to do this, call the software company's tech support line. I guarantee that the companies have all built this into their systems. If you cannot figure it out, or don't have the

patience, take it to a tax pro for the year in which you get this settlement. It will be well worth it to end up paying less tax.

Tip #141: SSDI

You're finally collecting Social Security Disability Income (SSDI), but you can't live on it. Are you allowed to do any work at all to supplement the income? Yes you are! You must earn less than $1,170 per month ($1,950 if you are blind) in 2017 **and $1,180 per month ($1,970 if you are blind) in 2018**. Visit https://www.ssa.gov/planners/disability/dwork2.html to see what the limits are in the current year (the year in which you read this).

Tip #142: LLC Strategy

You're not disabled but want to collect Social Security early anyway. Someone asked me if it's possible to structure an LLC with his wife so he could start collecting his benefits at age 62, while he keeps working. It's an interesting concept. And it can be risky. However, if they form an LLC in a non–community property state, it can be owned by the spouse who is not collecting Social Security. Then this arrangement just might work. She can pay his wages for the part-time work. She can provide retirement plan contributions and medical benefits to reduce the profits. Then she could keep the profits as her own self-employment income. This could potentially help to increase her own Social Security account for her future retirement.

There are two potential drawbacks to this—aside from the tax considerations:

1. Turning over your business to your spouse is only a good idea if you have a really solid marriage.

2. If your business requires a specialized license that can only be assigned to a person, not to a business (like a contractor's license), . . . well, that might prevent this whole plan from working.

Tip #143: Nonreturnable

When don't you have to pay anything back? People who don't need to work, people who have investment income (any kind at all—interest, dividends, rentals, royalties, capital gains, pensions, etc.), can receive an unlimited amount of investment income while collecting SS benefits early. For those with the wherewithal (and who bet on this loophole never being closed), you can start your savings and investment programs early so you can be among those who have investment income.

Tip #144: Control Earned Income

Can you control your earned income? Yes you can. Many years ago I was a speaker at a CPA dinner meeting. One of the CPAs there was saying that she had just started to collect her Social Security benefits early. Because, clearly, she was still working, I asked about the repayment requirement. She said she doesn't have to worry about that. Her CPA practice was in an S corporation. She could keep her wages under the earnings limit set by the SSA, and all the rest of her profits would come to her as dividends. This strategy would also work with a C corporation. It won't work in a partnership. But beware if you have been operating a business and continue to do so. If you continue to work as much as before, but your earned income (wages) suddenly drops and becomes dividends, you can expect an audit. And you can expect to lose that audit, with respect to the level of wages. So don't bring yourself to the attention of the IRS needlessly.

Tip #145: Repayment Options

We mentioned that sometimes you get too much money from Social Security and have to pay it back. There are four ways to deal with this repayment:

1. If the repayment is less than the benefits you're still getting, you don't need to do anything. The SSA-1099 for the year in which you make the repayments will show the net benefits in box 5. You will only pick up that amount on your tax return. Easy peasy.

2. Your repayments are more than the benefits you receive. The amount in box 5 is negative, and it is $3,000 or less. You must deduct that amount as a miscellaneous itemized deduction, reduced by 2 percent of your AGI.

3. Suppose the repayment amount in box 5 shows a negative number that is more than $3,000. In that case, you are allowed to deduct it on Schedule A. In this event, you won't have to reduce it by that nasty 2 percent of AGI. You would put this on a different line—line 28 instead of line 23.

4. But when the amount is more than $3,000, you have another option. Read Tip #229, where we explain "claim of right," to learn how to get a tax credit instead of a deduction. Your best bet is to try both ways. (Yes, I know it's a pain!) Generally, the more complicated credit computation will give you more money back. It boils down to refiguring your income as if the money had been paid back in the year it was received. You won't actually have to amend that prior-year return. You may need some help with this. (Warning: Not all tax pros understand how to deal with this concept. So if you do go to a pro, ask if the person has ever prepared a return with a "claim of right" computation.)

Tip #146: Not Enough?

We talked about getting too much Social Security income, but what if you don't have enough? There are lots of people who worked for themselves, cleverly showing the lowest possible taxable profits to keep their taxes low. Or they came to the United States later in life. Perhaps they worked for employers who did not participate in the Social Security system. Suddenly, they look up and realize they haven't worked in the Social Security system for the full 40 quarters (10 years). What do they need to do to catch up? It's time to get a job with an employer who pays into the system, or start a business where you have self-employment profits. For 2017 (**2018**), the wages or profits must be at least $5,200 (**$5,280**) per year or $1,300 (**$1,320**) per quarter. You can look up the annual minimum earnings requirement on the Social Security website (https://www.ssa.gov/oact/cola/QC.html).

Tip #147: Taxable Profits

Suppose you are, and have been, legitimately self-employed, but your taxable profits just don't reach that level. Is there something you can do? You bet there is. Take a look at Part II of Schedule SE's Schedule B (https://www.irs.gov/pub/irs-pdf/f1040sse.pdf). It's on the bottom of the second page of this form. There are two "Optional Methods"—one for farmers and one for other businesses (nonfarm). When your profits are too low, you have the option of paying the higher amount of self-employment taxes to ensure that you meet the Social Security Administration's 40-quarter earnings requirement. Most people either overlook it or simply don't understand it and never ask. Take a look and see what I mean: https://www.irs.gov/pub/irs-pdf/f1040sse.pdf.

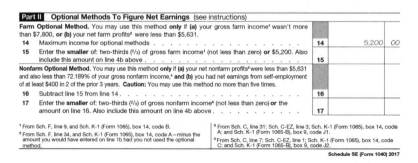

Tip #148: Increase Your Account

OK, you do have your 40 quarters in, but the income isn't very high. How can you raise the income in your Social Security account? Here are some ideas:

- **Get a new job.** People who have held the same job for 10 years or more often aren't valued as much as new employees (at least, not in terms of compensation). Companies often pay new hires more than current employees. So start looking at your company's competitors to see where you would be more valuable.

- **Get a second job.** The additional income will be added to the earnings for your regular job, thereby showing that you are earning substantially more each year.

- **Start a business**—even if it's on the side. Follow your passion. So many people who start a blog, or sell their handicrafts, or provide a service start making more money than they had ever imagined. After all, even a profit of $10,000 can increase your Social Security benefits over your lifetime.

- **The passive alternative.** Don't start collecting Social Security early (age 62) or at your regular retirement age (age 67 and above). Wait until you are age 70 to get a higher payout each month. This is worth doing if your family has a history of living into their late eighties or nineties and you don't have any deadly or debilitating medical issues.

Tip #149: Earnings History

For how long must you earn the additional income in order to raise your Social Security benefits? It all depends on your overall earnings history.

- The Social Security Administration looks at your highest 35 years of earnings. It first recomputes your annual earnings to index them for inflation, then adds up the earnings for the 35 years with the highest numbers and divides by 35 years. You can see an example here: https://www.ssa.gov/oact/progdata/ retirebenefit1.html. Look at the "Indexed Earnings" column. See how $9,870 in 1978 translates to $45,481 in 2018?

- To see where you stand, start by requesting your report from the Social Security Administration. You can do this online, or you can file Form SSA-7004 to get a free copy (https://secure.ssa .gov/RIL/SiView.do; https://www.ssa.gov/myaccount/materials/ pdfs/SSA-7004.pdf). This can take several weeks, so try the on-line option.

- Now that you have the information, add up your 35 highest earnings years and see what the average is. How much should you raise your income each year to increase the benefit? Use the benefit calculators (particularly the Online Calculator) that the SSA provides to help you see what happens when your in-come increases (https://www.ssa.gov/planners/benefitcalcula-tors.html). This will help you decide if it's worth it to sacrifice the irreplaceable precious hours you have with your family and friends.

Tip #150: No Early Withdrawals

We've been talking about putting money away for retirement, but what about using some of the money before you retire? You may have heard that you can draw out money as a down payment on your home or to pay education expenses without paying taxes. *This is not true.* Before you ever take money out of any account that is meant to be a retirement account, invest in two hours with your tax professional.

Tip #151: Taxes Always

When you draw money out of any retirement account (except a Roth-type account), there will always be taxes. When you draw money out before you reach age 59½, there are ways to avoid the 10 percent early withdrawal penalties that the IRS assesses, plus the state penalties. But these exceptions only work if you draw the money out of an IRA. When you draw the money from your 401(k) or other pension plan, everything is still subject to penalties. Therefore move the money you will need to an IRA account. It's not a simple process, but if you don't, you will waste the money on penalties, needlessly.

Tip #152: 25 Percent Penalty

Add about 25 percent to your draw. You can add 25 percent plus your state tax rate. You've moved the money you will need to your IRA, but the draw will still face full taxation from both the IRS and your state. In fact, the administrator is required to withhold 20 percent of your distribution and to send it to the IRS. So right off the bat you're only going to get 80 percent of the money you are expecting. The rest goes to your IRS account to pay some of your estimated taxes. Does that mean you will owe nothing in April, at least? No! Once the full amount of your draw is added to your wages, you will probably end up owing more than 20 percent. So here you are, drawing this money and only getting 80 percent of it, but you are paying taxes on 100 percent of the money—money you never got. Even without the penalties, this is not a good deal. By the time all the tax issues are taken into account, you end up paying around 30–40 percent in taxes on the net cash you receive. So if there is a way to get the money elsewhere . . . do it. Even credit cards are cheaper than drawing money out of your IRA or retirement account.

Tip #153: Draws You Can Take

Where is the list of draws you can take while you're still young that won't cost you an early withdrawal penalty? See this table on the IRS's Retirement-Plans website: https://www.irs.gov/retirement-plans/plan-participant-employee/retirement-topics-tax-on-early-distributions. *Note: You will need a code number or letter to use on line 2, Form 5329 (https://www.irs.gov/pub/irs-pdf/f5329.pdf)—the form number to use this information on and the code number for the specific exclusion from the penalty.*

Tip #154: Exceptions

What are the most commonly used exceptions? There is so much information in this one area, so for more details, read the instructions for Form 5329 (https://www.irs.gov/pub/irs-pdf/i5329.pdf) and work with a tax pro. Meanwhile, here are some of the more commonly used, or useful, exceptions to the penalties:

- **Code 03:** Total and permanent disability. This must be provable with a letter from a doctor. A temporary disability does not qualify.
- **Code 04:** Death.
- **Code 06:** Qualified Domestic Relations Order (QDRO). Ironically, this distribution may *not* come from an IRA. It may only come from a qualified retirement plan. This may only be used in a divorce to split the retirement account by order of a court.
- **Code 08:** Funds are used to pay for qualified education expenses. If you have scholarships, grants, or Coverdell ESA funds, make sure you have enough educational expenses to cover this draw as well.

- **Code 09:** $10,000 for the down payment on a first home. (You may not have owned a home for at least three years.) *Note: To draw out $20,000, you and your spouse must each draw up to $10,000 from your separate IRAs. You may not draw the $20,000 from one IRA just because you're married.*

Tip #155: Phantom Income

Beware the phantom income. One of the best ways to get your hands on money from your pension plan is to borrow from it. Not all companies make this available. But when they do, you are allowed to borrow up to 50 percent of the balance of your qualified retirement account, or up to $50,000 (whichever number is lower). The great part about this is that there are no tax consequences. There is no early withdrawal penalty. They don't hold back any of the funds to pay to the IRS for estimated taxes. So if you draw $50,000, you actually get $50,000—not 80 percent of that amount. And the fees are minimal, around $100 or so. Best of all, you pay yourself back at a very low interest rate. But there are some caveats.

If you leave the company before you pay all the money back, you will have to pay taxes and possibly early withdrawal penalties on the unpaid balance. It doesn't matter if you were laid off, fired, or quit.

Be sure you know how much you owe before you leave so you can settle the account. Often, the plan administrator will give you three to six months to secure a loan so you can pay the employer back. After all, if you still owe $30,000, you will be adding this to your income, which will probably push you into at least a 25 percent bracket (if you were not already there). Add the state taxes of about 10 percent. Then add the early withdrawal penalties of, say, 12.5 percent (IRS + California). You will need to come up with nearly 50 percent of that $30,000 in taxes and penalties. So be super diligent about finding a way to pay back your employer. At least if it's your decision to leave, you have time to plan some strategy (like to request a huge hiring bonus from your new employer) to come up with the balance due.

Good news. The TCJA has a provision to give you extra time to pay back this loan when you leave a job. Essentially, as long as you pay back the outstanding loan balance before the due date of your tax return (including extensions), you can avoid the taxes and penalty. Just deposit the loan balance to the IRA where you rolled over your 401(k) account (as this book went to press, this had not become law, but we expect it to!).

Tip #156: Internet Millionaire

What is the best deal on the list but the least understood? Code 02, a series of substantially equal payments. This is the Internet millionaire provision. This is the provision that lets Internet mavens build up substantial retirement accounts, roll them over to IRAs, and start collecting their retirement benefits in their thirties instead of waiting until their sixties. It's called a Section 72t election (https://www.irs.gov/Retirement-Plans/Retirement-Plans-FAQs-regarding-Substantially-Equal-Periodic-Payments). You basically turn your newly stuffed IRA into an annuity. You recalculate the withdrawals each year based on the growth or losses in the account. This is quite tricky, so work with a retirement professional who understands the process well. Otherwise you will suddenly find yourself facing IRS and state withdrawal penalties on all the money you have drawn for years.

Tip #157: Professional Advice!

Retirement planning is very complex. Even with all the information in this chapter, we have only scratched the surface (we didn't even discuss self-directed IRAs). I recommend you see a tax professional before acting on anything in this chapter on your own. Getting good advice can save you thousands of dollars—and put more money into your pocket than you can imagine.

CHAPTER 10

Long-Term Savings and Retirement Tax Issues for the Actually Young

T HE BEST STRATEGIES FOR young people? Follow Warren Buffett's advice to save early and save often, even if it's just a little at a time. As he is quoted, "Someone's sitting in the shade today because someone planted a tree a long time ago."

Tip #158: Start Small

It's never too early to start saving for retirement. If you are starting a family, a good time to start is when your first baby is born. There are all kinds of ways to start to build savings. All of them have advantages and disadvantages. But so does everything in life. The DRIP Investment site (it used to be the *MoneyPaper* magazine) shows how much security you can build up for your children with as little as $25 per month for 62 years (https://www.directinvesting.com/index .cfm). You start with a small investment and teach your children to keep adding to it as soon as they are old enough to understand numbers. Naturally, you can put the money into savings accounts, brokerage accounts, or dividend reinvestment programs (DRIPs), or save up for US Savings Bonds. But if you want your children to learn secure investing, the DRIP site helps you find no-fee or low-fee DRIPs where you can buy the shares directly from the company, sometimes for as little as $10 or $25 (https://www.directinvesting.com/25_dollar_drips .cfm). Take a look at their "kid's portfolio" (https://www.directinvesting .com/drip_learning_center/starter_portfolio.cfm?from=kids).

Some companies still provide "perks" to shareholders. Kimberly Clark stockholders still get an annual gift box of goodies for about half the retail price (http://www.kcgiftbox.com/). Ford shareholders who can prove ownership get discounts on vehicle purchases. Some cruise lines offer onboard discounts. Berkshire-Hathaway shareholders who attend the stockholders' meetings can get a whole array of discounts and goodies in their meeting packet. There's a list of companies that provide gifts to investors at TheBalance.com: http:// iTaxMama.com/InvestorGifts.

Note: To learn how much your investment would be worth in the future, Google this phrase to find a calculator to help you: "future value of monthly deposit."

Time VS. Money

Patient long-term investors will amass wealth by following the simple strategy that direct investment plans (DRIPs) make accessible to almost everyone.

Use our quick calculator below

Assuming a 10% average return over the long term, see how much your assets can grow over the years.

| $25 | / mo. | **For** | 62 | / yrs. |

(Note: As you reduce the number of years, you must increase the amount you invest in order to achieve a simliar result.)

Submit

Your investment would be worth: **$1,476,148.69**. Your cost was: **$18,655.00**
Click to see presumptions and calculations

Tip #159: No More My Retirement Account

The Treasury Department decided to phase out the myRA (a program for those without a retirement account at work) and is no longer accepting new participants (https://myra.gov/how-it-works/). However, those who have already made contributions can still use these accounts and earn the comparatively high rate of interest.

Tip #160: Coverdell

Coverdell Education Savings Account (ESA). This is another IRA-type account with no tax break at the time when you fund it. This is often called the Education IRA (https://www.irs.gov/publications/p970/ch07.html). Folks may contribute up to $2,000 per year into the ESA for each designated beneficiary as long as the contributor's modified adjusted gross income (MAGI) is less than certain annual limits, which change each year (http://iTaxMama.com/MAGI_ESA). You may contribute to your offspring, your grandchildren, even the children of your employees or just for a friend. The purpose of this account is to set aside money to help fund a person's education someday. While there is no deduction for the contribution, the earnings in the account grow tax-free. So if you can find a stable investment that can generate a decent rate of return, these accounts can be a valuable way to grow college funds tax-free. If you don't have the skills or contacts to find secure investments paying more than a quarter of a percentage, skip it. Just put the money into a savings account for your child. It won't have any strings attached to the withdrawals. And the earnings will be low enough each year that the annual taxes will be insignificant, or there won't be any at all.

Tip #161: Coverdell Withdrawals

Strings on the Coverdell ESA withdrawals. There are restrictions on how the money can be used. For this account, the restrictions are not too burdensome. Let's explore them:

- The educational institution must be "qualified." The IRS says, "This is any college, university, vocational school, or other postsecondary educational institution eligible to participate in a student aid program administered by the US Department of Education." It includes virtually all accredited public, nonprofit, and proprietary (privately owned profit-making) postsecondary institutions.
  › This includes certain overseas educational institutions.
  › Did you notice that this also includes "vocational" schools? You can train to become an auto mechanic, plumber, long-haul trucker, master chef, esthetician, hairdresser, dress designer, deep sea diver—or whatever your heart desires.
  › However, if the educational institution simply provides continuing professional education, or isn't accredited with the US Department of Education, you cannot use the ESA funds for those schools.
- Eligible higher education expenses include:
  › Tuition and fees.
  › Books, supplies, and equipment, including computers and related supplies.
  › Room and board—either the actual amount charged by the school if the student is staying in school housing or the budget amount determined by the school's financial aid folks if the student is residing off campus.
  › For special needs students, only those additional costs related to making it possible to enroll in and attend the school.
- **You can also use these funds for an eligible elementary or secondary school. The limit is $10,000 per year, as a result of the TCJA. This includes any public, private, or religious school that provides elementary or secondary education (kindergarten through grade 12) as determined under state law. In fact, the TCJA allows the money to be used for certain homeschooling costs—see Chapter 1.**

› When you have friends, employers, and relatives funding these accounts, this is a great way to tap into the money to cover the high costs of private schools.

• Eligible K–12 education expenses include all the above, plus these additional costs:

› Academic tutoring

› Transportation

› Uniforms

› Extended daycare programs or other supplementary costs

Tip #162: Coverdell Myth

Coverdell ESA limit. The main drawback is that we may only deposit up to $2,000 per child, per year, no matter who provides the funds. Even if you start the account the year the child is born, by the time he or she turns 18 there will only be $36,000 in the account, plus the earnings. At 3 percent per year, that would be about $50,000 (http://www.hcuonline.com/HCU_Calc_PeriodicSavings.html). That might be enough to cover higher education costs for a year or two. But if you use the funds for private school (K–12), the money would be depleted before it even earned any interest.

Periodic Deposit Calculator

This calculator will help you to determine the value of putting money away in to savings on a regular basis. **Note: Your actual amount saved may vary from these calculations.**

To calculate the future value of a periodic investment, enter the beginning balance, the periodic dollar amount you plan to deposit, the deposit interval, the interest rate you expect to earn, and the number of years you expect to continue making monthly deposits, then click the "Compute" button.

Enter the initial investment (optional):	2000
Enter the Annual ⇕ deposit amount:	2000
Enter the annual interest rate: see our rates Enter 0.5% as 0.005	.03
Enter the number of years:	18
Compute Reset	
Future value:	$50,233.74
Interest earned:	$12,233.74

Tip #163: Direct Gifts

No harm, no foul. Consider direct gifts of educational costs. Did you know that when you pay someone's education costs directly to the school, there is no gift tax consideration and no limit on how much you may contribute or pay on his or her behalf? Talk to all those nice people who would have been willing to chip in toward the Coverdell ESA. Instead of limiting their combined contributions to $2,000, they could pay any amount at all directly to the school. True, there's no tax deduction for this. But they also won't have to file any gift tax returns, regardless of how much they contribute. And this doesn't deplete the lifetime unified estate and gift tax exclusion for those really wealthy relatives.

What is the value of this to the recipient? More than you can imagine. When families, religions, or communities require that their children attend private schools, the costs can be overwhelming. Even with scholarships to help out, there are still funds the parents must pay. In absolute dollar terms the additional costs might not seem high. But when you look at the supplement cost in terms of a percentage of the budget—especially if you must pay for more than one child—this can cause severe hardship.

Tip #164: Get Help

The consequence of not getting financial help when needed. While educational expenses are extremely worthwhile, don't put yourself in financial jeopardy by taking out more loans or spending more than you can afford. Ask family for help before selling your house or taking other drastic measures. Your future self and your heirs will thank you!

Tip #165: Qualified Tuition Program

Another way to save is the Qualified Tuition Program (QTP), also known as the Section 529 plan (https://www.irs.gov/publications/

p970/ch08.html). Why is it called the Section 529 plan? Simple. That's the Internal Revenue Code section where you will find all the details. As with the other plans we have been discussing, there is no tax deduction for your contribution to the 529 plans. These plans were designed to allow family members to put a lot of money into a college savings plan, quickly. Essentially, the first year's contribution to the plan is designed to be quite large. In the first year, family and friends may contribute up to five times the annual gift tax limit, which is currently $14,000 (**$15,000 in 2018**). Five times that amount is $70,000 (**$75,000 in 2018**). If the maximum amount is contributed in the first year, no contributions may be added for five years. After that, contributions are limited to the annual gift tax limit. When these plans became popular, I made up a detailed Benefit and Drawbacks list on the TaxMama.com site (http://iTaxMama.com/TM_529).

Julie Garber, TheBalance.com's gift and estate planning guide, provides the updated annual gifting limits from 1997 to the current year (https://www.thebalance.com/annual-exclusion-from-gift-taxes -3505637). This large initial contribution was valuable in several ways:

- Having a lot of money in the plan made it possible to invest in securities with higher returns than you could buy with lower balances—depending on the provisions of the particular plan document.

- The big benefit of plans that were tied to specific educational institutions was that if you paid in a specified amount, your college tuition was guaranteed to be covered, regardless of the increase in fees over the years. (Of course, that guarantee was only valid at that institution or in that state. What if the student didn't want to attend that college, or wanted to study in a differ-ent state, when he or she grew up?)

- You could fund the account quickly for a student who would be starting college in just a few years.

- Some states may offer incentives that the IRS doesn't offer. They are well worth looking into.

- Funds could be used for tuition, books, and supplies as well as housing.

The drawbacks?

- Once that large initial deposit was made, the generous relative could make no more gifts to that person for five years.

- When you fill out the FAFSA (Free Application for Federal Student Aid) form for financial aid, the balance of the Section 529 plan owned by the student or the student's parents is taken into account (https://fafsa.ed.gov). *Note: If the trustee, who controls the plan, is a grandparent, you might not need to show the whole balance on your application.*

- Funds not used for educational purposes would face penalties when withdrawn from the account.

The details of these accounts have evolved over a decade or two. Read the IRS overview in Publication 970 (https://www.irs.gov/publications/p970/ch08.html). Better yet, explore the excellent information on the Saving for College website (http://www.savingforcollege.com/college_savings_201). It can answer all your questions.

Tip #166: ABLE

Moving on from Section 529 to Section 529A—ABLE. Young or old, sometimes you face disability issues. Have you ever heard of the Achieving Better Life Experience (ABLE) Tax-Advantaged Accounts for Disabled Individuals (IRC Section 529A; https://www.law .cornell.edu/uscode/text/26/529A)? Most people have not because this is a new plan. You will find an excellent explanation by Steve Hopfenmuller, CPA, at http://www.smbiz.com/sbspec518.html. Let me give you a summary. Essentially this allows for contributions of up to $15,000 per year (the annual gift tax limit) to go into a special bank account to help the person with a qualified disability. The "advantage" part of this account is that Medicaid and other aid programs won't take this bank account into consideration when they determine if the person is qualified for state aid. However, as with all tax benefits, there are drawbacks:

- The balance in the account can never exceed $100,000.
- Anything over that amount will be taken into account to reduce government aid and benefits.
- Excess annual contributions are subject to a 6 percent excise tax for each year until the excess amounts are removed.
- The funds may only be used for medical and support costs for the beneficiary.
- Any funds left in the account at death must be paid back to the various state aid programs up to the amount they contributed to the care of the individual.

Some benefits of the account include:

- There are no complicated legal processes to set up an ABLE account as there are in special needs trusts and the like.
- The funds may be used for funeral costs.
- You may pay legal and financial administration costs.
- The account balance may be transferred to another close relative who is disabled.
- **If you need more money in the fund, the new TCJA allows you to roll money into your ABLE account from your Section 529 college savings account—up to the allowable limit for funds held in the ABLE account.**

Tip #167: How to Qualify

The IRS issued new rules to simplify how people can qualify for these accounts: https://www.irs.gov/pub/irs-drop/n-15-81.pdf. The guidelines were open to comment, and commenters noted that three of the requirements for qualified Achieving Better Life Experience (ABLE) programs in the proposed regulations would create significant barriers to the establishment of such programs. So the IRS simplified them. Please read the notice. These ABLE plans are brand new. States still need to establish guidelines, so check with the experts before trying to set these up on your own. Meanwhile, here are the changes:

- **Categorization of distributions not required.** ABLE programs need not include safeguards to determine which distributions are for qualified disability expenses, nor are they required to specifically identify those used for housing expenses. Commenters noted that such a requirement would be unduly burdensome and that, in any case, the eventual use of a distribution may not be known at the time it is made. Designated beneficiaries will still need to categorize distributions when determining their federal income tax obligations.

- **Contributors' TINs not required.** ABLE programs will not be required to request the taxpayer identification numbers (TINs) of contributors to the ABLE account at the time when the contributions are made if the program has a system in place to reject contributions that exceed the annual limits. However, if an excess contribution is deposited into a designated beneficiary's ABLE account, the program will need to request the contributor's TIN. For most people, the TIN is their Social Security number (SSN).

- **Disability diagnosis certification permitted.** Designated beneficiaries can open an ABLE account by certifying, under penalties of perjury, that they meet the qualification standards, including their receipt of a signed physician's diagnosis if necessary, and that they will retain that diagnosis and provide it to the program or the IRS upon request. This means that eligible individuals with disabilities will not need to provide the written diagnosis when opening the ABLE account, and ABLE programs will not need to receive, retain, or evaluate detailed medical records.

• **Location of account.** The ABLE account doesn't need to be established in the state where the beneficiary is a resident. This may make it easier for trustees to manage the account.

Watch for updates here: http://iTaxMama.com/529_ABLE.

Tip #168: Save via Whole Life

Using whole life insurance to save up for college (or anything at all). This is something you can consider. You start funding the whole life policy for the child when the child is born or is very young. At that time, there are no health issues. The insurance companies are happy to take your money, knowing they will hold it for decades. The policy will build up value. When children are ready to go to college, they simply borrow the funds. They can use the money for anything they choose without having to track the costs of books, fees, and so on. They won't have to care if the institution is accredited or not. There are no taxes on the borrowed funds. Either they can pay themselves back over the years, or they can get a lower payout when they die or cash out the policy.

CHAPTER 11

Tax Savings for Education

THE MOST VALUABLE THING in the world is a good education. It doesn't really matter what the education or major is; it's all about learning: learning how to think, how to research, knowing that you must ask questions and not take everything at face value. A free college education has even become a campaign issue. Will we get that throughout the United States? Not anytime soon. But we are hopeful that we will get ever more high-quality free colleges and universities, at least those operated by the cities and states. The state of New York announced that the State University of New York (SUNY) will be offering free tuition to in-state students who meet certain criteria in the fall of 2017. At the other end of the country, in California, the city of San Francisco raised money to make the City College of San Francisco tuition-free to all residents. **This trend is just starting. And it's growing. More and more colleges have stepped up to offer free tuition: https://www.google.com/search?q=free**

+tuition+in+colleges&oq=free+tuition+in+college. We hope it's the wave of the future. Because without this kind of help, higher education is expensive.

For example, at present, the city college system in Southern California is expensive. A student carrying a full load (12 to 16 units) would pay about $550–$750 per semester at the Los Angeles City College or Pierce Community College, plus the costs of books, parking, and fuel or transportation. Add it all up, and the cost for nine months' attendance, if students live at home, comes to $12,000 per year—more than $20,000 if they have to pay for housing (http://www.piercecollege.edu/pierce_fees.asp). The cost is five times that amount if the student is from out of state or from out of the country.

Clearly, we need some help. So where do we start? Let's look at tax benefits.

Tip #169: Scholarships

Scholarships are great, but they are not always tax-free (https://www.irs.gov/taxtopics/tc421.html). You can use scholarship funds to cover the costs of tuition, fees, books, supplies, and mandatory course equipment. But if the scholarship covers more than that, like food, housing costs, travel, or optional equipment, you now have taxable income. This applies to grants, stipends, and even funds to Fulbright scholars. What's even worse is that if the scholarship is taxable, students will pay tax at kiddie tax rates—in other words, at trust tax rates, which start at 10 percent, but hit 37 percent when income exceeds $12,500.

Tip #170: Tax-Free Benefits

Tax-free education benefits at work. All employers can pay up to $5,250 of your education costs without the benefit being taxable to you. Anything over that, and you pay tax on the benefit. It will be included in your wages (http://iTaxMama.com/Pub970_Chap_11 .html). Is there a way around that? Maybe . . .

Tip #171: Working Benefit

Working benefit fringe. That's a nice little secret. When the education payments qualify as a working benefit fringe, none of the payments are taxable to you even if your employer pays out $30,000 or more. How do you get that? Well, it must be a written plan. The benefit must be available to all employees, without favoring "highly compensated employees," and it covers practically all costs except for tools and supplies that employees get to keep after the course ends. It cannot cover the owners of the business. But even small businesses can offer this benefit, say, to family members who don't meet the definition of "related parties" when it comes to ownership of the business. Read this information carefully and discuss it with the boss (http://iTaxMama.com/WorkingBenefit_Education.html). Incidentally, you cannot convert part of your wages to the education reimbursement. That would violate the provision that "the program does not allow employees to choose to receive cash or other benefits."

Tip #172: Work Off Loans

Don't pay off your student loans; work them off instead. There are federal and private programs that will pay off your student loans in exchange for a few years of your time (http://iTaxMama.com/Pub970_LoanRelief.html). Now think about this and ask yourself these questions:

- How long will it take for you to pay off all your student loans? For many people, it could take 10 to 20 years.
- During all that time, the loan is sitting on your credit, pushing down your FICO score. How do you feel about your credit?

- A big chunk of your wages goes toward the student loan payments, which means your standard of living is reduced—unless you spend like there's no tomorrow and just get deeper into debt. (This is dumb, but done.)

- Do you really need all that stress?

- How bad would it really be to go on an adventure for two or three years? You might even build up savings, meet the partner of your dreams, or at least learn more about life. And hey, think about all the great stories and pictures you will have!

Tip #173: Default?

Let your student loans go into default. Yup. You might be able to give up and do that. Only it's not easy. Did you know that you cannot even bankrupt student loan debt? But let's say that you could somehow get the debt cancelled. Not only does that totally mess up your FICO score; it generates taxable income for cancellation of debt. So you are suddenly going to add $30,000, $50,000, or $200,000 to your income in the year you default on the loan. Talk about messing up your entire future. Instead, when you're having a tough time with the student loan, call the company, and work out more manageable payment arrangements. If you don't, the IRS will start grabbing your tax refunds—so you'll be force-paying your loan and racking up collections fees in addition to the loan and interest.

Tip #174: When You Pay

You're paying your student loan. Deduct the interest expense (http://iTaxMama.com/Pub970_Student_Interest.html). You may deduct up to $2,500 of your interest payment. There are lots of strings on this deduction, including a limit to the amount of MAGI (modified adjusted gross income) you may have before your deduction is reduced or eliminated. In fact, suppose you felt the interest rate was too high and you were able to refinance the loan at a better interest rate. You might have just changed the nature of the loan from a student loan to a personal loan. Interest on personal loans is not deductible at all. So be very careful—run the numbers. If you can get a low enough interest rate, you might be better off without any tax benefit at all.

- For instance, if you're paying 7 percent on a $60,000 loan, you're paying $4,200 in interest, right?

- Assuming you can save 30 percent (IRS and state tax rates) on $2,500 of that interest (or $750), your net interest expense out of pocket would be $3,450.

- Let's say you were able to refinance the loan to 4 percent. Your interest expense would be $2,400.

- Even without the interest deduction, you are more than $1,000 ahead.

Incidentally, I found a really interesting article in *Forbes*, by Nancy L. Anderson, telling you, "Why Your Kids Should Take out Student Loans, Even if You Can Afford to Pay for College" (http://iTaxMama .com/GettingStudentLoan). One of the main things I like about it is the concept of evaluating the return on investment in that particular course of education.

Tip #175: Deductions

Now we come to the education deductions and credits. The nice thing about my professional tax software is that, for decades, I have been able to enter all the education and income data and tell the computer to select the best deduction or credit available to my clients. That doesn't mean the computer is always right. Sometimes I have to make some major adjustments and overrides to get the numbers to work because the computer isn't taking into account some key element. (Like one year, when my taxpayer's daughter ended up with a taxable scholarship and the software wasn't picking it up correctly.)

Most of the time it works just fine. In recent years, the major consumer software houses like TurboTax, H&R Block, eSmart Tax, and TaxAct seem to have added this feature to their systems as well. If you are going to file your own tax return, make sure your tax preparation software offers you this benefit if you have education expenses.

Tip #176: MAGI

The tuition and fees deduction is worth $4,000 per tax return before it is reduced by your MAGI, or modified adjusted gross income (http://iTaxMama.com/Pub970_Tuition_Fees.html). I find that this deduction is often less useful than the two main tax credits. The main benefit of using the deduction instead of a credit is to reduce your adjusted gross income (AGI). By bringing the AGI down, you might free up a few more deductions on Schedule A, increase some other tax credits, or even reduce the impact of the Alternative Minimum Tax (AMT). I am not sure if tax software takes all these attributes into account all by itself. So if you find yourself generating AMT, or losing deductions or credits, see what happens if you use this deduction instead of an education credit.

The Bipartisan Budget Act of 2018 extended this deduction through December 31, 2017. The deduction limits and income phaseouts are as follows: The deduction is capped at $4,000 for an individual with AGI up to $65,000 ($130,000 for joint filers) or $2,000 for an individual with AGI does up to $80,000 ($160,000 for joint filers).

Tip #177: AOC

The American Opportunity Credit (AOC) is worth up to $2,500 per eligible student on the tax return (http://iTaxMama.com/Pub970_AOC.html). The credit is computed as 100 percent of the first $2,000 of qualified education expense, plus 25 percent of the next $2,000. You must be working on a degree to use this credit and in school at least as a half-time student for at least one full academic period during the current year—or the first three months of the following year. This is a favorite credit because it's partially refundable. That means even if you have no taxes due at all, you can still get back up to $1,000 per eligible student (or up to 40 percent of the total credit if less than $2,500). This credit is only good for four tax years. They don't need to be consecutive years. As one IRS agent explained to me, plan out in advance which four tax years will give you the highest benefit for each student in the household. Oops. A student who has a felony drug conviction is not eligible for this credit. Good news: This credit was made a permanent part of the Internal Revenue Code as Section 102 of the PATH Act of 2015. So we can stop wondering if it will be there each year.

Although the House of Representatives wanted to tinker with this credit, in the end, the TCJA did not change any of these provisions.

Tip #178: LLC

The Lifetime Learning Credit (LLC) is worth up to $2,000 per tax return (http://iTaxMama.com/Pub970_LifetimeLearning.html). It is computed as 20 percent of the first $10,000 of qualified education expenses. No need to pursue a degree to claim this credit. All types of courses will qualify. No minimum number of courses is necessary, and no worries about felonies or drug convictions. Even former criminals are encouraged to learn. Although this credit is not available per student, one of the reasons it's worthwhile is that this credit can be used to educate you in every year of your life. So if you're taking classes each year to improve your business skills, use this credit before taking a deduction for employee business expenses. Whatever part of your education expenses you cannot use here, apply them toward your job if the courses are applicable.

Alas, it's a nonrefundable credit; if you have no tax liability, this credit is wasted. But good news: If one family member (spouse or dependent) qualifies for the AOC and another family member qualifies for the LLC, you may use them both on the same tax return—separately for each household member—up to the various limits.

As with the AOC, the House of Representatives wanted to tinker with this credit, but in the end, the TCJA did not change any of these provisions, either.

Tip #179: MAGI Computation for Tuition and Fees

For the purpose of education, how do we modify the adjusted gross income (AGI) to arrive at the modified adjusted gross income (MAGI)? Here is an overview of the computation. It shows the items that are added back into income (mostly foreign income and housing exclusions) to arrive at the MAGI to be used for the tuition and fees deduction.

1. Enter the amount from Form 1040, line 22	1. _____
2. Enter the total from Form 1040, lines 23 through 33 . . . . 2. _____	
3. Enter the total of any amounts entered on the dotted line next to Form 1040, line 36 . . . . 3. _____	
4. Add lines 2 and 3	4. _____
5. Subtract line 4 from line 1	5. _____
6. Enter your foreign earned income exclusion and/or housing exclusion (Form 2555, line 45, or Form 2555-EZ, line 18)	6. _____
7. Enter your foreign housing deduction (Form 2555, line 50)	7. _____
8. Enter the amount of income from Puerto Rico you are excluding	8. _____
9. Enter the amount of income from American Samoa you are excluding (Form 4563, line 15)	9. _____
10. Add lines 5 through 9. This is your **modified adjusted gross income**	10. _____
Note. *If the amount on line 10 is more than $80,000 ($160,000 if married filing jointly), you cannot take the deduction for tuition and fees.*	

Tip #180: MAGI Phaseout Levels

We mention MAGI (modified adjusted gross income) in several places in this chapter (and elsewhere). However, please be aware that, thanks to the brilliant minds in Congress, MAGI has a completely different phaseout level for each and every tax deduction, credit, and attribute.

- ## MAGI student loan interest

  http://iTaxMama.com/Pub970_Student_Interest.html

Table 4-2. Effect of MAGI on Student Loan Interest Deduction

IF your filing status is...	AND your MAGI is...	THEN your student loan interest deduction is...
single, head of household, or qualifying widow(er)	not more than $65,000	not affected by the phaseout.
	more than $65,000 but less than $80,000	reduced because of the phaseout.
	$80,000 or more	eliminated by the phaseout.
married filing joint return	not more than $130,000	not affected by the phaseout.
	more than $130,000 but less than $160,000	reduced because of the phaseout.
	$160,000 or more	eliminated by the phaseout.

- ## Tuition and fees deduction MAGI

  http://iTaxMama.com/Pub970_Tuition_Fees.html

Table 6-2. Effect of MAGI on Maximum Tuition and Fees Deduction

IF your filing status is...	AND your MAGI is...	THEN your maximum tuition and fees deduction is...
single, head of household, or qualifying widow(er)	not more than $65,000	$4,000.
	more than $65,000 but not more than $80,000	$2,000.
	more than $80,000	$0.
married filing joint return	not more than $130,000	$4,000.
	more than $130,000 but not more than $160,000	$2,000.
	more than $160,000	$0.

- ## American Opportunity Credit MAGI

  http://iTaxMama.com/Pub970_AOC.html

Limit on modified adjusted gross income (MAGI)	$180,000 if married filing jointly; $90,000 if single, head of household, or qualifying widow(er)

- ## Lifetime Learning Credit MAGI

  http://iTaxMama.com/Pub970_LifetimeLearning.html

Limit on modified adjusted gross income (MAGI)	$128,000 if married filling jointly; $64,000 if single, head of household, or qualifying widow(er)

Tip #181: Education Expenses

Unreimbursed work-related education expenses. While you may not generally deduct the cost of a degree, if you can prove that specific expenses are job related, do claim them on your Form 2106 as employee business expenses. Read this Tax Court case, *Lori Singleton v. Commissioner*, from 2009 (http://www.ustaxcourt.gov/InOpHistoric/singleton-clarke.sum.WPD.pdf). It's quite interesting to read the story of this nurse who took a $14,787 deduction for the cost of her MBA/HCM (Health Care Administrator) on her 2005 tax return. She was able to prove that the new degree did not necessarily prepare her for a new job. It helped her maintain her skills for the job she already had. Singleton handled her own case and fought her own battle. She did a great job. That's why I am including her story. Generally, I would not have been so aggressive as to deduct the actual cost of the degree. But I would have taken the deduction for each individual course that helped a taxpayer maintain skills for his or her present job or business. Keep your mind open to the possibilities (that are available within the law). And keep excellent records, as Singleton did. In fact, there have been other successful Tax Court cases with taxpayers who fought for their rights to deduct their education. So the Singleton case is not a one-shot win. We now have a trend. Again, the key is—excellent records.

Tip #182: Deduction Will Be Back!

Save this information. For now, this deduction is suspended until after 2025. But expect this deduction to return in the future. After all, education is America's most valuable long-term resource.

Tip #183: Summary

Need a summary? Due to the complexity and inconsistency of the variety of tax credits and deductions related to education, it really helps to have a scorecard. Actually, in a way, the IRS does have such a thing. It's called Appendix B, "Highlights of Education Tax Benefits for Tax Year 20XX." This appendix is updated in each new year's edition of Publication 970. Alas, it's not available as we write this. But that doesn't mean you can't pull up the PDF version of this publication and click on Appendix B in the table of contents when you are working on your tax return (https://www.irs.gov/pub/irs-pdf/p970.pdf). Really, seeing the overview of the various benefits, rules, and limits side by side will help you understand which ones you can use for yourself and your family.

Tip #184: Homeschooling

While we're talking about education, let's take a quick look at homeschooling to see if there are any tax benefits at all. For families who prefer to homeschool their children, consider getting a group of families together to share the responsibilities. If you can get state accreditation for the parents and for the school, it will be recognized as a school by the state. As a result, the IRS won't consider the teachers, principals, counselors, or aides to be homeschoolers. All accredited teachers may deduct their unreimbursed, class-related costs on line 23 (up to $250; see Tip #219) and the rest of the balance of costs on Form 2106 as itemized deductions. Remember, each "teacher" still has to meet the 900-hour test. For a 10-month teaching cycle, that's about 21 hours per week—or about three hours per day of a seven-day week. This wouldn't be easy to accomplish. A lot depends on why you are homeschooling. If it's to preserve security and your particular ideology, and you share it with others in the community, this may work for you.

Great news! The TCJA is allowing up to $10,000 worth of distributions from Section 529 plans, per student, to cover certain costs of homeschooling.

- **The funds may be used for the following homeschooling costs:**

1. **Curriculum materials—to develop the lesson plans**

2. **Printed or electronic instructional materials**

3. **Online educational materials**

4. **Tuition for tutors or outside educational courses—as long as the instructor is not related to the student**

5. Simultaneous enrollment in an institution of higher education

6. Educational therapy for students with disabilities

CHAPTER 12

Tax No-No's

HAVE NEVER BEEN ABLE to figure out why people make financial decisions based on what they hear from strangers in grocery lines, at bars, at Starbucks, or from what they see in cute pictures on Facebook, while ignoring their own financial advisors. This is especially true for really radical advice about ways to cut your taxes dramatically. Why aren't you getting your information from someone who can see your entire financial picture and give you advice based on your particular situation—not just on one piece of the picture or on urban myths?

Did you know that tax professionals around the country talk to each other? It's true. We are connected in closed groups on LinkedIn, Facebook, and other social media outlets where we share stories about your exploits. Of course, none of us actually names any of our clients. We just tell our stories. Sometimes we laugh, sometimes we cry. Often we ask each other for advice. The truth is, even though you come to us after you're already in trouble, we really, truly want to help you.

OK, let's start the no-no's with the nightmare stuff. Have patience and work your way down to the routine things you never want to do.

Tip #185: Audit Roulette

Don't play audit roulette. The odds are with the house (the IRS). It's really tempting to claim a large deduction for something that you didn't spend. Or to overvalue something that you sold so the profits are lower. Or to avoid reporting income that you got in cash or without a W-2 or 1099. After all, who's going to know? You're right. There are times you can get away with falsifying the information on your tax return—for a while. But the problem with this is that, as with winning when you gamble, it gets addictive. You get away with it once, looking over your shoulder all year . . . maybe for two years. No one comes after you. So let's try it again. The second time you do it and nothing happens, you're not quite as nervous. So you keep doing it. Sooner or later you will get caught. Yup. The IRS has better and better methods of cross-referencing information in your tax return with where you live, your lifestyle, your spending, and even your social media posts. The very deductions that you take tell the IRS when you are living above your reported means. Or when you keep getting away with it, it's tempting to brag to a friend. Great friend. Uh-huh. Your friend turns you in. People snitching on (former) friends, lovers, spouses, and neighbors are a big source of leads for the IRS. When the IRS does audit, and you have scammed on your taxes for several years, the IRS will start auditing previous years and give the information to your state(s).

Tip #186: Be Smart

If you are going to play audit roulette, be smart. Keep your under-reported tax reductions to below 25 percent. That way, the IRS may only audit you for up to three years. (Your state may have an extra year or two, though.) When you underreport more than 25 percent of your income or tax liability (or your asset values), your exposure to audit is for at least six years. If the IRS can prove you were not just mistakenly underreporting but filing fraudulent tax returns, it may audit you as far back as it pleases. No limits. Not fun. This can even lead to criminal penalties and jail time.

Tip #187: No Amateurs

Don't fall prey to amateur tax geniuses. Friends who know everything and push tax advice on you will get you into trouble, and you will end up coming to a tax professional quaking in terror. Why? The IRS is auditing that genius—and everyone with whom that person shared his or her wisdom. You will end up paying a tax professional who will try to smooth over the truth and convince the IRS not to charge you penalties or bring criminal charges. There is nothing we can do about the taxes you will owe for doing something that was clearly not sensible. But the penalties and the interest on those penalties can run to the thousands of dollars. We can help prevent, reduce, or reverse those for you. Sometimes.

Tip #188: Too High

Avoid the refund mills, those tax preparers in your community that have a reputation for generating really high refunds. How do you think these people are able to generate refunds that are so much higher than everyone else can? Do they look smarter than your current tax professional? Do they even have a degree in accounting or taxation? Do they have an excellent reputation for integrity, known throughout the community as an expert? Heck no! Many of them are fly-by-night operators who will be long gone by the time the IRS comes to you asking for its money back. These kind folks not only rip the IRS off; they steal from you. Many of them give you one version of your tax return but file a different version. Their version has a higher refund. They have the part of the refund that you don't know about being deposited directly in their bank accounts. You will have to pay all that money back to the IRS even though you didn't know it was happening.

Don't believe me? Think this is far-fetched and TaxMama is exaggerating to scare you? Drop by the IRS's Criminal Investigation website. Click on the link to "Examples of Abusive Return Preparer Investigations," http://iTaxMama.com/CriminalPreparers.

Tip #189: Penalties

Speaking of penalties, don't waste your money getting saddled with tax penalties. Not only are they annoying and irritating, but you have to pay interest on the penalties. Practically all the time, if you are conscious of your responsibilities, you will have no reason to get a penalty. Of course, if you consort with tax wildcatters, watch out!

What are some of the regular penalties (which keep rising!) (https://www.irs.gov/uac/Newsroom/Eight-Facts-on-Late-Filing -and-Late-Payment-Penalties)?

- $135, or 100 percent of the unpaid tax if you file more than 60 days past the due date or extended due date of the return, whichever is lower

- 10 percent for substantial understatement (§6662) or $5,000, whichever is greater

- 20–40 percent for accuracy-related penalties, specifically for gross undervaluations (§6662), in some instances rising to 400 percent of undervaluations, or $20,000, whichever is greater

- 25 percent for delinquency (§6651), with a minimum of $205 (increased by inflation adjustments) if the tax return is up to 60 days late

- 25 percent, or 5 percent per month until you reach 25 percent, for late filing

- 25 percent, or ½ percent per month until you reach 25 percent, for late payment

What are the biggies?

- 75 percent for fraud (§6663)

- 75 percent for fraudulent failure to file (15 percent per month, up to 75 percent) (§6651)

- $5,000 minimum for filing a frivolous tax return (§6702)

These are just the civil penalties. You don't even want to begin to get involved with the criminal penalties.

Tip #190: Waive Penalties

Don't pay IRS penalties. If you find yourself facing large IRS penalties, get the penalties waived. Unless you're a tax criminal or a habitual tax delinquent, there are often ways to get the IRS to forgive penalties. For folks who've never gotten hit with penalties before and suddenly face really large penalties, there is a special provision for you. It is called the First Time Penalty Abatement (FTA). You will find the details on the IRS website (https://www.irs.gov/Businesses/Small-Businesses-&-Self-Employed/Penalty-Relief-Due-to-First-Time-Penalty-Abatement-or-Other-Administrative-Waiver). Here are the three main qualifications to convince the IRS to waive your penalties:

1. You didn't previously have to file a return or you have no penalties for the three tax years prior to the tax year in which you received a penalty.

2. You filed all currently required returns or filed an extension of time to file.

3. You have paid, or arranged to pay, any tax due.

Tip #191: If Penalty Is Small

If you owe a small penalty for something like not paying enough estimated taxes or withholding, just pay that penalty. Save the FTA for the big mistakes. Sometimes, with the complexity of the tax laws, even the most diligent Tax Vigilante will get hit.

Tip #192: Protect Your SSN

Don't disclose your Social Security number (SSN) when not absolutely necessary. Naturally, you need to provide it to your employer, your medical care providers, and your bank. But really, unless you are in business, think twice, OK, three times, before giving it to anyone else. Do not have that number printed on your checks. And do not carry anything in your purse or wallet with your SSN. In my research for a MarketWatch.com article several years ago, I learned two disturbing sources of Social Security numbers theft (making identity theft possible):

1. SSNs were stolen when people applied for jobs.
    * Recommendation: Don't give prospective employers your driver's license number or SSN until you are among the final candidates. Even then, make sure this is a legitimate employer, one that has been in the community for some time.
2. Baby's SSNs were stolen in the hospital. The hospital needs to file paperwork when the baby is born. The family would not be filing any tax returns for the baby or applying for credit for years, right? So someone in the hospital was selling the numbers. Parents would learn of this when opening savings accounts for their children, often years later.
    * Recommendation: Get a family account, if possible, with your favorite credit bureau, preferably one of the big three—Equifax, Experian, Trans Union. Check the credit activity

for each family member's SSN at least four times a year. The bureaus also offer a service where you can get access to all three bureaus, combined, as part of your account. Or simply freeze each child's credit until he or she needs to use it. The bureaus have information and tools related to child identity theft:

› **Equifax:** https://www.equifax.com/personal/identity -theft-protection (Disclosure: I wrote a tax column for Equifax for several years: https://blog.equifax.com/ author/eva-rosenberg/.)

› **Experian:** http://www.experian.com/data-breach/ newsletters/child-identity-theft.html

› **Trans Union:** https://www.transunion.com/fraud-victim -resource/child-identity-theft

Tip #193: SIRF

Don't become a victim of Stolen Identity Refund Fraud (SIRF). According to an August 2015 report by the Treasury Inspector General for Tax Administration (TIGTA; https://www.treasury.gov/ tigta/auditreports/2015reports/201540026fr.pdf), approximately 1.1 million fraudulent tax returns were filed in 2011 that showed evidence of identity theft. TIGTA's words: "That have the same characteristics as IRS-confirmed identity theft tax returns." As a result, the IRS has started a campaign to make you aware of the issues, to solicit your help to stop this widespread fraud, and to help you become more active about protecting yourself. The campaign is called "Taxes. Security. Together." Get the details from the new IRS Publication 4524 (https://www.irs .gov/Individuals/Taxes-Security-Together). While most of the recom- mendations are common sense, it seems people are far too trusting and don't bother with precautions. Please don't think you are immune. You are not.

In the intervening years, the IRS has worked with TIGTA to develop better methods for resolving the flood of identity theft cases. As a result, taxpayers are getting faster resolutions when they file an identity theft report with the IRS. What does faster mean? According to a TIGTA report on June 6, 2017 (https://www.treasury.gov/tigta/auditreports/2017reports/201740036fr.pdf), that means the IRS is closing out identity theft cases in 166 days instead of 278 days. And the IRS's error rate in these cases dropped from 11 percent to 7 percent. Still, that means if you fall victim to identity theft, you have to wait nearly half a year to get your refunds. So take sensible steps to protect yourself!

Tip #194: Scams

Don't give out any information over the telephone to anyone who calls you about any identity, bank account, or tax or financial details. Even if (especially if) the caller seems to know a lot about you, do not answer or confirm the information. The best thing to do if the call is not from someone you actually know is to just hang up. Don't start a conversation at all. Professional confidence scammers know how to trick information out of you. If you feel that it might be a legitimate call, call the organization the person claimed to be from, and ask if there are outstanding debts or medical or insurance issues. *Please, please, please, tell your parents and other elderly friends to hang up, as well. Help them avoid being victimized. Remember, you cannot be bullied if you hang up.*

For instance, even though I deal with the IRS all the time, if I am not expecting a call and someone calls me saying he or she is from the IRS, I won't discuss my client. I ask the caller his or her name, employee ID number, campus/location, and group number. I do get his or her phone number. Then I call the IRS directly. I do some research within my sources to determine if this person or phone number is legitimate. Hint: Google the phone number you were given to see if it is an IRS phone number. That saves time. If that doesn't work, you will need to call the IRS's main phone number, 1-800-829-1040. Tell the caller that you will call him or her back in a couple of days. If the person tells you it's urgent and that you're about to be levied . . . beware. You would have gotten mail from the IRS if there were a levy notice. Another place you can call or visit is your local IRS office, where there are what's called Taxpayer Assistance Centers (TACs). Visit the IRS website to contact your local IRS office: http://iTax-Mama.com/IRS_Office. These days, you can schedule appointments to speak to someone, in person, at a TAC.

If you don't have the time or patience to track down the information, get in touch with your tax professional. We can do this for you.

Don't worry; we're going to give you more guidance on dealing with the IRS in Chapter 14.

Tip #195: Phone Threats

Never send money to anyone who calls you on the phone. If someone calls and tells you that you owe money to the IRS or the state or for any outstanding bill, call that entity to ensure that you do owe the money and that the balance is correct. You can reach the IRS at 1-800-TAX-1040 (1-800-829-1040). Send your money directly to the IRS, state, or your creditor, not to someone who calls you and threatens you—especially if the person wants cash, money order, debit card, or cashier's checks. First of all, the IRS doesn't make calls like that. Second, the **IRS never asks for cash, money order, debit card, or cashier's checks—or for funds to be placed on gift cards or store cards.** There are some very aggressive callers who may threaten you with police action or even harm (http://iTaxMama.com/IRS_Suspicious_Calls). Although there have been some significant arrests of scammers in India and the United States, the calls continue. Truly, the easiest way to deal with them is to hang up. Many of my clients have gotten these calls but were smart enough to call me before sending money. I have at least one of these calls on my answering machine. Do not call these people back and think you're going to play with them. If they are close enough to you to collect cash, they are close enough to do physical harm. If you do feel they are nearby and will harm you, call the police immediately.

People do give these scammers money. They have collected over $20 million, according to a TIGTA estimate. The average amount people are bullied into giving them is $5,000. The highest payment reported, believe it or not, is *half a million dollars!*

Tip #196: Frivolous Arguments

The last big scam: the IRS and the US Tax Code are unconstitutional. Of course not. If that were true, do you think anyone would still be paying taxes? Yet lots of smart people fall for the scam. The IRS has devoted an entire section of its website to help you understand the issues and why the "tax protester" movement is totally off base. The IRS puts these actions under the label of "Frivolous Arguments" (https://www.irs.gov/Tax-Professionals/The-Truth-About-Frivolous -Tax-Arguments-Introduction). This behavior earns criminal penalties, prosecution, and jail time (http://iTaxMama.com/IRS_ Frivolous).

I was once privileged to spend about three hours with the new IRS District Director in Los Angeles, Steven Jensen, interviewing him for an article for the *Los Angeles Daily News*. Our conversation ranged across many topics. This was one of them. I pointed out to him that these tax protesters generally cited specific Tax Code sections or sections in the US Code of Federal Regulations (CFR). Jensen asked if I had ever looked them up. The answer was no. So he proceeded to prove that their citations were generally meaningless. They made up cases and code sections to make their argument appear to have weight. But when you look them up, they are not even related to the point at all.

Even famous people fall for this.

In 2017, we have a new celebrity in trouble. In April of 2017, the IRS indicted Michael "The Situation" Sorrentino and his brother

Marc on charges of tax evasion and falsifying records (https://www
.irs.gov/pub/foia/ig/ci/ci-2017-04-07-a.pdf). And in the same month,
there's another Michael in trouble. Michael Theil, a Louisiana criminal defense attorney, was convicted of tax evasion for over $1 million
in unpaid income and employment taxes (https://www.irs.gov/pub/
foia/ig/ci/ci-2017-04-19-b.pdf).

Tip #197: Disclose

Don't assume the IRS will understand your tax return. TaxMama's
other mantra: *disclose, disclose, disclose.* Whenever you have anything
complicated or confusing in your tax return, explain it in detail. If you
had to estimate something, include an explanation of why you don't
have the actual amount and what source of information you used
to come up with your estimate. If you needed to do a computation,
include the detailed worksheet. Include information about account
numbers and other specific information. When you provide details
like this, it limits the IRS's audit powers to three years instead of six.
Use the Form 8275 Disclosure Statement and add your attachments
(https://www.irs.gov/pub/irs-access/f8275_accessible.pdf). If it turns
out that you made some wrong assumptions, the full disclosure could
eliminate penalties. If you relied on the advice of a tax professional,
that surely will help eliminate penalties.

Good news: We are done with the nastiness. Let's get on with
normal Tax No-No's!

See Tips #247 and 248 for a lot more information about disclo-
sures and Form 8275.

Tip #198: Net Operating Loss

**Whenever you have a net operating loss (NOL), don't file your tax
return without first deciding whether or not to waive NOL carryback** (https://www.irs.gov/publications/p536). This is a very common mistake, or oversight. Not making a decision about this can be
extremely costly and could lead to audits. The average person doesn't

realize this is necessary. In fact, in the rush to file on time, many tax professionals overlook this decision as well. It will be up to you to bring it up and ask about this if you see a negative AGI on your tax return. What the heck is TaxMama talking about? Good question.

The way the Internal Revenue Code is written, when you have an NOL (say in 2017), you are required to carry that loss back to your tax return two years earlier (to 2015). Once you use up that loss, you carry what's left to the tax return one year before the NOL year (to 2016). If there is still anything left, you carry it to the tax return for the year after the NOL year (to 2018). No, you don't have the right to choose to carry it back only one year. It's two or nothing. No doubt, our legislators thought that making this an automatic requirement would be helpful to taxpayers. But most people don't understand it and rarely use this provision. Because this requirement isn't understood, and because it is ignored, most people just take that loss and use it to reduce the next year's taxable income (2018). And this is what causes the audit. Since that's the wrong year, the IRS knows that when it audits, it is guaranteed to generate additional taxes. So what's a good taxpayer to do? Let's look at the next tips, shall we?

Well, this is no longer a consideration for tax years after December 31, 2017. The TCJA removed the ability to carry losses to prior years. (For more details, read Chapter 2 on the business updates of the TCJA.) However, this still affects 2017 calendar year and fiscal year businesses. And it still affects losses generated on tax returns from earlier years.

Tip #199: Carryback

Don't carry the loss back. Waive your right to the carryback. If you could carry that loss back for two years and get refunds fairly quickly, why wouldn't you want to do it? Or why shouldn't you? Here are some reasons taxpayers may not file backward:

- As we discussed, most people just don't know about it, so they don't do it.

- Sometimes you have very little income in the earlier years and won't get enough of a tax reduction to make it worthwhile to file an amended return, so you would rather not bother.

- When you carry the loss back, you lose quite a bit of the loss because it gets eaten up by a variety of tax attributes. Besides, if your tax return for the carryback year shows losses, you get no benefit at all; you lose some or all of the value of the NOL by carrying it backward.

- Some people have concerns over some tax issues in their returns in prior years. By filing an amended return, they open up that year's tax return to IRS scrutiny. They are afraid of an audit.

Again, this is no longer a consideration for tax years after December 31, 2017. The TCJA removed the ability to carry losses to prior years. However, this still affects 2017 calendar year and fiscal year businesses. And it still affects losses generated on tax returns from earlier years.

Tip #200: Election Statement

Don't forget to include the "election statement" in your tax return in the year the NOL is created. What statement? The statement must be attached to your timely filed tax return, including extensions. It must read something like this: "I am choosing to waive the carryback period for tax year 20*XX* under Section 172(b)(3)." This tells the IRS that you will be using the loss in future years only.

Your tax software has this built in for you to use. You just have to know where to find it. If you cannot find the checkbox for it, call tech support and ask. Otherwise, file your tax return on paper and include that election. Feel free to use my wording.

You won't have to worry about this for tax years after December 31, 2017. The TCJA removed the ability to carry losses to prior years. However, this still affects 2017 calendar year and fiscal year businesses. **So if you have an NOL on your 2017 tax return, this may be your last chance to carry losses to earlier years.**

Tip #201: Amended Return

Oops, you forgot to make the election, or didn't know. Can you still fix it? No worries . . . uh, well, no worries if it is less than six months since you filed the tax return. Here's what you do. The IRS explains it beautifully: "If you filed your original return on time but did not file the statement with it, you can make this choice on an amended return filed within six months of the due date of the return (excluding extensions). Attach a statement to your amended return and write, 'Filed pursuant to section 301.9100-2' at the top of the statement" (http://iTaxMama.com/Waive_NOL_CB.html).

Tip #202: Form 1045

Supposing you do want to use the carryback, don't forget to file Form 1045 before the end of the year. Most people, when they think about filing an amended personal tax return, think about Form 1040X. But when it comes to NOLs, there is a special form, Form 1045, Application for Tentative Refund (https://www.irs.gov/pub/irs-access/f1045_accessible.pdf). This form is special for several reasons:

- It is primarily designed to use when you have an NOL.
- It lets you include amendments for several years on one form. (This is especially important in certain years when you are able to carry losses back for up to five years.)
- It is meant to generate a refund more quickly than if you had filed Form 1040X—instead of having to wait for four months or

more, this should be faster—but only if you attached absolutely everything to explain your NOL and your adjustments to the prior years.

- It must be filed by December 31 of the year in which you file the tax return that generated the NOL. For instance, suppose you file the 2017 tax return by October 15, 2018. You must use Form 1045 by December 31, 2018. If you miss the deadline, no worries. You simply have to file the separate Form 1040X for each carryback year.

- A tax pro recently posted in a Facebook group that he missed the filing deadline by one day. As a result, he had to prepare and file separate amended returns (Forms 1040X) for each year, instead of combining the filings.

Tip #203: Pet Policy

Don't deduct costs related to pets, no matter how strongly you feel that they are part of your family. The IRS doesn't accept them as dependents. Yet. Huh? Why *yet*? Believe it or not, in 2009, Representative Thaddeus McCotter, who represented a Detroit-area district, introduced the HAPPY (Humanity and Pets Partnered through the Years) Act (http://www.newsmax.com/InsideCover/mccotter-pets-taxes/2009/08/25/id/334603). It was designed to authorize a deduction of up to $3,500 a year for "qualified pet care expenses," including veterinary care. Of course, it was not successful. But expect more of this thinking as the population ages.

Tip #204: Service Pets

Don't overlook allowable deduction for service pets. Seeing eye dogs, hearing dogs, and other service pets' costs are fully deductible as medical expenses. Naturally, you need a prescription from your doctor. The pet must be specially trained to help you with your particular medical need. You can find more information about

service animals at Assistance Dogs International (ADI; http://www
.assistancedogsinternational.org/about-us/types-of-assistance-dogs/
service-dog). ADI is overseen by the Americans with Disabilities Act
(ADA). You can find ADI's FAQs on the ADA site (https://www
.ada.gov/archive/animal.htm).

Tip #205: Pools/Tubs

**Don't take your swimming pool or hot tub energy costs into
account when applying for the Residential Energy Credit on Form
5695.** The rules say, "Costs allocable to a swimming pool, hot tub,
or any other energy storage medium which has a function other than
the function of such storage do not qualify for the residential energy
efficiency credit" (https://www.irs.gov/pub/irs-pdf/i5695.pdf).

Tip #206: Medicine

**Don't deduct the cost of over-the-counter drugs or certain
non-Western medicines.** They are not deductible **or reimbursable**
in Flexible Spending Accounts, Health Savings Arrangements, or
itemized deductions on Schedule A. Nowhere. People argue and try.
However, there is one exception: when the over-the-counter drugs are
prescribed by a doctor (in writing) for the treatment of a specific condition. Certain non-Western or nontraditional medical practitioners
are recognized by the IRS. You will find them in IRS Publication 502
(https://www.irs.gov/publications/p502). Keep a copy of the prescription. Get a new copy every year. Have the doctor's office write
a letter, each year, explaining why these over-the-counter drugs are
prescribed instead of behind-the-counter drugs. Here are the IRS's
FAQs about this issue: http://iTaxMama.com/IRS_Over_Counter_
Meds. Regardless of other limitations, insulin is always deductible,
whether purchased over or behind the counter.

Here are some nondeductible drugs, even with prescriptions: lae-trile, medical marijuana, and other drugs bought outside the United States that are not approved by the FDA. Incidentally, in the 2015 budget bill, Congress quietly stopped all prosecution for businesses selling medical marijuana in states where that is legal.

And, although medical marijuana is not deductible on an IRS tax return, you are allowed to deduct it on a state tax return, if you file in one of the 25 or more states where medical marijuana is legal (http://www.governing.com/gov-data/state-marijuana-laws-map-medical-recreational.html).

While we may lose medical expenses on the IRS tax return, states where medical marijuana is legal will accept those deductions—so remember to enter the additional medical expenses on your state tax return.

Tip #207: Cosmetic Surgery

You may not deduct the cost of cosmetic surgery if the surgery is for purely personal reasons (http://iTaxMama.com/Cosmetic_Surgery.html). However, if there is a medical reason for the cost, you may claim the deduction. What is the best way to prove there is a medical reason? If your health insurance company provides all or partial reimbursement, there's a good chance there is a medical reason for the procedure. Still, it's a good idea to get a copy of the prescription or doctor's paperwork showing the medical need for the surgery. Common acceptable reasons include reconstructive surgery after an accident (a fire), an earlier surgery (like breast removal), or a birth defect (cleft palate). Sometimes the medical reason might be psychological—severe depression, perhaps even threatening suicide, because of a visible defect.

Tip #208: 401(k)

Don't withdraw money from your 401(k) or other retirement plan to pay for education, your first house, or other exclusions. You may have heard that there are a few expenses that are exempt from the early withdrawal penalty, but that only applies if the money is drawn from an IRA—not from any other retirement account (see Chapter 9).

Tip #209: Mileage

Never deduct commuting mileage (http://iTaxMama.com/Commuting. This is the mileage from home to your office or your job, a trip you take regularly. (I found this out, early in my career, the hard way. During an audit. It was embarrassing, but we had a good laugh.) However, if you drive from home to an alternate work location, or to class, or to training, and so on, that is not commuting. You may also track the mileage from the office to those other locations, or to a second or third job location in the same day. This rule applies equally to people with jobs and businesses.

Tip #210: Loans

Paying off a loan is not a deduction, no matter how big that loan is. A long time ago I had an angry discussion with a client who was also my roommate. She had borrowed about $50,000 to buy Nautilus equipment for her gym. We took a depreciation deduction for all that equipment. One day, a new boyfriend came along and paid off her loan. He insisted that she must get a deduction for that payment. Despite my explaining patiently three or four times, and even providing detailed worksheets about how the numbers worked, he didn't believe me. They stalked out of my office in fury. I haven't heard from them since. Over the years, I have had similar discussions with other clients. All the rest understood the concept after a while. I hope you do, too. If there are deductions to be had, the deductions were used when the loan was first obtained and the assets were purchased. If it was a business loan, the interest was deducted each year as the payments were made. But the payoff? No deduction. The journal entry on the books would be:

Debit—Loan Balance (a liability)—to wipe the debt off the books
Credit—Cash (the bank account)

Tip #211: Modification

You may not claim a deduction for the cost of fees relating to loan modification documents and/or IRA transfers. When it comes to loan modifications, if the loan is on a home, you might be able to add it and the other costs to the basis (tax cost) of the home. There is no deduction at all for fees related to student loans and other loans. For investment loans, you may take a deduction under miscellaneous itemized deductions and reduce the cost by 2 percent of your adjusted gross income.

Tip #212: IRA Fees

Don't claim a deduction for the annual IRA fees or transfer fees unless you paid the fees with money outside the account. Most people let the fees come from the funds inside the IRA. That means you are reducing your investment each year. It's wiser to pay the costs with money out of your pocket, especially if the fees are relatively low. If you are able to use miscellaneous deductions, you will be able to deduct the fees. Even if you cannot benefit from the deduction, your IRA balance will grow just that little bit more.

Since these deductions have been suspended by the TCJA until after 2025, consider paying these fees with funds inside the IRA account. You won't be out of pocket with respect to your current cash flow. But it will reduce your IRA balance and the related growth. If the account is growing nicely, you may not want to use that money. But if it's only earning 1 percent or so, let the account pay the fees.

Tip #213: Again?

Don't let the IRS audit you year after year. It's actually the IRS's own rule about "Repeat Examinations." If a return was examined for the same items in either of the two previous years and no change was proposed to the tax liability, contact the IRS immediately and the examination will likely be discontinued. This policy is in accordance with IRC Section 7605(b) of the Internal Revenue Code, which states that no taxpayer shall be subjected to "unnecessary examinations" (https://www.law.cornell.edu/uscode/text/26/7605). So what do you do if the IRS invites you back to the dance again? If it's for the same issues—and the IRS found nothing the first time—just call the IRS and politely explain that they need to cancel the audit. Please, do be polite. Being rude, arrogant, and pushy will only get you into trouble. After all, Martha Stewart didn't go to jail because of a small amount of insider trading profits. She went to jail because she was rude to the investigators and brushed them off. They had power. They used it. Had she cooperated, most likely she would have simply been embarrassed, slapped on the wrist, and fined.

Tip #214: Second Opinion

Do not rely on the IRS instructions, written or verbal. There is an excellent article by attorney Robert W. Wood on Forbes.com: http://iTaxMama.com/Forbes_Dont_Rely_on_IRS. Wood provides a long list of taxpayers who relied on the IRS's instructions and lost in court. If you're going to take a position on a tax issue that you think is a little borderline or aggressive, get a written opinion from an Enrolled Agent, Certified Public Accountant, or attorney. That will give you standing. The IRS's public information will not.

Tip #215: Money on the Table

Don't leave your tax refunds on the table. You only have three years to file a tax return after the end of the tax year. If you don't file . . . whoosh! The money is gone. Every year, the IRS posts its announcement about unclaimed refunds (http://iTaxMama.com/IRS_UnclaimedRefunds). Millions of dollars go unclaimed. In 2017, the IRS announced that there was about $1 billion sitting there, waiting for you. Sure, it's nice to make a large donation to the coffers of the US Treasury. But . . . you don't even get a donation deduction for this. And do you really want your government officials just wasting your tax refund? Heck no! File on time, before the three-year filing deadline passes, and waste that money yourself.

Tip #216: Unclaimed Assets

Don't leave assets unclaimed. Visit the unclaimed property sites in the states where you or your family have ever lived. Start at the USA.gov (https://www.usa.gov/unclaimed-money) site to look up your states—that way you know that you are dealing the real states' websites, not someplace bogus. (Warning: If people call you or send you an email saying they have found assets for you, do not give them any money or information. If they refuse to provide you with details, visit the unclaimed property sites yourself. There is a lot of fraud out there.) You would be surprised what family members may have left behind in bank accounts, insurance policies, wages, security deposits, and so on. After the entities lose touch with the account owners, they are required to turn the assets or money over to the state. I found several thousand dollars that belonged to my deceased aunt.

Tip #217: Too Good

Never fall for a "too good to be true" tax preparer or investment offer. If it looks too good to be true, it probably is. Sure, you like to believe in Santa Claus, Peter Pan, and fairy tales. The fantasy world is a delightful escape, and I go there often. But when you enter that world, please leave your money and your tax returns behind.

CHAPTER 13

Adjusting or Itemizing—What's the Difference?

W̲E̲ ̲A̲L̲L̲ ̲K̲N̲O̲W̲ ̲T̲H̲A̲T̲ people try to increase their tax deductions as much as possible to reduce their total tax hit. The truth is, tax deductions are actually quite troublesome and have a whole raft of disadvantages and limits. What's wrong with itemized deductions (which are reported on Schedule A)?

- You already have a substantial standard deduction (2017): $6,350 for single and married filing separately, $9,350 for head of household, and $12,700 for married filing jointly and qualifying widow(er). (You can find the most recent standard deduction numbers at the Tax Policy Center: http://www .taxpolicycenter.org/statistics/standard-deduction.)

- **The deduction is much higher, starting in 2018: $12,000 for single; $18,000 for head of household, married filing** separately, and qualifying widow(er); $24,000 for married filing jointly.

In addition, you still get the extra standard deduction for folks aged 65 or more and the blind. This is your total standard deduction for 2018–2025 under the TCJA, which will be increased by inflation each year.

- In order to get any benefit from your itemized deductions, they must be higher than the standard deduction associated with your filing status. This means you lose the benefit of the automatic deduction provided by the IRS in the first place.

- Most of your deductions have limits or reductions. For instance:

  › Medical deductions are reduced by **7.5 percent** of your AGI.

  › If you deduct the state income taxes that you paid, you may have to pay taxes on any state income tax refunds the following year (see Tip #7).

  › **Most miscellaneous itemized deductions which are reduced by 2 percent of your AGI have been eliminated in the new Tax Act.**

  › Investment interest deductions have always been limited to your investment income. And if you do use the investment interest deduction, it might cost you the special capital gains rates on some, or all, of your capital gains and dividends. *Note: The TCJA doesn't specifically address the treatment of investment interest. It does discuss business interest limitations and carryforwards.* We talk more about that in Chapter 2, on the business changes in the TCJA.

- Mortgage interest deductions are limited on several levels:

  › **You may only deduct the interest on the original mortgage on the home, increased by loans for repairs and remodeling.**

For 2017, taxpayers may still deduct the interest up to $100,000 of a home equity line of credit (loans in excess of acquisition debt), in addition to the $1 million loan limit. This interest deduction is subject to the Alternative Minimum Tax (see Tip #12). After 2017, the Tax Cuts and Jobs Act eliminates this extra deduction—at least until December 31, 2025.

› If you refinance the mortgage, you may only deduct the interest on the balance of that original mortgage. So if you took cash out . . . you might not be able to deduct the mortgage at all.

› If you are rich and have a very high original mortgage, you may only deduct the interest on the first **$750,000** (or $1 million if your acquisition debt was in place before December 31, 2017). You'd be surprised at how many people get caught in this trap and deduct all their mortgage interest. With the new version of Form 1098 (starting with 2016), the IRS now gets to see any changes in your mortgage balance (see Tip #12).

• Itemized deductions are further limited by a phaseout. Your deductions are reduced as your income rises above $261,500 or more ($313,000 for married couples filing jointly) in 2017. This is adjusted for inflation each year. **This is suspended for 2018–2025.**

• To make matters even worse, your itemized deductions are apt to be reduced by the Alternative Minimum Tax (AMT) in 2017. **However, since the HELOC deduction is suspended for 2018–2025, the AMT on interest expense won't be a consideration on that deduction for a while.**

• Last but not least, with high itemized deductions, you increase your chances for audit.

So you can see why you actually want to avoid those deductions, if possible, and aim for adjustments to income instead of itemized deductions. That way you can keep the full benefit of those standard deductions and reduce your audit risk. For 2017 and future updates, phaseouts, and so on, look for the information at the SMBIZ site—at http://www.smbiz.com/sbrl001.html.

Tip #218: 1040

Adjustments are the Form 1040's best kept secret. Let me show you something that most people working on their own taxes often overlook. These are the "above the line" deductions called Adjustments to Income. The "line" is the bottom line on page 1 of Form 1040—usually, line 37. Line 37 is also generally referred to as your AGI.

37	Subtract line 36 from line 22. This is your **adjusted gross income** . . . . . ▶	37	

Tip #219: Above the Line

There appear to be *a dozen or so* deductions you can use above the line. Although this is the usual list, in the past, two of these deductions had be renewed by Congress each year—the $250 educator deduction (line 23) (this was) and the $4,000 tuition and fees deduction (line 34) (this was extended through December 31, 2017 only). Just as we went to press, Congress passed the **Tax Cuts and Job Act and the Bipartisan Budget Act of 2018. Some of these deductions were lost—others were retained**.

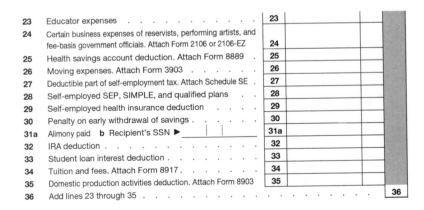

23	Educator expenses	23		
24	Certain business expenses of reservists, performing artists, and fee-basis government officials. Attach Form 2106 or 2106-EZ	24		
25	Health savings account deduction. Attach Form 8889 .	25		
26	Moving expenses. Attach Form 3903	26		
27	Deductible part of self-employment tax. Attach Schedule SE .	27		
28	Self-employed SEP, SIMPLE, and qualified plans . .	28		
29	Self-employed health insurance deduction	29		
30	Penalty on early withdrawal of savings	30		
31a	Alimony paid **b** Recipient's SSN ▶	31a		
32	IRA deduction	32		
33	Student loan interest deduction	33		
34	Tuition and fees. Attach Form 8917	34		
35	Domestic production activities deduction. Attach Form 8903	35		
36	Add lines 23 through 35			36

Tip #220: Line 36

Line 36, total adjustments. Shhh . . . don't tell anyone. More secrets for you. Although the 2017 Form 1040 shows 13 items you may deduct "above the line," line 36 lets you use another 10 adjustments. Who knows—some of them might just apply to you. After the next tip, we will discuss the key adjustments that might affect your financial life. Meanwhile, here's the information about the hidden adjustments straight out of the IRS instructions for Form 1040, line 36 (http://iTaxMama.com/AGI_Line36).

- Archer MSA deduction (see Form 8853). Identify as "MSA."

- Jury duty pay if you gave the pay to your employer because your employer paid your salary while you served on the jury. Identify as "Jury Pay."

- Deductible expenses related to income reported on line 21 from the rental of personal property engaged in for profit. Identify as "PPR."

- Reforestation amortization and expenses (see Pub. 535). Identify as "RFST."

- Repayment of supplemental unemployment benefits under the Trade Act of 1974 (see Pub. 525). Identify as "Sub-Pay TRA."

- Contributions to section 501(c)(18)(D) pension plans (see Pub. 525). Identify as "501(c)(18)(D)."

- Contributions by certain chaplains to section 403(b) plans (see Pub. 517). Identify as "403(b)."

- Attorney fees and court costs for actions involving certain unlawful discrimination claims, but only to the extent of gross income from such actions (see Pub. 525). Identify as "UDC."

- Attorney fees and court costs you paid in connection with an award from the IRS for information you provided that helped the IRS detect tax law violations, up to the amount of the award includible in your gross income. Identify as "WBF."

- Nontaxable amount of the value of Olympic and Paralympic medals and USOC prize money reported on line 21. Identify as "USOC."

Tip #221: Main Adjustments

In IRS Publication 17 on Table V, the IRS provides a list of the main adjustments to income, linked to the places where you can find more details. The table (http://iTaxMama.com/Pub17_AGI) also includes some of the adjustments we mentioned in the previous tip. We discuss the adjustments in the various chapters about education, investment, retirement, and so on. *Note: We won't be covering any of the business deductions (lines 27–29 and line 35) though—that's a whole other book. I just wanted you to be aware that you can use these special deductions.*

Table V. **Other Adjustments to Income**
Use this table to find information about other adjustments to income not covered in this part of the publication.

IF you are looking for more information about the deduction for...	THEN see...
Certain business expenses of reservists, performing artists, and fee-basis officials	Chapter 26.
Contributions to a health savings account	Publication 969, Health Savings Accounts and Other Tax-Favored Health Plans.
Moving expenses	Publication 521, Moving Expenses.
Part of your self-employment tax	Chapter 22.
Self-employed health insurance	Chapter 21.
Payments to self-employed SEP, SIMPLE, and qualified plans	Publication 560, Retirement Plans for Small Business (SEP, SIMPLE, and Qualified Plans).
Penalty on the early withdrawal of savings	Chapter 7.
Contributions to an Archer MSA	Publication 969, Health Savings Accounts and Other Tax-Favored Health Plans.
Reforestation amortization or expense	Chapters 7 and 8 of Publication 535, Business Expenses.
Contributions to Internal Revenue Code section 501(c)(18)(D) pension plans	Publication 525, Taxable and Nontaxable Income.
Expenses from the rental of personal property	Chapter 12.
Certain required repayments of supplemental unemployment benefits (sub-pay)	Chapter 12.
Foreign housing costs	Chapter 4 of Publication 54, Tax Guide for U.S. Citizens and Resident Aliens Abroad.
Jury duty pay given to your employer	Chapter 12.
Contributions by certain chaplains to Internal Revenue Code section 403(b) plans	Publication 517, Social Security and Other Information for Members of the Clergy and Religious Workers.
Attorney fees and certain costs for actions involving certain unlawful discrimination claims or awards to whistleblowers	Publication 525.
Domestic production activities deduction	Form 8903, Domestic Production Activities Deduction.

Tip #222: Jury Duty

Jury pay. When you do jury duty, always make sure to ask for mileage reimbursements at the outset. If your court system allows for mileage compensation, generally the only time to secure that is at the very beginning. When you are paid for your jury duty by the court, you will get a 1099 even though the compensation is often quite minor. Some employers are kind enough to pay you while you are off on jury duty. They usually require you to turn over the jury pay to them as a token repayment. If your company has you do that, deduct that amount on line 36 and write "Jury Pay."

Tip #223: Rental of Personal Property

PPR. Deductible expenses related to income reported on line 21 from the rental of personal property engaged in for profit. This requires a bit of translation. "Personal property" is anything you rent out that is not real estate or a vehicle (there are other places to report those rentals). What are some examples? You work in the film industry and get a rental fee for your camera. You are a set designer and keep a supply of all kinds of furniture, accessories, fabrics, and other unique items you have collected over the years, so you get a "kit fee." You work in construction and have a special set of your own tools or equipment. What do you rent to your employer?

You report the rental income for your personal property on line 21 of Form 1040 as Other Income. You can deduct any costs related to the personal property rental here. Such costs might include depreciation, repairs, refurbishment of the asset, cleaning fees, and storage fees. Keep a good record of the costs and related receipts in your tax return file for the year. Deduct those amounts on line 36 and write "PPR."

Tip #224: Unlawful Discrimination Claims

UDC. Attorney fees and court costs for actions involving certain unlawful discrimination claims, but only to the extent of gross income from such actions. Generally, attorney fees are only deductible as itemized deductions. You can't even imagine the unfairness of this! Because of this requirement in the Tax Code, some people who win judgments end up owing more in taxes than they netted after paying legal fees, administrative costs, and medical costs. However, when it comes to unlawful discrimination, you are allowed to deduct the legal fees here, above the line, up to the amount of your gross income from the settlement. What is "unlawful discrimination?" It includes all these types of discrimination: age discrimination, sex discrimination, and employment discrimination.

If you received such a judgment and paid attorney fees, consider reading the IRS's "Lawsuits, Awards, and Settlements Audit Techniques Guide": http://iTaxMama.com/IRS_Lawsuit_Settlements.

Tip #225: Whistleblower Award

WBF. Attorney fees and court costs you paid in connection with an award from the IRS for information you provided that helped the IRS detect tax law violations, up to the amount of the award includible in your gross income. This is the "whistleblower award." If you turn someone in (see the following tip) and the IRS ends up paying you, you are allowed the privilege of deducting your attorney fees and costs above the line. If turning someone in also costs you jail time, it's not clear if you are permitted to include those attorney fees here. You may want to pay a good tax professional to research that for you. Why? Is it even possible for you to get an award but still go to jail? You bet! Read on.

Tip #226: Reporting Fraud

Did you know that you can get a substantial award for turning in someone you know is cheating on his or her taxes? Yep. In fact, there is a special form for that, Form 211, Application for Award for Original Information (https://www.irs.gov/pub/irs-pdf/f211.pdf). Bradley Birkenfeld earned about $104 million for turning in his employer, UBS, in 2008 (http://www.marketwatch.com/story/irs-whistle-blowing-for-fun-and-profit-2012-09-19). (Probably the biggest award ever.) The IRS was able to examine the finances of major tax evaders who stashed their funds in secret Swiss accounts and collected a fortune in back taxes, penalties, and interest. Birkenfeld was paid a percentage of the amount the IRS collected. But . . . he went to jail for his own participation in the bank fraud. He's done his time and feels great about the $104 million he received from the IRS (http://www.newsmax.com/Newsfront/ubs-whistleblower-birkenfeld-arrest/2015/11/08/id/701199). How does this affect you? If you know of individuals who are cheating on their taxes to the tune of a couple of million dollars or more, you can report them to the IRS using Form 211. When you do, be sure you can tell the IRS where their assets can be found. After all, if the IRS cannot collect on the judgment, you cannot get paid. If the IRS decides to investigate and is able to locate the tax evader's funds, you will get a percentage of the recovery. Naturally, that award is taxable—report it on line 21 as "Other Income." Sometimes a tax evader is violent and vengeful. In that case, consider remaining anonymous. Use an experienced IRS whistleblower attorney to represent you. Regardless, many people do get these judgments. If you do, and you have attorney fees and court costs, deduct them on line 26 and write "WBF."

Tip #227: Medicare

Medicare. One extra adjustment not mentioned in the IRS publication is legal fees paid for a private cause of action under the Medicare Secondary Payer Act (http://www.teaguecampbell.com/private-cause-action-medicare-secondary-payer-act). What does this mean? Sometimes when people are injured or ill, they turn to Medicare to pay their medical expenses. Suppose they have workers compensation, other insurance coverage, or employer coverage, and Medicare determines that one (or more) of those coverages should reimburse Medicare. If Medicare does not get reimbursed, the government will file a conditional reimbursement lien and collect from the taxpayer. The taxpayer can then sue the various other providers. When the taxpayer wins and gets a settlement, that settlement will be taxable. You are permitted to deduct these legal fees above the line. Since the IRS doesn't provide a code, consider using "Medicare." Be sure to include an explanation with details. File this tax return on paper, not electronically.

Tip #228: Consult a Pro

The other obscure stuff for line 36. If any of those things apply to you, do consider sitting down with a tax professional who is an expert in those areas. They are not generally common issues in self-prepared returns.

Tip #229: Claim of Right

Repayments more than $3,000 under a Claim of Right. This isn't really an adjustment. It can be an itemized deduction, or, best of all, it can be a tax credit. What does this mean? Well, let's start with the easy part. "Repayments" are anything you have to repay on which you paid tax. This could be unemployment income, if the state found out you were actually working; wages or sign-on bonuses repaid to an employer; excess Social Security income because your earned income was too high; and so on. You would think that since you paid tax on this income in a prior year, you should simply be able to deduct the reimbursement on line 21 as negative "Other Income," right? If only that were the case. Alas, no. When the repayments are under $3,000, you are forced to deduct the amounts as miscellaneous itemized deductions on Schedule A. These deductions are reduced by 2 percent of your AGI, like most miscellaneous itemized deductions through December 31, 2017. You get no benefit from these deductions if you can't itemize. In fact, starting in 2018, as a result of the Tax Cuts and Jobs Act, you won't even have this option for 2018–2025.

When the reimbursement is more than $3,000, you get to take a tax credit instead of a deduction (or you may use the deduction but not have it reduced by 2 percent of your AGI). Tax credits are better than deductions. They reduce your taxes, dollar for dollar.

OK, here's the complicated part. To get that tax credit, you need to go back to the tax return for the year when you originally reported this income. Deduct the amount you are paying back and recompute the tax return. Print it out. The difference between your original total tax liability and your reduced income is the tax credit you will use. IRS Publication 525 has some examples of how this computation works—look for "Repayments" in the index (http://iTaxMama.com/IRS_Replay_Claim_of_Right.html). If you must reimburse funds that cover several tax years, you might have to do several years' worth of recomputations and claim the credit in the year in which you pay back all the money. (No, you would not amend those earlier years.) If the credit is significant, do file your tax return on paper and include copies of all the revised prior-year tax returns, each marked "COPY." Incidentally, sometimes the deduction works better than the credit. Compute the repayment both ways. Better yet, get a tax pro who understands this claim or right to help you. (Warning: Very few tax pros know about this credit option.)

Tip #230: PATH

On December 18, 2015, Congress passed sweeping legislation in the form of the Protecting Americans from Tax Hikes Act of 2015 (or PATH). This bill makes some tax provisions permanent, so taxpayers will not have to wait in suspense until the end of every year. Here is a link to the House Ways and Means Committee's summary of the key provisions of the proposed PATH Act: http://iTaxMama.com/PATH_Act.

Although this law made many former extenders a permanent part of the US Internal Revenue Code (Title 26 USC), Congress allowed many tax breaks to expire between December 31, 2016, and December 31, 2019. TCJA overrode some of the provisions in the PATH Act—some temporarily, some permanently. Those tax provisions have been incorporated into the various tax tips in the book. Some of them are summarized in the second chapter. But the TCJA didn't take into account several tax provisions that expired.

Congress passed the Bipartisan Budget Act of 2018 (http://iTaxMama.com/BudgetAct2018_Extenders). Many of the tax breaks that needed to be extended, were extended. However, only for one year. The extensions to these tax breaks were effective, retroactively, to January 1, 2017—and ended on December 31, 2017. We will need another round of extenders for 2018 and forward.

CHAPTER 14

The IRS
Noticed Me!

ONE OF THE MOST dreaded things that happen to us is getting correspondence from the IRS. Even when it turns out to be good news or a check, we feel a frisson of fear—that chill going down the spine. For some people, just seeing the envelope is so daunting that they simply ignore it. And ignore the next one—and the next. Until . . . oh no! The IRS takes all the money in their bank account. Or hits their paycheck. Or their pension check. This really does happen. In fact, in July 2017, "RandomIdiot" wrote to TaxMama about that very problem. You are welcome to read that conversation: http://iTaxMama.com/Random_Idiot.

The knottiest tax problems arise when people ignore communications from the IRS or state or local agencies. Often the missives are inquiries, to clarify something that was or wasn't reported on a tax return or information return. If you respond, the issue can be solved instantly—before it ever becomes a problem. Each communication comes with a deadline, specified in the letter. As long as you respond by that date (often 30 days), you can clear up the question and nothing bad happens. Or you agree the IRS is correct, and just work out the correct balance due.

Think about this. How do you feel when you send notes or letters to family, friends, clients, or customers—and they flat-out ignore you. You get more and more angry and resentful—and eventually, this affects the way you deal with them. After all, when someone has a history of ignoring *your* reasonable communications, when he or she finally does contact you, you are mistrustful and wary. So are the IRS and the state, when you finally contact them.

In this chapter, we're going to cover three topics. This chapter, all by itself, will be worth at least 10 times the price you paid for this book:

1. You'll learn what to do if you managed to miss filing a few years of tax returns. (See Tips #231–#241.)

2. We'll talk about what to do when you get an IRS notice. (See Tips #242–#245.)

3. We're going to look at ways to avoid these problems in the first place. (See Tips #246–#249.)

So, let's start talk about filing tax returns—current and/or past returns.

You Didn't File Tax Returns for a Year or Many

Tip #231: Always File

File all tax returns, even when you have refunds coming. Let's start by looking back at Tip #215, about not leaving your tax refunds on the table, and TaxMama's Truism (Appendix A) about always filing a tax return whether you need it or not. "RandomIdiot" (he chose this handle, not me) didn't file tax returns for many years when he had refunds coming. He figured it didn't matter, since he didn't owe the IRS anything. But the IRS doesn't know that you have refunds coming unless you tell it. Unfortunately, there are consequences to shrugging off your filing responsibilities. By not filing, he lost refunds for all years before 2014. And the IRS is now attaching his Social Security benefits and his pension. What's even worse is, if he had thousands of dollars in refunds coming to him, but owes money for some of those unfiled years, he probably won't be able to use those old refunds to pay those balances due. He's not alone. TaxMama hears from people all the time, crying because they've lost thousands of dollars in refunds by missing the filing deadline. Let's not let that happen to you. If you have unfiled tax returns in your past—get filed, now!

Tip #232: Tax History

You want to file those old tax returns but don't really know where to get started. The first step is to know as much about your tax history as the IRS knows about you. Here is the list of information you want from the IRS in order to prepare your unfiled tax returns:

- All W-2s and 1099s filed under your Social Security number (SSN) or federal identification number (FEIN) or employer identification number (EIN).

- W-2Gs—gambling income reports sent by casinos at the time of your winning.

- Form 1099-R—distributions from IRAs, pension plans, or annuities. This also includes loans from 401(k) accounts (or similar accounts) that were not paid back on time, or when you left your employment (or retired).

- Any 1098s filed (for interest payments on mortgages and loans).

- Any K-1s on record—for partnerships, S corporations, or trusts.
- Form 5498—contributions to IRAs, Roth IRAs, SEPs, SIMPLEs, with information about rollovers, life insurance, and other key data.
- Form 8300—report of cash over $10,000.
- Anything else the IRS has gotten from third parties.

Tip #233: Account Records

Aside from income and expense information, you want your account records. Since you haven't been filing tax returns, the IRS has built up a whole file on you. (Yes, another of those dreaded government files!) It might contain tax returns that the IRS made up for you, called SFRs (Substitutes for Returns); there would be assessments for penalties and interest; and of course, since the IRS has been levying your bank accounts, wages, pensions, etc., there will be a record of payments it has collected on your account. What are these records called? There are two primary records you want: the Account Transcript and the Record of Account. In the past, these records contained mystical codes. You needed your superhero decoder ring to understand the arcane data in your files. Or—you needed to pay a tax professional a fortune to interpret it all for you. Not anymore. Now, the IRS lists the explanation right next to the code number. Of course, the explanation is somewhat cryptic. But it does give you a good starting point to understand what happened to your account—and when.

Tip #234: How to Get Your Tax Info

Where do you get all that information, if you don't have it at home or in your files? There are a few ways to get that information without having to pay anyone to do it for you—and without paying any fees.

- Form 4506-T (https://www.irs.gov/pub/irs-pdf/f4506t.pdf) is called a Request for Transcript of Tax Return. But it's much more than that. This will give you transcripts of all the third-party reports and account records you need (use line 8). For records of account, check every box in item #6 (a–c) to get everything available for the years shown on the form. Alas, this will only provide account transcripts for the current year and the last three years—although you might be able to get copies of the third-party reports (W-2s, 1099s, etc.) for several more years. There is no charge for the information.

- Form 8821 (https://www.irs.gov/pub/irs-pdf/f8821.pdf) is called a Tax Information Authorization. It's designed for you to give someone the authority to request information from your tax files, like transcripts of tax returns, account records, and so forth. But I don't find a limit on the number of years of data that you may request. So why not use and name yourself as the authorized recipient of the data (line 2)? (OK, you're not really supposed to do that, but . . .) This form doesn't lay out the specific reports and forms you want to get as well as Form 4506-T does. So use Form 4506-T as your guide to list the things you need in the boxes on line 3. Again, this service is free.

- Go to the IRS in person. You can set up an appointment to visit a local IRS Taxpayer Assistance Center (TAC) these days (http://iTaxMama.com/IRS_Office). You no longer need to stand in line all day. Expect to go through security, just as you do at the airport. Be prepared with good identification—like your driver's license and Social Security card—for your appointment. Bring information that shows your current address. You might need to update your mailing address with the IRS so you can get current correspondence. The agency will probably be able to print out the most recent records for you on the spot. (Say, about three to four years' worth.) Any older years will have to be mailed to you. Those could take about 10 weeks or more.

- Call the IRS at the phone number on the most recent notice or at 800-908-9946. You will have to answer questions to prove your identity. The people there might be able to handle your request on the phone. But don't count on it.

Incidentally, find out how to get the same information from your state. You can look up your state tax authority on this website: http://iTaxMama.com/StateAgencies.

If you keep running into stumbling blocks trying to get the information or to understand it, you just might have to turn over the research to a qualified tax professional. An Enrolled Agent (EA) (http://taxexperts.naea.org/) or Certified Public Accountant (CPA) (https://www.aicpa.org/forthepublic/findacpa/findacpa.html) can help you. We have our ways! With a valid power of attorney from you, we can perform miracles.

Note: You can also get help from an attorney—but those fees will be higher than you need to pay for this information.

Tip #235: Get Transcript

A terrific tool that you cannot use—yet. You have an online option with the IRS's Get Transcript system: http://iTaxMama.com/GetTranscript. (Yes, it was hacked a while back, and the IRS shut it down. The agency reactivates it and shuts it down to new users whenever there are security issues. So set up your account now, if you qualify.) This is a really nifty way to look up a great deal of information—and even to solve some tax problems. So why can't you use it yet? Because you haven't filed a tax return recently. To verify your identity, the system asks you for information like the address on your most recent tax return, your adjusted gross income on last year's tax returns—and other things related to recent filing activity. Without that, you cannot log in. We'll get back to this tool shortly, when we discuss handling responses to IRS notices for people who have been filing tax returns.

Tip #236: Report All

What about the income you earned that the IRS doesn't know about? I know, you have two questions about this. (1) Should you report it if the IRS doesn't know about it? (2) What if you, yourself, don't know how much more income you earned? The answer to the first question is easy. Yes. Report all your income. Believe it or not, the IRS has a way to determine, statistically, how much you would have earned based on where you live, your profession, and your lifestyle. It's much easier to address it yourself in the first place. And it cuts down the audit risk. The harder question is how do you reconstruct income when you don't have a clue how much money you earned? Let's tackle that problem next.

Tip #237: Guesstimates

I don't know how much I earned in some of my unfiled years. What do I do? When you are self-employed, freelancing, or just getting paid cash, the IRS database doesn't have a record of W-2s or 1099-MISCs issued to you. So how do you figure out how much income to report on your tax return? You need to back into the numbers. If your lifestyle was pretty much the same for all the unfiled years, this process can be pretty easy. But if you were married for some of those years; divorced for others; rented a place sometimes; owned a home in other years; were essentially homeless in some years; had a job and a business in some years; had just a business in other years, etc.—you will need a separate worksheet for each year. You may as well do this and keep these worksheets in each year's tax return file. If you don't do this, the IRS will estimate a much higher income level based on statistical income levels for your occupation, license, or source of income.

All years are the same. I owned my home, was single, and had a business. How much was my income? So, let's look at what it cost you to live in your home and to support your lifestyle. Enter approximate monthly amounts for each cost listed. If it doesn't apply to you—ignore that line. If there are costs you know about, but I didn't list—there are blank lines. Include some realistic expenditures for the "Other" category. In other words, how much do you normally spend per month on just "stuff?" You can look at your current spending habits to get an idea.

❏ Mortgage payment   _____

❏ Property tax   _____
    (if not included in mortgage)

❏ Homeowner's insurance   _____
    (if not included in mortgage)

❏ Association dues   _____

❏ Utilities   _____

❏ Maintenance   _____
    (like gardener, pool, etc.)

❏ Food and supplies   _____

❏ Clothing and basics   _____

❏ Entertainment   _____

❏ Travel   _____
    (if you remember taking trips)

❏ Education   _____
    (if you took any courses)

❏ Transportation   _____
    (car payments and/or fuel and maintenance)

❏ IRS taxes paid   _____
    (You can find that in IRS transcripts)

❏ State taxes paid   _____
    (You can find that in state transcripts)

❑ Luxuries   _____
  (if you lived high on the hog)
❑ Health insurance   _____
❑ Life insurance   _____
❑ RA or retirement
   contributions   _____
❑ Other   _____
❑ Other   _____
❑ Other   _____
Total   _____

This total is what you lived on per month. Multiply that by 12 to get your net business profit. You can use this to figure out your taxable income and self-employment taxes.

All years are the same. I rented my residence, was single with a teenaged child, and had a business. How much was my income? So let's look at what it cost you to live in your rented residence and to support your child and your level of expenditures. Enter approximate monthly amounts for each cost listed. If it doesn't apply to you—ignore that line. If there are costs you know about, but I didn't list—there are blank lines.

❑ Rent   _____
  (Did you pay each month?)
❑ Rental insurance   _____
❑ Utilities   _____
❑ Maintenance   _____
  (like gardener, pool, repairs, etc.)
❑ Food and supplies   _____
❑ Clothing and basics   _____

❏ Child's school supplies   _____

❏ Entertainment   _____

❏ Travel   _____
  (if you remember taking trips)

❏ Education   _____
  (if you took any courses)

❏ Transportation   _____
  (car payments and/or fuel and maintenance)

❏ IRS taxes paid   _____
  (You can find that in IRS transcripts)

❏ State taxes paid   _____
  (You can find that in state transcripts)

❏ Luxuries   _____
  (if you lived high on the hog)

❏ Health insurance   _____

❏ Life insurance   _____

❏ IRA or retirement
  contributions   _____

❏ Other   _____

❏ Other   _____

❏ Other   _____

Total   _____

This total is what you lived on per month. Multiply that by 12 to get your net business profit. You can use this to figure out your taxable income and self-employment taxes.

All years are the same. I was essentially homeless, was single, and picked up cash work here and there. How much was my income? So let's look at what you must have spent to stay alive. And yes, this is not an absurd scenario. Many people who have come to TaxMama as non-filers had actually spent a year or more in a homeless condition. They may have camped out on friends' couches, lived in their cars, or been on the street for several months—or more. In some cases, they paid rent for a month or two, or paid friends some money to chip in on groceries. Or even paid for gym memberships so they had a place to shower and clean up. I even knew one guy who was homeless and got a membership in the Beverly Hills Country Club so he could shower, get some food—and make business contacts. (They didn't know he was homeless.) As it happens, 20 years later, he is a millionaire. Enter approximate monthly amounts for each cost listed. If it doesn't apply to you—ignore that line. If there are costs you know about, but I didn't list—there are blank lines.

❑ Rent   _____
    (if any—average out your cost for the year)

❑ PO box
    (for mailing address)   _____

❑ Utilities   _____

❑ Food and supplies   _____

❑ Clothing and basics   _____

❑ Entertainment   _____

❑ Gym membership   _____

❑ Transportation   _____
    (car payments and/or fuel and maintenance)

❑ IRS taxes paid   _____
    (You can find that in IRS transcripts)

❑ State taxes paid   _____
    (You can find that in state transcripts)

❑ Luxuries   _____
    (if any)

❑ Other   _____

❏ Other   _____

❏ Other   _____

Total   _____

This total is what you lived on per month. Multiply that by 12 to get your net business profit. You can use this to figure out your taxable income and self-employment taxes.

Incidentally, getting handouts at freeway off-ramps counts as income. Gifts from family and friends—those are gifts and not taxable.

Tip #238: Complex Business

We've been showing you how to figure out the net income for a Schedule C. But backing into the gross income is a little bit more complicated when you have a complex business. After all, depending on the nature of your business, you may have to use a higher level of gross income. For instance, if you were in the business of selling retail or wholesale merchandise, you had to buy your inventory. Then you had a profit margin on that inventory. So if your net profit is $30,000, your gross income might be $250,000—but you spent $220,000 on the inventory that you sold (COGS—cost of goods sold). Or you might have had employees—in which case, the IRS and state should have payroll tax records you can get.

When your income is based on services you provide, your costs are not as high. But you might have some costs specific to your service— like licensing or specific software (Realtors have Multiple Listing Service costs, tax pros pay for tax preparation software, engineers pay for design software, and so forth).

Clearly, if you were homeless and living on handouts, you probably didn't have any business costs. Maybe supplies for a sign?

You really should work with a tax professional to reconstruct income when you operate a business.

Tip #239: Get Organized

So now you know how to figure out your taxable income. What's next? Easy, just get ready to prepare your tax return. You learned how to get your transcripts from the IRS—and our hope is that you followed up with your state. The information on those transcripts will include your income tax withholding to the IRS (and the state, if you got those transcripts). The transcripts will include the mortgage interest you paid. (Unless you paid a private party.) It might include the property tax paid, if your lender collected that from you as part of your mortgage payment. Otherwise, you can get that from your property tax assessor. You should be able to get auto registration fees paid over the years from the DMV, as long as you have the license number of each vehicle (include Sea-Doos, motorcycles, boats, RVs, etc.). Or the DMV might be able to find records based on your name. If you actually have proof of any other deductions, like contributions, mortgage insurance, union dues, medical expenses, or other large costs, organize them by year—and include them in the appropriate year's tax return file.

Tip #240: Forms You Need

Where do I get the forms to file a prior-year tax return? Folks who only need to file the last two or three years' tax returns can usually use the major tax software companies, like TurboTax and H&R Block. You might even be able to file the last couple of years electronically. Anything older than two or three years must be filed on paper. Where do you get the forms to do that? Well, you can go to the IRS website and find the prior-year forms (http://iTaxMama.com/IRS_PriorYear). The only two problems are—you need to prepare all forms by hand, and you need to figure out which forms you need to file each year. The IRS site doesn't have all the forms organized in such a way that you can know which forms to gather together for a given year. Typically, if you had a business, here are some common forms you might need in your IRS tax return:

- **Form 1040:** The main form—the Individual Tax Return
- **Schedule A:** If you had a mortgage or high medical expenses or union dues
- **Schedule B:** For dividends or interest
- **Schedule C:** Your business tax return
- **Schedule F:** If your business is a farm or a ranch
- **Schedule SE:** Self-employment taxes—(Social Security and Medicare on your business profits from Schedule C or F (or partnership K-1s)
- **Form 4562:** Depreciation—for your car or business equipment

Once you have all the forms, you would have to fill them out by hand. If you've never prepared a business tax return by hand, you're in for a big surprise. You need to know which numbers move from one form to another—and sometimes to several forms. And if you make a change on one form, it might cascade and affect three or more other forms. Have a good, clean eraser handy.

But wait! There might be an easier way to do all this—rather than trying to find each form and working everything out on paper. There is a website called FreeTaxUSA: http://iTaxMama.com/FreeTax_Prior. *Note: I do not know these people at all. But FreeTaxUSA is a member of the IRS Free File Alliance (see Appendix C). So the IRS knows who it is.* It has software going back to 2010 for you to use. Great news! The website says it doesn't charge you for the federal tax return. The fee for the state is only about $15. That's an amazing deal. (After all, filing current-year returns with the major software companies costs more than that.) You will still have to file your tax return on paper. But at least you'll have the software to coordinate all your data and handle your computations.

Of course, if you're still overwhelmed, turn to a tax professional who has experience working with multiple unfiled years—and has the relevant software for those years. (No, not everyone knows how to handle this—or wants to.) On the other hand, those who are experienced have certain tricks and shortcuts to make your life easy.

Tip #241: Balance Due

Uh-oh! I prepared six years' worth of tax returns—and I cannot afford to pay. As it happens, that's less of a problem than you might think. The IRS has several options to help you address the daunting balance due. You can get an Installment Agreement (http://iTaxMama.com/IRS_IA), or an Offer in Compromise (http://iTaxMama.com/IRS_OIC). In addition, there are a variety of other ways to deal with an IRS or state balance due that you cannot afford to pay. It will take a whole other book to cover the details. In the meantime, you can follow the links in this tip to get more details from the IRS. Or drop by TaxMama.com to ask specific questions about your own situation and get answers for free. Or if you actually want to learn how to handle these kinds of problems—perhaps even start a whole new career representing taxpayers in trouble—sign up for TaxMama's Tax Practice Series (http://www.cchcpelink.com/teamtaxmama). For less than the price of a consultation with a tax professional, you can learn to solve your own IRS problems.

You Got an IRS Notice

Tip #242: IRS Notice

Oh no! That envelope with the IRS logo! What do you do now? Open it. Pure and simple. Does that sound too simplistic? Believe it or not, most people who have tax problems get to that point because they don't open those letters. When they come to see me, or another tax professional, they often bring us stacks of letters—sometimes boxes full of letters—that have never been opened. We're not even talking about people losing the correspondence. Or moving and never getting the correspondence. No. That's not the case. They have all the letters. Not a single one has been opened. Ironically, not even the letters with the checks. Of course, those checks are often too old to be cashed. Getting them replaced can take months—if they can be replaced at all.

Never mind. OK, first step—open the envelope.

Second step—read the letter.

Don't understand what it's about? No worries. You can look up the purpose of the notice on the IRS website: http://iTaxMama.com/ IRS_Notices. Just enter the letter number into the search box. The letter number can be found on the top line of the right-hand corner of the letter, or the bottom right-hand corner.

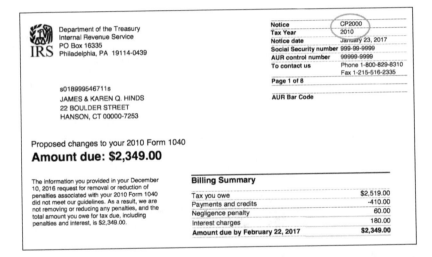

For instance, one of the most common notices is the CP-2000. Here's what the IRS says about it: "The income or payment information we have on file doesn't match the information you reported on your tax return. This discrepancy may cause an increase or decrease in your tax, or may not change it at all."

What this means is, the IRS received a W-2 or 1099 or K-1 with your Social Security number on it, but you didn't report it on your tax return.

The second page of the letter will start listing all the income sources that the IRS computer didn't find on your tax return. Please look at pages 2 and 3 of the IRS's sample CP-2000 letter to see what I mean: http://iTaxMama.com/CP-2000.

Don't get worried yet. Quite often, that income is actually reported somewhere on your tax return. But you didn't put it on the form or schedule where the IRS expected to find that information. On the other hand, if you are missing the information, sometimes the income comes with related withholding. So things work out. Of course, it might turn out that you really did omit something from your tax return. That's not the end of the world. That takes us to our third step.

Tip #243: Response Deadline

Third step—respond to the IRS notice. When you get a notice, pay close attention to the response deadline. Generally, the notice will tell you how many days you have (10 days, 30 days, 90 days, or more) on the first page. It might even tell you the date by which the IRS is expecting your response. When you respond by the due date, the issues raised by the notice can be resolved without fuss—and often without penalties. In fact, responding on time can help avoid having the IRS post an assessment at all, if the proposed assessment was in error. Procrastinating and missing the deadline is costly. It takes much more time and work to remove an assessment (or a lien or levy, if you've waited that long). Often, by that time, things have gone so far that you really do need the help of an experienced tax professional to untangle the knot of problems your procrastination has created. You can respond by phone—call the phone number on the notice. Or you can respond by mail to the address on the notice. For instance, if you got one of those CP-2000 notices, the IRS has a page that tells you exactly how to respond. Read these instructions— https://www.irs.gov/taxtopics/tc652.

Tip #244: Be Sure

Warning! In all cases, before responding, make sure the notice really is from the IRS or your state agency. There is so much identity theft and phishing going on, that it's easy to get caught in those ugly traps. Thieves really are getting hold of people's information and sending out notices that look as if they come from the IRS. They have collected millions of dollars from unsuspecting taxpayers.

What's even worse is that the IRS is turning over hundreds of thousands of unpaid accounts to four professional collection agencies whose workers are not IRS employees. You can read more about who they are and how to identify these people on the IRS website: http://iTaxMama.com/IRS_Private_Collection.

The best ways to make sure the notice is really from the IRS is to call the IRS's main phone number, 1-800-TAX-1040 (1-800-829-1040), log into your Get Transcript account on the IRS website (see Tip #235), or have your tax professional find out for you.

Obviously, trying to call the IRS's main phone to have someone look up your account to determine if the IRS sent you a notice can take hours. Yes, it really can. So never try to call on a Monday, or on a Friday morning. If you are going to call, the best time to call is on Tuesday or Wednesday in the early afternoon in your time zone.

Better yet, set up your access to your GetTranscript account: http://iTaxMama.com/GetTranscript. If the IRS sent you a notice, that information (or at least the notice number) will appear in your account. To make this work instantly, you will need a mobile phone account (not a prepaid phone). Otherwise, the IRS will need to send you information in the mail. That could take 5 to 10 business days. Of course, you'll also need information about your most recent tax return, and certain credit history information. The IRS computer cross-checks your information with one of the credit reporting agencies. So if you have frozen your credit, the IRS cannot verify your identity and you won't be able to create the account. *Note: I changed cell phone numbers, and now I have to wait for the IRS to send me a snail mail code. So don't change cell phone numbers once you set up your account. Although it took nearly two months to make this work, I now have access. Here's a tip—use Internet Explorer to set up your account, and it might work the first time.*

Of course, if you're running up against that response deadline and you don't have the patience to sit on IRS hold for hours, and can't get the GetTranscript system to let you in—get hold of a tax professional who has experience dealing with the IRS. We can usually get through to the IRS that same day—either electronically or through the private phone line reserved for tax professionals. Of course, you will have to provide a signed power of attorney to the tax professional. But don't worry. Tax professionals can have you sign electronically, or you can provide a faxed or scanned signature.

Tip #245: Notice Types

What kinds of notices are you apt to get? You have already become familiar with the CP-2000 notice. The IRS has a variety of other routine CP or LTR notices. You can get one for good reasons—like the IRS found withholding or estimated payments you left off, and you're getting a larger refund. Yes, that really does happen. We learned about a $20,000 payment a client had forgotten to mention. In fact, sometimes these notices bring another happy surprise. How can that be? Well, this is especially true with older folks whose faculties are dimming, or family members dealing with a dead relative's taxes. The notices from the IRS provide information about banks or other financial accounts that were forgotten or no one knew existed. In fact, one woman who was handling her sister's finances got a notice showing unreported interest on two bank accounts. They turned out to be two certificates of deposit for $100,000 each. Talk about being happy to get that IRS notice! Sometimes there is a math error—in either direction. One of the most common notices is for penalties and interest assessed due to paying late. And then there are the surprising notices. The IRS tells you that you have a balance due, even though you have proof that you paid it to the IRS via its own online payment system—http://iTaxMama.com/IRS_Direct_Pay. That happened to me. I got that notice in September. I responded the same day via snail mail. (Since I had copies of my payments handy, it only took me about five minutes to respond.) I finally got verification from the IRS that it had found the payment in mid-November. Two months later. So make sure you keep printouts and/or electronic copies of all paper and electronic payments to the IRS's and other taxing agencies. Your payments might not get coded to the correct tax form or year. While I urge you to respond to the IRS or state's notices, I don't want you to just pay the balance shown without making sure you owe it.

Avoid Tax Problems in the First Place

Tip #246: Sweat the Details

Sweat the details. Slow down and make sure you've included all the correct information on the tax return or on your payments. Read the tax return information to see if you have entered all the data on the correct form or schedule. If you're not sure, contact support for your tax software—or ask a tax professional where something belongs. Of course, you can always Ask TaxMama (www.TaxMama.com). When preparing your own tax return, review it in detail before clicking the button to transmit it electronically. Don't perform your review on the same day that you finalize all your entries. Your brain has a funny habit of seeing what you meant to do, not what you actually did. I know. It happens to me all the time. So here's what I have figured out. (And my students tell me this works for them, too, once they implement this practice.) Whenever I cannot have someone else review my work, I set the file aside for two days before doing the review. That way, the brain sees everything as if it's the first time. Errors jump out at me that I wouldn't have seen if I had done the review on the same day. Usually, the errors are minor. But sometimes, I find important errors—like the temporary entries I made in order to figure out how much to pay with the extension. Things like that result in doubling deductions (usually) or sometimes doubling certain types of income. In other cases, you might see tax savings opportunities you missed when you were busy focusing on getting the details right. For instance, a self-employed gentleman faced over $5,000 in Obamacare repayments because his income was higher than he expected when he applied for insurance in the Marketplace. He was going to have to pay back his premium credits. After thinking about it for a day or two, I realized that having him deposit some money into a retirement account would do so much more than just reduce his income tax balance. Depositing the right amount of money would also wipe out the entire $5,000 premium credit repayment. It turned out that he needed to deposit $20,000 into his SEP-IRA. Frankly, even if he had not had that amount of money available, it would have been worth it to borrow the funds. (Borrowing a $20,000 cash advance on a 0 percent deal from your credit card company costs about $600 in cash advance fees—usually about 3 percent. Those 0 percent deals are good for anywhere from 12 to 18 months.) Overall, between IRS, state, and premium repayments, that $20,000 contribution to his own retirement account saved him more than $12,000.

Tip #247: Explain Yourself

Explain yourself. You may need to clarify complex issues in your tax return, unlike Sergeant Friday's admonition on the old *Dragnet* TV show, "Just the facts, ma'am. Just the facts, please." For instance, when you have to estimate a cost or the basis of an asset or stock that you just sold, it's important to tell the IRS how you arrived at that estimation. Did you look up the value online, based on the approximate date of purchase? Print out the source and put it in your tax return file for the year. Explain exactly how you arrived at that date and amount in your tax return. Did you start depreciating a car or equipment you bought several years ago and just started to use for business? How did you find the value on the date it became a business asset? Again, print out the source of the information. Did you donate a painting to your favorite charity? How did you determine the value? Did you get a written appraisal? Was it the price the charity was able to get when it sold the painting at auction? Did you look up the value in some guide? Print out the details. (*Note: If the painting is worth $5,000 or more, you do need to attach a signed appraisal to the tax return, on the back of Form 8283.*) Are you claiming a dependent whose status might be in dispute? Explain how you determined that you have the legal right to claim that dependent on your tax return, instead of the other parent, or guardian. (Or did you get a signed release from the other parent on Form 8332?) Do you have a net operating loss (NOL) this year that you don't want to carry back to last year—you would rather use it on next year's tax return? (See Tips #200 and 201.)

How do you explain yourself? Sometimes, as with the donation of the painting or release from a parent, there is a specific form that must be attached to the tax return. When it comes to making choices about how to handle an issue, you need to make an "election." An election is a formal statement referencing an Internal Revenue Code section or regulation or an IRS procedure. For the more common elections, your tax software probably already has the information built in. You just have to find it and check the box—and maybe answer some related questions. Call your software's tech support folks if you cannot find the checkbox.

When there is no form or election to make, you can include an explanation on Form 8275—the Disclosure Statement: https://www .irs.gov/pub/irs-pdf/f8275.pdf. This is where you can explain your logic, how you arrived at estimates, what other decisions you may have made, within the bounds of the law. You may need to include another page or two for the complete explanation. Or not. You don't need to include copies of the documents or printouts that back up your explanation. But you do need to include enough detail that the IRS can follow your computations or adjustments. For instance, you get a 1099-INT for $6,000 of interest on an investment account that is owned by you, your mother, and your sister. You don't want to pay tax on all that interest yourself. After all, $4,000 of that belongs to your mother and sister. How do you handle this? On Schedule B, you report the full $6,000 on one line. On the next line you write "See Form 8275" and deduct the $4,000 that belongs to Mom and Sis. On Form 8275 you provide Mom's and Sis's names, addresses, Social Security numbers, and the amount of interest that each of them should be reporting. (Be sure to let them know that they must report their respective $2,000 share of this interest.)

Tip #248: Form 8275

Why bother with Form 8275? There are three strong reasons for handling the clarification this way. First, by using Form 8275, the IRS is sure to get your explanation, even if you file electronically. (You won't have to file on paper.) Second, when your estimate, adjustment, or computation might be challenged by the IRS, providing a clear explanation about your thought process on Form 8275 protects you. It forces the IRS to limit its objection to a three-year audit window. If the detailed clarification isn't sent with the tax return, and the IRS feels that there is an error that reduced your tax liability by more than 25 percent, or that increased the basis of a sold asset by more than 25 percent, the IRS is permitted to object, or audit, for up to six years. You don't want to give the IRS those three extra years, while you sweat it out, waiting to see if the IRS disagrees with you. And the reason is the best of all. When you include a good, short, clear explanation, you might avoid being audited at all. You see, the IRS computer pulls a lot of tax returns to audit. Before the files get assigned to an examiner, someone looks through the tax returns to see which ones will give the IRS the highest odds of collecting a lot of money. Kind of a tax triage. (Yes, really. The IRS doesn't just want to audit—it wants to make its audits profitable.) When agents see that you have all those detailed explanations in the tax returns for the very issues that caused the computer to flag your return—your tax return will most likely get dropped from the audit selection list.

Tip #249: Get It Right

Sweating more details—getting the payment information right.
This is another thing that you might think is totally obvious. Make
sure that the IRS knows exactly what you're paying with that check or
electronic payment that you sent in. Yet, payments are misapplied all
the time. And usually it's not the IRS's fault. It's taxpayer error. How
can you avoid this problem? Let's talk about paper payments. When
you send a check, you also include a voucher (like a 1040-ES for
quarterly estimated tax payments). What you probably don't realize
is, the check and the voucher get separated when the mail is opened.
So if you don't put all the information on the memo line (or someplace) on that check, the person entering the payment into the IRS
computer won't know how to code your payment. So always include
the following information directly on each check (I call it FYTIN):

- *F.* The form number.

- *Y.* The tax year you're paying (use a separate check for each year).

- *TIN.* The taxpayer identification number (TIN)—your Social
  Security number (SSN) or employer identification number
  (EIN)—to credit with this payment. If you are paying money in
  toward a married filing jointly return, list both SSNs.

One more thing to consider noting on the check. When your balance due for the year includes penalties and interest, the IRS can
apply your payment to the penalties and interest first, instead of
toward the taxes. So if you want to pay taxes only—be sure to write
that on the check. Or even include a cover letter to specify that you
want your payment applied to taxes only. After all, we can often get
penalties and interest waived.

Incidentally, the IRS tells you not to staple the check to the payment voucher or to the first page of your tax return. Well the IRS is
going to hate me for telling you this. But do staple the check to the
voucher. Why? Suppose the IRS misapplies the payment, saying, for

instance, the person entering it couldn't read the year clearly on your check. Well, those staple holes in the copy of the check can prove that you sent it in with the voucher or the tax return. Of course, you've made a copy of the check and the voucher, or the check and page 1 of the tax return.

Paying electronically is a breeze these days. The IRS's DirectPay system (and the EFTPS option for businesses and investors) lets you pay from your bank account, without any fees. When you pay electronically, be very careful to select the correct year and form number for your payment. Back out of the payment or cancel it before you finalize it if you find an error. Trust me on this. Several people have contacted TaxMama because they entered the wrong year or the wrong form— and only realized it (if they ever did) after they printed out the receipt. It's not all that easy to get this corrected—and might require hours on the phone with the IRS. Or if you don't notice you've done this, you won't know why the IRS is showing that you haven't paid your taxes, when you know the money left your bank account.

One last problem with payments. Make sure the bank account you're paying from is the correct account—and that it has enough money to cover the payment. The IRS charges a 2 percent bounced check fee with a minimum of $25. That can be significant. One of my clients wrote a $40,000 check for an estimated tax payment on a closed account— resulting in an $800 penalty. Clearly, that was an error. He replaced the payment as soon as he got the notice (using a good account). In instances like that, you can probably get the IRS to waive that first-time penalty. And I was willing to do that. But my client insisted that he deserved it for being so stupid. (His words, not mine.)

Sigh, there is so much more I could tell you about IRS notices, audits, and collections problems. It would fill an entire additional book. And it just might. In the meantime, if you have questions, areas of confusion, or problems, please, don't guess. If you don't want to engage the services of a tax professional, do come to www.TaxMama.com and click on Ask a Tax Question.

How to Get the Most Out of This Book

N O ONE CAN BE expected to know everything in the Tax Code. Not you, not your tax professional (or tax expert), not the IRS—no one. We've all heard the statement, "Ignorance of the law is no excuse." So what's the secret to getting it right?

TaxMama's Secret is *R & R*—Reliable sources and Research. We know whom to ask. We know where to look.

My goal is to teach you those two things: whom to ask and where to look for accurate answers.

Along the way, you'll get tips, ideas, and strategies that you can implement immediately.

Please understand that not everyone will agree with everything in this book. Nor will all the provisions help you. Some of the provisions will change as tax laws change. I guarantee that you will find enough practical information to save you hundreds or thousands of dollars—and even some ideas on how to earn some extra money.

Here are some of my hard-won insights and truisms to help guide you throughout your tax journey.

TaxMama's Tax Truisms

Philosophy about taxes. Lower taxes, achieved ethically = higher profits and increased joy.

Mantra about tax return records. Document, document, document! In other words, get a backup for everything!

Philosophy about people in general. There's never a bad time to be nice to someone. There's never a bad time to say something nice to someone. In fact, say or write something nice to someone right now!

Philosophy about dealing with IRS and state officials. Always be gracious and polite to IRS, state, and other tax officials. They can either help you or do you great harm. While it's illegal to give gifts to government officials, you are welcome to write a letter of commendation to thank them for helping you. Send it to them with a copy for their superiors. These letters go into the employee's file and help with promotions, commendations, and other advancements. Besides, it always feels good to get a compliment.

Philosophy about getting even. What's the best way to get even with people who are really mean and nasty? Smile and be super nice to them at all times. It will totally confound them.

Philosophy about burnout. Sometimes, even when you love doing something, too much of a good thing becomes a burden. Take a break.

Philosophy about tax filing when you think you have no taxable income. Always file a tax return whether you need to or not. Why? Because TaxMama said so. You never know what future trouble you will forestall. If you don't file, you will find out in about five years—and it will be hell. If you do file, you will never know the trouble you've missed.

Philosophy about not filing when you have refunds due. Never leave money on the table. Not filing because you have a refund coming and will collect it later is . . . how can I say this diplomatically? I can't. It's *stupid*! After three years, you lose your refund. I actually had a client who lost more than $100,000 because he didn't file his tax return for more than 10 years and had five-figure refunds each year. It can happen to you, too!

Philosophy about caregivers who don't want to report their income. If childcare providers are cheating on their taxes and lying to the IRS, do you really want them being your children's caregivers? If they refuse to provide a Social Security number to you, what will they teach your children about right and wrong?

Philosophy about people who want to work outside a system. If people are ripping off their suppliers or marketers (like hosts going around Airbnb's rules, or house cleaners who want you to hire them without their agency), can you trust them not to cheat you, too?

Philosophy about extending credit to people who don't pay proper taxes. If people have avoided paying the IRS for years, do you really think they will be afraid of your bill collections efforts?

Philosophy about finding treasure. Search the Unclaimed Money site at least once a year (https://www.usa.gov/unclaimed-money). You never know what treasures you will find. I found money for my cousin that had been left unclaimed by her deceased mother.

Philosophy about admitting errors. Stop worrying about the worst that can happen. Just admit you made a mistake and face the consequences. The punishments or penalties are usually far less than you have imagined. Besides, by being a mensch (mensch is a Yiddish term for someone with character; good character—not humorous) and admitting you're wrong, you are apt to get sympathy and help.

How to Use This Book

This book is designed to give you some tips you probably won't find anywhere else.

It isn't intended to regurgitate the tax laws and deductions that you already know and are, quite frankly, bored with.

"I try not to use an acronym in a chapter without explaining it in that chapter. And you will see one—AGI—used throughout the book relentlessly. It is the heart of the of the entire income tax computation. It stands for adjusted gross income. This is a specific amount that you will find at the bottom of page 1 of your long-form 1040. (The same amount is found at the top of page 2 of the long-form 1040.)

Regardless, if you encounter a term or acronym that is unexplained, a quick Internet search should provide you with the information you need.

Part of TaxMama's philosophy is, "If it's too good to be true, it probably isn't true."

So when I give you a tip or guidance that is too good to be believed, you will find a reference. In the print book, you will be given an IRS publication number, a code section, a Tax Court case, or some other useful reference. In the electronic version of the book, you will find links directly to that part of the publication or links directly to the specific source of the information. Since some of the links change frequently, you will find that some links start with "http://iTaxMama.com/." This allows me to update the underlying link when the IRS or other resource changes the URL. If you find outdated links in this book, please let me know. Send your note to trumptaxbook@gmail .com. We'll fix them in the e-book and next printings.

You would be wise never to take advice on faith. Please look things up; research them. Learn how to read and understand what is happening in your tax life. After all, when you sign a tax return or other tax form, you are attesting that you have read it, you understand it, and you are responsible for the contents.

Naturally, researching, reading, and learning take a lot of time. That's what tax professionals do—often, because we think it's fun. But perhaps you are like Isaac Asimov. Remember him, the famous scientist and mathematician best known for having written more than 500 books? He is known for his Three Laws of Robotics, and many of his works have become films—including the books *I, Robot* and *Bicentennial Man* and his chilling short story *Nightfall*.

One April, he devoted an entire editorial column in *The Magazine of Fantasy & Science Fiction* to tax season. The Good Doctor, as Asimov was known, explained why he used a tax professional: "I am sure I could understand income taxes if I put my mind to them. But if I took the time to do that, the world would be deprived of many of my books."

If a genius like Isaac Asimov needed us, perhaps you do, too.

Please make notes in this book. Dog-ear the pages, or use Post-it notes all over. When you're done, make a list of all the things you want to discuss further with your tax pro. In particular, make a list of the changes in the TCJA that you think might apply to you. List the changes that you are sure affect you—but add anything else that you are not sure affects you or your business. The new Tax Act could make a big difference in your personal finances, especially if you learn how to use the changes to your advantage. Or if you are armed with knowledge about those changes that will cause you to pay more taxes, you will have time to find loopholes to reduce the negative impact. This is especially important for small businesses. The special

20 perent business deduction adds much confusion to the potential benefits it brings.

Get a good tax professional who understands the tax laws related to things you want to accomplish. Most importantly, get a tax pro who will listen to you—as long as you are willing to pay for the time.

APPENDIX B

Record-Keeping Tips and Tools That Help Maximize Deductions

ARE YOU SERIOUS ABOUT paying less in taxes? I mean, really serious? Believe it or not, you are in control of how much you pay to Uncle Sam, your state, your property tax assessor, and your city—how much you pay in sales taxes and and in fact for all taxes. Look at it this way: you have three choices when it comes to taxes.

You can be a **Tax Pushover**, coasting along and paying out everything that's demanded of you without another thought. You can be a **Tax Vigilante**, fighting passionately to eliminate or reduce taxes wherever you can. Or you can be **Tax Aware**, doing the fundamental, logical things needed to keep your taxes legally low without becoming obsessed. This book will provide you with the information you need to fulfill any of those options. You'll get some routine ideas, but you will find special gems not found anywhere else. They are legal, but most people have never thought about using these strategies.

The foundation for all tax reporting is good record keeping. The concept is the same whether you're in business or simply dealing with your personal tax situation. In this book, we will focus on your personal records. It's not as hard to do as you think—especially with all the nifty apps available to you. We will talk more about apps in a few pages.

We won't go into detail on the various apps—that would require a whole other book. The tips that follow provide you with the names and URLs of the top apps that can help make your life easier. Some are free. Some charge a fee.

One of the big secrets to getting the best tax benefits is having complete records of all your financial transactions. That way, even if you didn't know about a tax break in your favor, you can take advantage of it at tax time because you have the records to prove you spent the money, drove the miles, or took the appropriate action.

Everyone should know at least a little bit about the household records. I often find that when it comes to married couples, only one person seems to handle all the household finances. It's important for both to be involved and to know where all the files and records are located. After all, heaven forbid, if you should become divorced or widowed, it's important to know how to take over and manage the household finances, pay bills, get organized for taxes, and so on. These events generally happen suddenly—with no warning at all. I have seen too many people in these situations become paralyzed and unable to manage. As a result, they stop filing tax returns and get into financial and credit trouble for five years or more. Please avoid that, OK? To learn a little bit about bookkeeping, painlessly—and perhaps for free—see the following (in alphabetical order, not by preference):

- Accounting Coach: https://www.accountingcoach.com/
- The Bean Counter: http://iTaxMama.com/BeanCounter

- The Open University—introduction to bookkeeping and accounting: http://iTaxMama.com/OpenU_Bkpg_Acct

- Saylor Academy—a complete series of business courses for free: https://learn.saylor.org/course/index.php?categoryid=6

Income requirements. Here's the information you must store in your records in order to satisfy the dreaded IRS when it comes to income (as it applies to your particular financial situation). We'll discuss many of these in the chapters to come:

- Paystubs—especially the final, year-to-date paystub at the end of the year (just in case you don't end up getting a W-2) or at the end of a job if you leave during the year.

- W-2s, 1099s, 1098s, K-1s, and all other third-party notifications.

- Bank and brokerage statements. Keep a paper or electronic copy of each statement for each and every bank account. That includes PayPal, ITEX, Bitcoin, and all other online accounts— including investment accounts.

- Securities trades—sales, purchases, short sales, straddles, and so on. You are the best source of information about the basis of your securities.

- Business income. Do not rely on 1099-MISCs. It's is your responsibility to keep *your* own books when you have a business. Just make sure the total of the 1099s you receive is less than or equal to the business income you report.

- Distributions from partnerships.

- Alimony, unemployment, state refunds, disability, and other miscellaneous sources—often forgotten, but generally taxable.

- Rental income—on your commercial or residential real estate, or your own home, or rooms in your home via private or commercial sources or places like Airbnb.

- Retirement income—Social Security, IRA and retirement account withdrawals or rollovers.

- Sales of assets. Not all sales are taxable, but all must be reported.

- Awards, prizes, scholarships—surprise, surprise, surprise. Not only are these things often taxable, but when children receive them, they might be subject to kiddie tax (at trust tax rates).

- Gambling income. Even if you lost the W-2G that the casino or gambling establishment gave you, the IRS has a copy of it. We'll teach you how to look up the information the IRS received from the casino (and elsewhere) on your account in Chapter 14.

- Barter income—whether through formal clubs or informal barter. Some of the transactions might be taxable. And some of the reported transactions might have deductible offsets.

- Inheritances and gifts. Often there is no taxable income until the assets you receive are sold or cashed out, but there may be some reporting required. However, when you inherit things like IRAs, annuities, US savings bonds, and certain other assets, income tax will be due on those assets.

- Hobby income. Sources could be eBay, ePages, Etsy, or other hobby income sites. There are special rules for reporting hobby income and deductions. You're going to hate these particular rules.

- Cancelled debt—on credit cards, real estate, and personal debt. I hate to tell you, but this invisible income is taxable.

- Jury pay. It's not much. And you often return it to your employer, but . . . remember to enter it because the IRS knows.

Expense requirements. Here's the information you must store in your records in order to satisfy the dreaded IRS when it comes to expenses (as it applies to your particular financial situation):

- Keep copies of all your cancelled checks—even if it's only a PDF copy.

- If you pay cash for something major, get a receipt and scan it into your online filing system or file it in your paper file.

- If you pay cash for something minor like parking, valet, tips, and so on, keep a small pad of paper handy (or 1" × 1" Post-it). Write the date, time, location, and amount on a separate page for each instance. File it or scan it by the end of each day.

- When it comes to charity, never pay cash. Always use a check, credit card, or online payment (like PayPal). Get a formal receipt for all donations of $250 or more. (More detail in Chapter 8, "Charitable Deductions.")

- Credit card statements are not enough to prove what you bought if you want to deduct it. You need the receipt as well. For big-ticket items, be sure to keep the receipts. (Besides, it helps for returns and warranties.)

- Save your property tax and vehicle registration bills with all the details they show. It doesn't hurt to copy the check or electronic payment and keep it with those receipts.

- Make a copy of every estimated tax payment you make for the IRS, state, or local taxes. Be sure to show the form number, year (or quarter), and type of tax you have just paid.

- Keep mileage logs for all driving so you can later deduct medical, charity, volunteer, moving, and/or business miles.

- When it comes to home improvements, always keep copies of all the invoices and proofs of payment. The details may come in handy for tax credits and warranties and for reducing profits when you sell the property.

- If you get tips on your job, keep the details about the tips you get and those you share with other workers at your job.

- For more details on how to keep records, read chapter 1 of IRS Publication 17, "Your Federal Income Tax" (http://iTaxMama .com/Pub17_Chapt1).

How long should you keep records? This is one of the most common questions people ask TaxMama.

You don't need to keep everything forever . . . but do keep tax returns forever. People are often shocked when the IRS or state pops up saying a tax return has never been filed for a given year, 5 or 10 years ago. Without a copy of that tax return, it's nearly impossible to prove that you did file. Tax returns don't take up much space. You can even scan them (preferably as PDF files), as long as you are certain that the copies are clean, readable, and retrievable a decade from now. Do you need all the backup records that went with the tax return? Not necessarily. But keep those for at least six to seven years.

The IRS is generally only permitted to audit for up to three years after you file a tax return. However, if you have underreported gross income or overreported expenses, or you have overstated the basis of assets by 25 percent or more, the IRS has the right to audit for up to six years. If there are criminal omissions or overstatements, the IRS may audit forever. But that should not apply to you. Add one to two years for state deadlines.

What about other records?

Keep the following records until at least six years after the contracts or terms expire or assets are sold:

- Copies of all contracts, warranties, original insurance contracts, and loans. You will need these to ensure that the terms are met in the event you need to file a claim or a dispute. The (annual) invoices aren't enough. The original contracts contain the terms.

- Purchase documents for real estate, and all improvements to the real estate. These will help you when you sell the property—or if you want to convert it to a rental.

- Copies of the original property's purchase and sale, and the tax return reporting of the rollover if you ever rolled over gains—in either tax-free exchanges or the sale of a home—before 1998. (If you don't have the records, start digging.)

- Purchase information and all splits of all stocks or securities that you are still holding (or sold this year). If you reinvested dividends, don't forget to add those reinvestments to the cost. If you don't have all the details, but know approximately when you originally bought the stock, www.netbasis.com can reconstruct the entire history of your ownership and compute your basis for a small fee. If you are an active trader and need more complex analyses of your trading, you may even want a full-blown account here, instead of the one-shot reconstruction.

- Deductions for funding a regular Individual Retirement Account (IRA). Sometimes, though, you make after-tax contributions. Be sure to track those, since those funds won't be taxable when you withdraw your money. Also, states may have a different allowable IRA deduction. So you might have a tax basis for the state. (More details in Chapter 9.)

Keep tax preparation records for at least six years. That means all the cancelled checks, receipts, mileage logs, and records that were directly used in the preparation of your tax return. This should include copies of all your notes, work papers, and correspondence with your tax professional or tax software company. Keep them with a copy of the tax return, so if you're ever audited, everything is right there, right at hand.

TaxMama's Record-Keeping Law of the Universe. You won't need to look at most of your records for years. But as soon as you throw something out—you will need it desperately.

The benefits of mobile applications:

- They let you scan documents, checks, and receipts on the spot and let you upload them to your application instantly instead of spending your entire evening tediously entering data into a traditional print or electronic system. Yawn.

- They generally integrate with other tools to help you organize the data—or to have someone else organize the data for you (like Shoeboxed: http://iTaxMama.com/ShoeBoxed).

- The information can be stored in the Cloud, so you don't need to worry about data loss, fires, messy desks, and so on.

- When the documents are linked to specific lines in your books and records, you are creating an "audit trail." That means if the IRS or state wants to see the receipt for a particular deduction (or category of deductions), you can just click and give it to whoever is making the request or print out all the data in the category.

- Some of the tools will use GPS to track your mileage for each driving incident, allowing you to categorize the trip as personal, business, medical, moving, or charitable mileage. Others will require manual entries for each trip.

- **Most importantly—the IRS has new online tools for you to use. You can even log into your account and set up payment plans, download transcripts, and see if the IRS has sent you notices. (This is especially important when you get those threatening phone calls from someone pretending to be from the IRS. For security purposes (see Tip #244), the IRS tools all require that you have a cell phone that accepts texts. (*Note: It cannot be a pay-as-you go account.*)**

The drawbacks of mobile applications:

- A warning about free apps: Read the contract information carefully. You will learn that you generally don't own your data. The companies can shut down their apps at any time. Think about this: If they aren't getting paid, how can they afford to keep providing your free service? What are they selling to get the funds to keep their doors open? Are they selling your data to advertisers? Is there a paid upgrade? What about the security of your private information, especially when you link these free apps to your bank accounts and brokerage accounts? Do the companies have access to your financial usernames and passwords? Who owns and/or creates the apps? Do they have deep pockets to compensate you or help you in the event of identity theft?

- Security: Some of the data is often also stored on your mobile device. You don't generally have it password protected when you use it all day, so the data is at risk. If your device is lost or stolen, you must scramble to change all the passwords on all your accounts *immediately*.

Here are some of the top applications available to you for record keeping and mileage (listed in alphabetical order, not by preference):

- Deductr: http://deductr.com
- Expensify: https://www.expensify.com
- FreshBooks: http://iTaxMama.com/FreshBooks
- Metromile's mileage app: https://www.metromile.com/technology

Here are some of the top personal record-keeping systems that provide full bookkeeping (listed in alphabetical order, not by preference). Many apps are designed to integrate with these systems:

- Mint: https://www.mint.com
- GoDaddy Online Bookkeeping: http://iTaxMama.com/Outright
- QuickBooks: http://iTaxMama.com/QuickBooks
- Quicken: http://iTaxMama.com/Quicken

- Shoeboxed: http://iTaxMama.com/ShoeBoxed
- Xero: http://iTaxMama.com/Xero

Note: Of course you can use Excel if you know how. But if you don't already know how to use Excel, an app might be a better choice.

Not everyone lives in the Cloud. Some people still like the feel, texture, and smell of good, old-fashioned paper. Here are some paper alternatives for folks who like the tangible feel of paper records:

- Tax MiniMiser is a system with sets of monthly envelopes to hold all your receipts, invoices, and documents—and where you can record all money that you receive and money that you spend. Of all the paper systems, the Tax MiniMiser is the newest one, designed right around the turn of this century (2000) by Bob Whitaker after he got tired of being audited repeatedly. (All the other systems have been used for 50 to 100 years or more.) http://iTaxMama.com/EnUSA.

- Dome Record Books have books for a variety of industries that include bookkeeping information, bank reconciliations, payroll records, or whatever you need. https://thedomecompanies.com/record-keeping/.

- Wilson Jones has been producing columnar pads and binders in many shapes and sizes since 1893. You can design your own journals and ledgers based on the information you need to track. Pair these pads with loose-leaf notebooks and a set of tabs, and voila! You have your own customized accounting system. https://www.wilsonjones.com/us/us/2252/accounting-supplies.

- SafeGuard One-Write Systems combines ledger sheets with carbon-backed checks and receipts. So each time you write a check or make a sale, the entry appears on your ledgers without having to copy it over. This is how I first learned bookkeeping and how to reconcile books. https://www.gosafeguard.com/business-forms/.

- Accordion files can be paired with colorful labels, allowing you to customize your own filing system. Get a file with 24–31 pockets to store your receipts, invoices, and so on. Use a set with 12 pockets to store bank and brokerage statements. Or use the 12 pockets as a tickler file to remind you about monthly bills to pay, things to do, appointments or deadlines, or even birthdays and special occasions.

APPENDIX C

Should You Prepare Your Own Tax Return?

Whether you're a Tax Pushover, Tax Vigilante, or Tax Aware, the odds are better than 50-50 that you are among the 77 million-plus Americans working with a tax professional. But another 70 million or so folks are doing it themselves. In many cases, where your financial life is straightforward and uncomplicated, you're much better off preparing your own tax return. The IRS and all the major tax software companies even make free filing available for you. You will find two different free systems offered through the IRS right here at http://iTaxMama.com/IRS_Free_File. *Note: The main problem with these free services is that they don't maintain your data files from year to year. Or the company will charge you to get a copy of your prior-year tax return. So be sure to download and save all your data.*

File a tax return no matter what. Although the IRS discourages people from filing if they do not have taxable income, have refunds coming to them, or owe any write-in-type taxes, it is in your best interest to file every year. Why? For at least four reasons. Typically, you can file for free, so don't forgo filing.

1. When you file a tax return, the IRS has three years to question your filing. (Add another year or two for your state.) When you file a tax return, the IRS cannot come back to you years later saying you had income that should have been reported. It's hard to prove you didn't need to file when you no longer have records.

2. It's quite possible that you do need to file, to report and pay 2008 Homebuyer's Credit repayments of up to $500 per year, and this will stay in effect until 2024 or until you pay back your entire Homebuyer's Credit. You must also file to report your income information if you received any advance premium credits on your health insurance.

3. If there is a 1099 issued showing any income under your Social Security number that you have not reported, you will be notified by the IRS within weeks after you file. This system helped us find more than $100,000 in bank accounts belonging to a client's Alzheimer's-afflicted sister. Her sister was not in any condition to tell us where her bank accounts were.

4. Via the IRS notification, you will also learn about identity theft—illegal immigrants (or even relatives) using your Social Security number to work, or folks filing fraudulent tax returns to generate illegal refunds. The elderly are often targets because people know they won't be filing and won't know they have been targeted for identity theft.

You are a good candidate for preparing your taxes yourself if you fulfill the following requirements:

- Your only income is from wages, regular pensions, Social Security income, and interest income.

- You have routine dividends—nothing complicated.

- You have IRA contributions with no recharacterizations, and you've been keeping track of any basis (after-tax dollars contributed).

- You have a modest mortgage and uncomplicated property taxes.

- You have children with valid Social Security numbers and with documented childcare expenses.

- You have a receipt for every single charitable contribution you make.

- Your children are in college but don't have jobs or scholarships or income of their own that might prompt them to file their own tax returns.

- You can file your tax return without itemizing, using the higher standard deduction.

You *must* file a tax return if you received advance credits from the Health Insurance Marketplace system. A tax return may be required if you received the benefit of advance premium tax credit (APTC) payments. You must file a tax return to reconcile the amount of advance credit payments made on your behalf with the amount of your actual premium tax credit. You must file an income tax return for this purpose even if you are otherwise not required to file a return (see http://iTaxMama.com/IRS_MarketPlace_Issues).

The IRS's Free File Alliance system has teamed up with about a dozen major tax software companies to offer free filing of IRS and some state tax returns. Eligibility is generally based on certain income limits (around $66,000 or so), age, disability, and military service. You can find the list here at http://iTaxMama.com/IRS_Free_File_Members.

The reason I am telling you about this free service is that about 100 million American taxpayers are eligible; yet only about 50 million tax returns have been filed via the system since 2003. That averages out to less than 4 million tax returns each year out of the 100 million or so Americans that the IRS believes qualify to use these services. Under the new Tax Cuts and Jobs Act, millions more taxpayers will qualify. Many people who could use this entirely free service are wasting it. Yes . . . free. No up-sells, no product pitches, no strings, nothing.

The only potential charge? If your state doesn't participate in the program, you will have to pay to efile your state return. Though, by now, most states that have income taxes do participate in the program.

The only two drawbacks?

1. When you use the free services, none of the software companies let you roll over the prior-year data when you start your current-year tax return. So be sure to keep a copy of last year's tax return handy. You will need some of that information to prepare the current-year's tax return.

2. Suppose you start your tax return in the Free File Alliance database, and it turns out that your tax return is more complicated than you thought. Oops. Now you have to go to one of the paid services and start all over again. Even if you are moving to the same company's paid service. This won't happen if you start your tax return on the same company's website. They all offer certain free tax returns.

Meanwhile, if you know you have an easy tax return, get started here at http://iTaxMama.com/FreeFile_App.

Are you very computer savvy? You can get your IRS tax return filed for free without tapping into the commercial databases at

all. The IRS has a Free File Fillable Forms system that's a bit clunkier than the commercial software. It's harder to use. But engineers and tech wizards love playing with this system: http://iTaxMama .com/IRS_Free_File_Fillable. You won't get any state filing from this system, but you might want to explore your state's website and see if it has anything similar. Google your state's income tax department for more information, or call and ask if your state has online filing software.

The third free filing option comes from the tax software companies themselves. They all have a certain level of tax return they will file for free. You just start entering your tax return data at the free level. If all your information qualifies for the free service, you're all done. They will efile for free. Some states might be included in the process. Many are not.

If your entries start reaching the point where you need to pay for the tax return, you won't have to start over. You will get a notice that you have entered data on forms or schedules that require having you pay for the return. Then it's up to you to decide if you want to continue.

The good news is, even if you do continue and then decide not to use their services to file the tax return, you won't have to pay them. They only charge you when you get ready to file the return. As a result, you can use their systems to do some tax planning for the following year.

On the other hand, sometimes, by paying at the beginning, you can lock in early-bird discounts.

One of the big advantages of using paid services is that they retain your tax returns in their online database for at least three years. (Some companies archive the data even longer—just ask them if you need it.) You can roll over certain information into the new year— like all the names, addresses, dependents, Social Security numbers, childcare providers, and such. In addition, if you have carryovers from rentals, home offices, and other issues, the new file should have the prior-year amounts. This is one of the best reasons to select a software company and stay with it, year after year.

H&R Block. Its in-person services can come with high fees. However, its online services offer interesting benefits. For instance, all paid tax returns come with full audit protection, called "Free In-Person Audit Support." If you get audited, the company will not only guide you (like the other software companies do); it will provide an Enrolled Agent to represent you at your audit. (Most other companies offer a similar service if you pay an additional $40 or so per tax year.) The other interesting service is the company's "Tax Pro Review" product. You can add this service to any of its other online tax return products. This lets you get all the benefits of entering all your own data, paying a modest additional fee for the tax return (starting at about $50 for IRS and one state), with an H&R Block tax pro to answer your unlimited questions. The tax pro will review your tax return data and make corrections and adjustments, explaining what you did wrong or how to handle complicated issues. The person will sign your tax return and efile it for you. For complex returns, this service is much better than anything you can get in the H&R Block office. In fact, the whole process will probably cost you less than $150—much cheaper than an in-office appointment for a complex tax return. The tax pro will spend more time with you, if needed, than you would get in an office appointment; you will spend substantially less money; and it comes with the audit support.

TurboTax. TurboTax gives you access to your tax return files for at least four years. The company's claim to fame is that it has made it possible to upload data to its system from more than 300,000 financial resources—W-2s, 1099s, bank data, brokerage data, capital gains systems, and more. You can import data from Quicken, QuickBooks, and Mint.com. Better yet, practically everything can be started using your mobile devices. Extensions have traditionally been free. And

TurboTax claims that two-thirds of filers qualify to prepare their tax returns for free.

A few years ago, TurboTax started its "Ask the Tax Pro" service as a free service. It has evolved over the years. It's now called "Expert Service." Now, in order to get access to the Enrolled Agent or CPA who answers your questions, you will need to pay for your tax return first. Some of my friends and EA Exam Course graduates are working for this service—and they are passionate and dedicated to providing useful and accurate information.

In 2015, because there were so many problems with the new tax issues related to the Obamacare programs, everyone was very frustrated with the input. In fact, millions of people got bad data on their Form 1095-A, and the IRS announced that it would waive penalties for 2014 tax returns on this issue. Unfortunately, customers took out their anger on the TurboTax Answer folks, giving them bad evaluations. Please don't blame those who are helping you navigate the laws because you're angry with the laws. Congress passes them, and the IRS only enforces those rules. Let your representatives know. (See my website for information on how to contact all the key players: http://taxmama.com/special-reports/call-to-action.) Things went more smoothly during the 2016 tax return filing season, especially after President Trump's executive order to waive the Obamacare penalties. Read more about that in Chapter 7.

In 2018, for the 2017 tax return filing season, TurboTax added a new service called "TurboTax Live," starting at about $150. This is similar to H&R Block's "Tax Pro Review," which gives you access to an Enrolled Agent or CPA to answer all your questions and to review your tax return before you file. The differences? The tax professionals are freelancers, not regular employees of Intuit (which owns TurboTax). They don't sign the tax return and file it for you. Should you happen to get audited, they give you guidance, but won't assign an Enrolled Agent to handle your audit for you. However, you can buy an audit protection plan that will provide a CPA or EA to represent you for about $45 per tax year.

Your least expensive tax software option used to be TaxAct.com. It has raised its prices. Its highest-priced service now costs nearly $90, including one state, at the beginning of tax season. Most of TaxAct's support is via email or online chat. But the company has excellent resources. Its online Audit Assistance site is open to the public and gives you guidance you can access if you get a variety of IRS notices: https://www.taxact.com/support/audit-assistant. One other really great tool it used to have was for non-filers. The company's website used to provide access to prior-year software for individuals and businesses as far back as 2008. Now, it only goes back as far as 2014. (Shhh . . . don't tell anyone, but H&R Block tried to buy TaxAct several years ago. In 2011, the US Department of Justice prevented the purchase due to antitrust issues: https://www.justice.gov/file/498231/download.)

Your least expensive tax software option is FreeTaxUSA. The cost for an IRS return is –$0–, while the state costs under $13. Add another $7 for the Deluxe package, and it takes you to the front of the queue for support and provides audit assistance and unlimited amended returns for that tax year. Not a bad deal. I stumbled on this service while working on Chapter 14 looking for a resource that can help you if you had not filed tax returns for several years. TaxAct used to be my go-to service for consumers. Since it no longer offers its prior software for years before 2014, I had to find something else. (See Tip #240.) You can find software going back as far as 2010. The IRS return is free; the state costs under $15—http://iTaxMama.com/FreeTaxUSA.

Three other top software options. eSmart Tax (http://www.completetax.com/index.html; formerly called CompleteTax.com), 1040.com (https://www.1040.com; you have to scroll down to find the prices), and TaxSlayer (https://www.taxslayer.com/). Due to all the new complexities and reprogramming needed for Obamacare, as well as protecting against identity theft and fraudulent tax returns, their prices have risen to more than $50 to efile both a federal and state tax return. (Other than FreeTaxUSA, Taxslayer has the lowest prices mid-tax season—about $55 to prepare and efile a federal and state tax return.) These companies are all highly reliable and reputable, with solid tax research behind them—and they are members of the IRS Free File Alliance.

***Warning!* While you may find new companies popping up offering great prices for online tax preparation, please be careful.** The information you enter to prepare your tax returns is exactly the kind of information needed for identity theft. So if you have never heard of the companies and they don't spell out who is behind these great prices, avoid them. Try to stick with the list of companies on the IRS's Free File Alliance list (https://freefilealliance.org/)—even if you are using their paid services. You know the IRS has been working with them for years.

APPENDIX D

Choosing a Tax Professional

M ILLIONS UPON MILLIONS OF people can, and do, prepare their own tax returns. But should you? Let's explore criteria for why you may need to consult a tax professional, as well as what kind of tax professional you should hire if you need one.

Financial issues that require a professional. Don't prepare your own tax returns if you have these issues in your financial life:

- A business of any kind—whether it's as a sole proprietor, partnership, corporation, LLC, farm, ranch, multilevel marketing, network marketing, affiliate sales, pyramid schemes, and so on.
- Hobby income—whether you believe it's a business or not.
- Disability income, workers compensation, or other insurance proceeds that you're not certain are taxable.

- Lump sum income from Social Security Disability or SSI (after several years) or pensions.
- You are (or a family member is) age 70 or over and have IRAs and/or pension accounts. They require mandatory annual distributions (RMDs).
- Divorce, alimony, child support, family support, or disputes about dependents.
- Dependents who don't live at home, who are out of the United States, who don't have Social Security numbers, ITINs, ATINs, or other US-identifying numbers.
- Complicated investments including short sales, wash sales, stock splits, PFICs, flipped real estate, racehorses, and other things you may not understand all that well. If you don't know what the initials stand for or what something means, don't invest in it without consulting a tax pro first.
- Sales of any assets at all—especially real estate, business assets, collectibles, and eBay-type sales.
- Rental real estate of any kind, like taking in a roommate, bed and breakfast, short-term rentals (like Airbnb), studio rentals, time-share rentals, and so on.
- You are a first-time homebuyer.
- Complicated mortgage issues—you refinanced with balances higher than the original loan, loan modifications, balances over $1 million, multiple homes, private lenders, or your name is not on the loan, title foreclosures, short sales, or property abandonments.
- Scholarships, stipends, grants, prizes, winnings of any kind.
- Kiddie tax issues that you may not even realize you have.
- Gambling winnings and losses—casinos, clubs, bingo, lottery, and so on.
- Employee business expenses.

- Investment interest and other investment expenses.

- Complicated or high charitable contributions—especially for volunteer work, donations of high-value goods (art, vehicles, securities, more than $1,000 of clothing and household goods), and other things that require more substantiation, appraisals, or expertise.

- Military service—there are special benefits for both state and federal taxes you don't want to miss.

- Disasters, casualties, forced easements—whether personal or business, all have special benefits you can use to your advantage.

- Gifts that you made, or received, of $14,000 (pre-2018, or $15,000 in 2018) or more per person to/from any individual, including money you received from crowdfunding sources like GoFundMe, Kickstarter, and so on.

- You have ownership or signature authority over any financial accounts overseas—whether for yourself, your (elderly) parents or clan, your children, an estate, trust, or business. You own a share of the family business. You have a vacation home outside the United States.

- You have any extra taxes, like the Net Investment Income Tax (NIIT), the extra Medicare tax on wages or self-employment income, household employee taxes, excise taxes, and so on.

- You might be entitled to tax credits for your child(ren), low income, education, energy, retirement, or a whole raft of other things you might not know are available to you from the IRS and/or your state.

- You lived and/or worked in more than one state and need help filing two or more state returns.

- If you have any questions and really want to sit down and talk to a tax professional.

All paid preparers must have a Professional Tax Identification Number (PTIN). There are more than 750,000 US tax professionals with PTINs. In 2015, the IRS launched its database of all PTIN'd tax professionals. You can look up your tax pro here: https://irs.treasury.gov/rpo/rpo.jsf. If the tax pro you are paying is not in the database, you can contact the IRS Office of Professional Responsibility (OPR) by sending an email to epp@irs.gov and providing the name, address, business name, and any other specific information you have about this individual. The IRS will let you know if there is an error in the database or if this person is not operating legally. You can also contact the IRS OPR to get more information about a tax pro's status if he or she is not in the database.

Signature requirements. Sometimes tax professionals use TurboTax or some other consumer software to prepare your tax returns and don't sign your tax return as the preparer. That tax professional is operating illegally. You can report that person to the IRS by filing Form 14157. You can find more information on the IRS website here: http://iTaxMama.com/IRS_PreparerComplaint. Incidentally, if you think this person has been squirreling away a lot of money or preparing fraudulent returns, consider turning the person in to the IRS for a reward. Use Form 211: https://www.irs.gov/pub/irs-pdf/f211.pdf.

Volunteer tax preparation services. This is the one category of tax professionals who will not be in the database, who do not need valid PTINs, and who will not sign your tax returns. If you meet certain income and/or age criteria, you can get free in-person tax preparation and tax problem resolution from these sources. You may have heard about these programs. To find a VITA or TCE site in your area, please visit the IRS website at http://iTaxMama.com/VITA or call 800-906-9887.

- VITA—Volunteer Income Tax Assistance centers help people who earn less than $54,000 (indexed annually for inflation), are elderly, have disabilities, have trouble with English, or are military families. Volunteers can prepare and efile returns and help with fundamental returns, including a variety of credits like the Earned Income Credit, Child Tax Credits, and Retirement Credit.

- TCE—Tax Counseling for the Elderly centers will help seniors with all the same things as VITA does. In addition, TCE provides counseling on a number of issues related to retirement, Social Security, and other government-related issues—and can help seniors avoid scams. TCE centers are often run by AARP (American Association of Retired Persons) at its Tax-Aide locations. You can find them all over the country: http://iTaxMama .com/TaxAide_Sites. For more information, call 888-687-2277.

- AFTC—The Armed Forces Tax Council provides tax assistance specifically for members of the military and their families. It has on-base coordinators, worldwide, for the Marine Corps, Air Force, Army, Navy, and Coast Guard. Both the IRS and the states offer quite a number of special deferrals, allowances, and benefits for active-duty service people and their families. So if possible, use the AFTC advisors to help you. To get more information, ask your commanding officer or call the main IRS phone number at 1-800-829-1040.

- LITC—Most people have never heard of these Low Income Taxpayer Clinics. They are overseen by the National Taxpayer Advocate Service. Often affiliated with colleges or universities, LITCs offer free or low-cost services to taxpayers in trouble. They represent low-income individuals in disputes with the Internal Revenue Service, including audits, appeals, collection matters, and federal tax litigation. LITCs can also help taxpayers respond to IRS notices and correct account problems. Some LITCs provide education about taxpayer rights and responsibilities for low-income taxpayers and taxpayers who speak English as a second language (ESL). Use the LITC map to find one in your area at http://iTaxMama.com/IRS_LITC.

How many kinds of tax professionals are there? These are the main categories of tax preparation and consultation professionals you should choose from. (Numbers in parentheses are the PTIN holders in each category; http://iTaxMama.com/PTIN_Stats):

- Enrolled agents (EAs; more than 53,000). EAs are the nation's tax specialists, with the highest credential that the IRS issues to tax professionals. They are licensed to work anywhere in the country and overseas, with respect to your IRS and state issues. They must complete an average of 24 hours of tax education every year (30 hours if they are a member of the National Association of Enrolled Agents). They are a perfect choice if you need individual and business tax preparation, tax planning, or tax audit representation, or if you have tax debts. These are their areas of specialty. Some EAs also handle estates, trusts, and non-profit organizations. Many also offer bookkeeping and payroll services year-round.

- Certified public accountants (CPAs; more than 200,000). CPAs are the best-known tax professionals. They are licensed by their state CPA society and/or consumer affairs department. Their practice tends to be limited to their own state unless another state offers reciprocity. However, the IRS will accept their credentials anywhere in the United States or overseas. CPAs must also get continuing professional education, but there is no mandatory tax education requirement. Most CPAs prepare all kinds of tax returns. Some are adept at IRS audits, while a few are skilled at tax debt representation. So if you have that kind of problem, ask about their experience first. CPAs are great if you have a high-value business—especially if you are hoping to go public one day. For many CPA firms, write-up (accounting) is their lifeblood. Some firms primarily prepare tax returns for their business clients, related parties, and referrals. They are excellent if you have a nonprofit organization, which often requires an annual audit. Some offer certified audit services.

- Tax attorneys (more than 27,000). These people are also licensed by their state bar and/or state consumer affairs agencies. Like CPAs, their practice tends to be limited to their own state, unless another state offers reciprocity. However, the IRS will accept their credentials anywhere in the United States or overseas. Like CPAs, attorneys must also get continuing professional education, but there is no mandatory tax education requirement. You generally do not need an attorney to prepare your personal tax return. Some tax attorneys (often members of the American Bar Association Tax Section: http://iTaxMama.com/Bar_Taxation) will have extensive, complex, high-level tax backgrounds and continuing education. Use attorneys for estate and gift planning, business succession planning, and criminal tax issues. You need their help on all contracts and agreements, especially with respect to real estate, business agreements, trusts, wills, and so on. You don't generally need a tax attorney to help you with IRS debts. EAs and CPAs can help you with that. You might need an attorney to represent you on complex foreign bank account and asset issues. However, some EAs and CPAs can help with the noncriminal areas of foreign account reporting.

- State-licensed professionals. Of all 50 of the United States, only 3 have any solid licensing requirements for tax professionals. They are California, Oregon, and Maryland. Tax preparers in these states must pass a test and take a certain number of hours of continuing education in taxes and ethics each year. In New York State (NYS), tax preparers are required to register, and they have established minimum continuing education requirements. NYS is planning to create an examination. If you live in one of these states, make sure your tax preparer either is licensed by the state or is an EA, CPA, or attorney. *Note: Attorneys and CPAs licensed in other states, but practicing in CA, OR, or MD, may have to register with these states' tax preparer programs.* No one else may charge you to prepare a tax return. These tax professionals are limited to preparing a tax return and to answering the IRS's or state's questions about the tax return that they prepared. That's it. They are not permitted to represent you at any levels of the IRS with respect to balances due, collections, appeals, notices, or anything else. However, they may be able to help with some of your state tax department issues.

- Annual Filing Season Program Certificate of Completion (AFSP; more than 57,000). In 2014, the IRS instituted a voluntary program to allow unlicensed tax professionals in 47 states to demonstrate a higher level of training and expertise. These people may represent you at IRS audits on the tax returns they prepared, and they may respond to notices from the IRS about those tax returns. They cannot speak for you before the IRS collections or appeals divisions.

- Unlicensed tax professionals who have PTINs (more than 360,000). These people are permitted to prepare your tax return and to file your tax return electronically. Period. Some are highly experienced and do get a great deal of education and training throughout the year. Many are not, so beware. To determine if the unlicensed tax professional of your choice is reliable, here are some steps to take:

  › Check that IRS PTIN database I mentioned previously. If it shows that the person's PTIN is in good standing, that's good news.

  › Ask if the person is a member of any professional tax organizations. Some reputable organizations include the National Association of Enrolled Agents (NAEA), National Association of Tax Professionals (NATP), National Society of Accountants (NSA), National Association of Tax Consultants (NATC), and

American Society of Tax Problem Solvers (ASTPS), among others: http://taxsites.com/Associations2.html.

All these organizations require their members to maintain high standards of continuing education.

Avoid tax preparation outfits within certain retail establishments. Free or low-cost tax preparation services offered at car lots, stereo stores, and other high-ticket stores are often really designed to help you get a refund to use toward a store purchase. The preparers may be unlicensed, and untrained and only know how to generate high refunds in ways that may not be legal.

Avoid tax offices that push refund anticipation loans (RAL)— especially if they tell you that you must get one. With current IRS efiling protocols, you will probably get your refund deposited directly into your bank account **or on a special debit card** within about 10 business days or less. So there is absolutely no need to pay someone a high fee to get your own money. The IRS frowns on this practice and has posted alerts to the public about what to watch out for when being offered RALs: https://www.irs.gov/uac/tax-refund-related-products.

Read your tax return before you sign it. By law, all tax preparers must give you a copy of your tax return before you sign the Form 8879 or Form 8453 to file electronically. It doesn't have to be on paper; an electronic copy is OK. But do take the time to read and review it before you sign the electronic filing forms or before mailing in your paper tax return. After all, you are signing, under penalty of perjury, that everything on that tax return is true. If the preparer made an error, or deliberately falsified deductions or credits to give you a larger refund, it's your problem and your responsibility. So read the whole tax return and ask questions if you don't understand something.

Amazing and magical refunds are too good to be true. Some unscrupulous preparers attract clients by promising huge refunds. They make up numbers on Schedule A, Itemized Deductions—like mortgage interest (even when you don't own a home), tax credits like the American Opportunity Credit for education costs, or other credits that don't apply to you. If your refund is strangely high, ask them how it got that way. Do not file a fraudulent tax return. If you do, the IRS will catch you. You will face all the original taxes, plus high penalties and interest on the taxes and penalties. The preparer? He or she will be long gone and impossible to find.

Find a tax pro with whom you can establish a long-term relationship. Get to know this person and return to that firm year after year. In fact, since it's difficult to do tax planning during the tax preparation appointment, schedule a planning appointment for May or June so you can discuss your financial goals, planned large purchases, or expenses (home, dental work, college, retirement, etc.).

Always call your tax pro for a consultation before you take any large step financially. It breaks our hearts when you call after you have already done something. We can help guide you before the fact and often help you find a tax-free way to use your retirement funds or make investments or get credits. Once you've already taken the step, fixing it may be impossible—or time-consuming and expensive. Believe me, that one-hour consultation in advance may save you thousands of dollars later.

APPENDIX E

Five Best States
to Live In

FIVE BEST STATES TO LIVE IN

1. Delaware

2. Florida

3. New Hampshire

4. South Dakota

5. Montana

To CREATE THIS TABLE, we looked at lists of the most tax-friendly states and those with the best quality of life for retirees, according to WalletHub and Bankrate. In the case of taxes, the data reflect the total combined tax burden—what you pay in federal, state and local taxes. The quality of life ranking looked at weather, cost of living, culture, crime rates and other, similar factors. By comparing the two data sources we found that these five states—Delaware, Florida, New Hampshire, South Dakota and Montana—were the best in terms of both low overall taxes and highest quality of life for retired people.

Index

About TaxMama

The truth is, Eva never, ever, ever wanted to get involved with taxes. EVER!

Taxation is the most complicated area of accounting. The rules change several times a year. Sometimes, they don't change until after the year ends and you wait on pins and needles to learn the rules for last year's tax filings. It's like walking on black ice. You never know where the slippery spots are. If you step on one without realizing it, it can be deadly. Besides, there is just so much to learn. All the time.

But somehow, Eva ended up in a national CPA firm's tax department and became fascinated. Having a natural propensity for languages, once Eva realized that she could look upon taxes as a language. It all fell into place for her. The other attraction to this field came with helping people who were in trouble. Eva's problem-solving and trouble-shooting skills helped her see solutions other professionals missed. As a result, she became the go-to person for folks who hadn't filed tax returns for years; people who owed taxes through no fault of their own; people whose lives had devolved into disastrous situations. She even helped one client evolve from (practically) being a depressed, homeless, street person to being a happily married millionaire.

Her passion to help keep people out of trouble led her to set up the TaxMama.com website. It's meant to be a free, safe place to help people like you stay out of tax trouble. TaxMama and her wonderfully generous team answer all questions within about 48 hours. They don't do the computations for people—but they will point you to resources that will help you with your issues. They will provide guidance that might save you hundreds, or even thousands of dollars. They will help you avoid tax penalties—if you ask before you do things. However, in return, you are asked to search the database for answers to questions similar to your situation. Because, yes, there are repetitive questions—and dumb questions.

Another TaxMama passion is to educate tax professionals—in ethics and tax law and procedure. TaxMama was asked to start a school to train tax professionals to pass a rigorous set of Internal Revenue Service licensing examinations—the Special Enrollment Exams (SEE); also known as the Enrolled Agent (or EA) exams. You can find it at www.IRSExams.school. This is the only school of its kind. And it's all online—no driving; no sitting in traffic; no leaving home for a week or a few months. Just log in from your home or office. (Or like one fellow—who logged in from the McDonalds Wi-Fi outside the national park where he spent the summer.) While TaxMama's EA Exam Course includes training and software to help students pass the EA exams, its main purpose is to provide in-depth training on tax laws, tax research, tax practice tools, IRS procedures and taxpayer representation for IRS audits and tax debts. It even trains tax pros how to make a good living. It's like a 3–4 year tax course, all in six months. Students not only learn how to pass the SEE, they are entertained and inspired. The course is a lot of fun—and has been known to change lives—for the better. So if you're looking for a new career . . . if you're feeling like a Tax Nerd (www.TaxNerd.net), join us. Live classes run from May–October or November each year. Self-study classes are open year-round.

RateMyMemory
Powered by newsmax health

Normal Forgetfulness?
Something More Serious?

You forget things — names of people, where you parked your car, the place you put an important document, and so much more. Some experts tell you to dismiss these episodes.

"Not so fast," says Dr. Gary Small, director of the UCLA Longevity Center, medical researcher, professor of psychiatry, and the *New York Times* best-selling author of *2 Weeks to a Younger Brain*.

Dr. Small says that most age-related memory issues are normal but sometimes can be a warning sign of future cognitive decline.

Now Dr. Small has created the online **RateMyMemory Test** — allowing you to easily assess your memory strength in just a matter of minutes.

It's time to begin your journey of making sure your brain stays healthy and young! **It takes just 2 minutes!**

Test Your Memory Today:
MemoryRate.com/Tax

My RETIREMENT *Date*

How would you like to know the exact date you can expect to retire? Well, this **FREE** assessment will help you learn exactly that. And more importantly, we give you some fun tools that you can use so you'll retire quicker, safer, and wealthier than you ever imagined . . . along with simple investment strategies to help ensure you NEVER run out of money during your retirement. Enjoy!

Find out *your* retirement date!

Go To:

MyRetirementDate.com/Tax

 # Simple **Heart Test**

FACT:

▸ Nearly half of those who die from heart attacks each year never showed prior symptoms of heart disease.

▸ If you suffer cardiac arrest outside of a hospital, you have just a 7% chance of survival.

Don't be caught off guard. Know your risk now.

TAKE THE TEST NOW ...

Renowned cardiologist **Dr. Chauncey Crandall** has partnered with **Newsmaxhealth.com** to create a simple, easy-to-complete, online test that will help you understand your heart attack risk factors. Dr. Crandall is the author of the #1 best-seller *The Simple Heart Cure: The 90-Day Program to Stop and Reverse Heart Disease.*

Take Dr. Crandall's Simple Heart Test — it takes just 2 minutes or less to complete — it could save your life!

Discover your risk now.

- **Where you score on our unique heart disease risk scale**
- Which of your lifestyle habits really protect your heart
- **The true role your height and weight play in heart attack risk**
- Little-known conditions that impact heart health
- Plus much more!

SimpleHeartTest.com/Tax